THE
POWER
of
WOMEN

THE POWER of WOMEN

DR SUSAN NOLEN-HOEKSEMA

piatkus

PIATKUS

First published in the US in 2010 by Times Books, Henry Holt and Company, LLC
First published in Great Britain in 2010 by Piatkus

A CIP catalogue record for this book
is available from the British Library.

ISBN 978-0-7499-2883-4

Typeset in Minion by M Rules
Printed in the UK by CPI Mackays, Chatham ME5 8TD

Papers used by Piatkus are natural, renewable and
recyclable products sourced from well-managed forests and certified
in accordance with the rules of the Forest Stewardship Council.

Mixed Sources
Product group from well-managed
forests and other controlled sources
www.fsc.org   Cert no. SGS-COC-004081
© 1996 Forest Stewardship Council
FSC

Piatkus
An imprint of
Little, Brown Book Group
100 Victoria Embankment
London EC4Y 0DY

An Hachette UK Company
www.hachette.co.uk

www.piatkus.co.uk

To all the strong, powerful women in my life

Contents

For downloadable versions of the worksheets in the book, visit iamapowerfulwoman.com.

THE
POWER
of
WOMEN

1.

The Self-Help Revolution: What Women Do Right

If you could play God and create the perfect leader for our times, what would this person look like? You would want this person to be wise, able to comprehend many sides of complicated issues, and create novel and innovative solutions to problems. You would want the perfect leader to be working for the good of the whole group, not just for personal power or glory. The perfect leader would inspire others by understanding their perspectives, capitalizing on their strengths, and overcoming their weaknesses. And the perfect leader would persist until a job was done, even if it meant personal sacrifice.

You've just described a woman. Women lead with wisdom, integrity, and inspirational power every day, in their families, their workplaces, and their communities. They often aren't recognized for this leadership, because they don't wave their arms and ask for recognition. Instead, they simply harness their strengths to get the job done, fix problems as they arise, and help people in need.

I believe the strengths that women bring to every corner of their lives fall into four groups, and that every woman can harness these strengths:

- Women have *mental strengths*, namely, a particular form of mental flexibility that allows them to be creative and nimble in

finding solutions to problems they confront. They focus on getting things done, not just on doing things their way.

- Women have *identity strengths* that allow them to maintain a
  strong sense of themselves and their values in whatever situations
  they find themselves. They can deal with change and uncertainty,
  because their sense of themselves is not dependent on *what they
  do or have*, but *who they are*.

- Women have *emotional strengths*—the ability to understand their
  own feelings and those of others, and to use this understanding
  to cope with distressing circumstances. These emotional strengths
  also allow women to anticipate the emotional consequences of
  various life situations, which makes them particularly adept at
  making major decisions.

- Women have *relational strengths*—understanding others' perspectives, which then helps women create strong social networks
  that support them during stressful times. They seldom indulge
  in rage and arrogance, even when they are justified in doing so,
  and look for mutually satisfying ways of solving conflicts.

Every day, women utilize their strengths to lead others to better
lives, whether it be their children or partners, their neighbors and
friends, or their coworkers or employees. In quiet ways, and in bold
ways, they take others by the hand and lift them up, they build and
nurture lives, they create and inspire organizations, and they leave a
radiant mark on the world.

Transforming the World

Women are transforming the world and transforming the face of
power. Women-owned firms make up 40 percent of all privately held
businesses in the United States, employing 7.3 million people and generating $1.1 trillion in revenues per year.[1] In 1972, women held only
18 percent of managerial and administrative positions in the U.S. government, but by 2002, that percentage had increased to 46 percent. In

1979, only 3 percent of members of the U.S. Congress were women, compared to 17 percent after the 2008 election. Women have been elected to statewide executive offices in forty-nine of the nation's fifty states.[2]

Outside the United States, women are also making big political gains. Angela Merkel, the fifty-two-year-old physicist turned politician, became Germany's first woman chancellor in 2005, ousting the incumbent Gerhard Schröder. In 2006, Michelle Bachelet, a moderate socialist, was elected Chile's first female president. Reformer Ellen Johnson-Sirleaf became the first female president of an African country (Liberia). And Han Myung-sook, a former dissident once jailed as a political prisoner, was inaugurated as South Korea's first female prime minister in April 2006.

These trends in women assuming major leadership positions are inspiring. But women have been transforming the world for millennia by unleashing their strengths to meet the needs they see. Every day, in simple, unobtrusive, but powerful ways, women enrich their own lives and the lives of others. Let me illustrate with the story of Terri, a forty-two-year-old stay-at-home mom in the tiny town of Stonington, Illinois. Terri is the last person on earth to think she is powerful and strong, but she has had a huge impact on her community and the lives of hundreds of people. One day in early December a couple years ago, Terri ran into a woman she knew casually, named Annette, in the grocery store. The conversation naturally ran to what their families were doing for Christmas. Terri began to name the toys she had gotten her two kids when she noticed a twinge of sadness in Annette's eyes and a slump in her shoulders. It turned out that Annette's husband had been laid off a few weeks earlier, and the family was already desperate for money. There would be no toys for Annette's children this Christmas. Terri comforted Annette as best she could, and then the women went their separate ways.

The conversation niggled at Terri for the rest of the day, however. She knew there were a lot of other families in the area in the same position as Annette's family—farmers were struggling and manufacturing plants had been scaling back or moving out in recent years.

Terri imagined her own children waking up on Christmas day with no toys under the tree and her heart ached. Terri called her best friend, Rosanna, and the two women began putting together a plan to raise money for a toy drive. Terri and Rosanna made announcements for donations at their respective churches the following Sunday. They got local businesses to place donation boxes at every check-out stand. They convinced the elementary school's PTA to hold a bake sale to raise money to buy new toys. By December 18, Terri and Rosanna had raised nearly two thousand dollars. With this fund in hand, Terri visited the local discount stores and persuaded the stores' managers to sell her toys at cost.

On December 22, Terri and Rosanna laid out the dozens of toys they had acquired on tables in the American Legion Hall. At 6 p.m. the doors opened, and needy families, who had been identified by church leaders, school teachers and principals, and workers at the local food pantry, poured in. Excitement filled the hall as the children picked their toys. Parents beamed to see the joy on their children's faces and felt a bit of relief from the weight of their economic plight. In the years since that first toy drive, the community's involvement has grown, with nearly ten thousand dollars being raised and hundreds of toys being distributed to families in need.

Terri's success in organizing this toy drive was the result of the many strengths she brought to the task. Terri discerned that Annette was distressed by tuning into Annette's demeanor and what Annette was *not* saying about her Christmas plans. She took Annette's perspective and understood what it would feel like not to give her children toys for Christmas. Faced with the daunting task of organizing a toy drive in a few short weeks, Terri remained confident that she could pull it off and persisted despite the discouragement of others. She rallied her best friend and the huge social network she had built in her town and then devised multiple pathways toward reaching her goal of raising enough money to buy toys for the needy children.

Women like Terri can be found in every small town, sprawling suburb, and urban center in the world. They set their sights on doing things that express their personal interests and values and nothing stops them from accomplishing their goals. They connect with other people in ways that engender cooperation and support. They find creative ways to get around roadblocks. And they make their communities and worlds healthier and more vibrant by their everyday acts of leadership.

Transforming Adversity

For thousands of years, women have used their strengths to rise above even extreme adversity. There are famous examples, such as Mukhtaran Bibi, a Pakistani rape survivor who transformed her trauma into a movement to change traditional anti-woman laws in Pakistan. *Time* magazine recently named her as one of their 100 Most Influential People in the World. Around the world, women have organized to protect their families and themselves from injustices wrought by powerful governments, terrorists, and economic forces. During the "dirty war" in Argentina from 1976 to 1983, thousands of people were taken to detention camps and "disappeared," most likely killed by the military. The mothers and wives of these "disappeared" formed Las Madres del Plaza de Mayo (Mothers of the Plaza de Mayo) in Buenos Aires, silently demonstrating in the plaza outside the presidential palace to demand the return of their family members. They risked torture and death, but continued to demand information about their loved ones. Once democracy was restored in 1983, Las Madres called for the prosecution of the killers, despite death threats to themselves. These women, many of them uneducated and poor, helped to bring about major political change and justice by marshaling their own strengths and the strengths of other women on behalf of their families.

Others are not famous but are nonetheless heroines for their courage and resilience. One is Jody, a lovely brown-eyed woman whose son played goalie on my son's soccer team. Ten years ago, Jody had what many of us would think was the perfect life—two healthy, beautiful children, an attractive, successful husband she adored, and a thriving career as an executive at IBM. Then, when she was only twenty-nine, Jody's dream turned into a nightmare. Her husband, Len, who loved to bike, swim, and run cross-country, dropped dead of a heart attack at the age of thirty-three. Jody was initially devastated and overwhelmed at Len's death and her new role as a single mother. But within months, Jody mobilized a wide range of psychological strengths so that she could rise above her grief and reshape her life. She drew emotional support from her many friends and practical support from her family in getting her children's lives back to normal. Within a couple of years, Jody was leading support groups for young widows, helping them claim their identities as strong women, use the social networks they had available, and be creative about how to overcome the obstacles they faced as a result of the death of their husbands. Jody says, "Women are so much more resilient than they are given credit for. A tragedy like losing your husband can force women to recognize their power and learn how to use it."

Women's strengths don't only rise to the surface in response to tragedy, however. They are also demonstrated in the lives of the hundreds of thousands of women who ignore the real barriers to pursue their dreams with resolve and unswaying integrity. When Claudia Kennedy enlisted in the U.S. Army in 1968, women were not allowed to command men and there were no women generals. When Lieutenant General Kennedy retired in 2000, she was the nation's highest ranking female officer, a three-star general. Kennedy's first command was over a chaotic, drug-infested company in which an angry soldier threatened her life. She restored discipline and respect by relentlessly holding soldiers to the highest values of the army—loyalty, honor, and integrity. She eventually became the deputy chief of staff for army intelligence from 1997 until 2000, overseeing policies and operations affecting forty-five thousand soldiers stationed worldwide, with a budget of nearly one billion dollars.

Throughout her career in the army, Kennedy risked disapproval and outright punishment from her superiors by standing up for issues she felt she couldn't ignore, including the shameful living conditions of some army families. In 1996, as a two-star general, she was sexually harassed in her Pentagon office by another two-star general, Major General Larry Smith. She raised the matter internally after the army announced that Smith was to become the army's deputy inspector general, a post in which he would have overseen investigations of sexual harassment cases. After her charges became public in March 2000 and were substantiated in a subsequent investigation, the army quietly rescinded Smith's appointment. Since her retirement, Kennedy, who remains fiercely loyal to the army, has nonetheless exercised her integrity by speaking out on the issues that really matter to her, such as the Bush administration's decision to initiate and escalate the Iraq war. The kind of integrity Claudia Kennedy has displayed throughout the course of her military career and beyond earned her the respect and trust of her peers. It has also inspired her subordinates to work hard, take risks, and behave with integrity themselves.

Given what women, including Lieutenant General Kennedy, are up against around the world, it's astounding how much they have accomplished. Despite being ignored, dismissed, even beaten down, women have honed their many psychological strengths, breaking societal chains that have bound them for generations, emerging as superb leaders, entrepreneurs, innovators, and players of the game.

Claiming Their Strength

Over the last few decades, women's determination has led them to grab hold of opportunities to grow in strength, often by pursuing academic degrees. The result is a tectonic shift in the geography of education. For several years, girls and women have been outpacing boys and men on most indicators of academic success. Less than one hundred years ago, female students had to obtain permission to attend lectures and were not allowed to take degrees. Between 1998 and 2005, over 300,000 more women applied for university places than men, and today, girls have all but reached the U.K. government's target of 50 percent going on from school to study for a degree, while only 38 percent of boys go on to higher education at university.[3]

Women aren't just going to university in greater numbers than men; once they are there, they are performing better by many measures. The 2005 National Survey of Student Engagement, which questioned ninety thousand students at 530 institutions in the United States, found that women spent significantly more time than men preparing for class, while men spent significantly more time than women socializing or relaxing. Other studies find that women are less likely than men to skip classes and more likely to complete their homework and turn it in on time. As a result, women are getting better grades than men, are more likely to finish college once they start, and are earning a disproportionate number of honors degrees at universities. Recent statistics show that in the U.K., female graduates are more likely to enter employment after graduating.[4]

A great example of the ambition and drive of today's college women is Teresa, a senior at Yale who does research with my lab group. Teresa comes from a large, close-knit family in California. Neither of her parents went to college; instead they supported their seven children by running a small grocery store, doing housecleaning, and gardening. Fortunately, early in elementary school, teachers recognized Teresa's intellectual strengths and encouraged her to do well in school. She did so well that she earned a full scholarship to Yale. Still, she had to work to help pay for books and living expenses—this was how I was lucky enough to meet Teresa. She applied for a job in my research group to help run studies and enter data.

Teresa is a poised, articulate, and engaging young Hispanic woman with long brown hair and piercing brown eyes, and when she walked into my office for an interview, within five minutes I knew I wanted to hire her. In the two years she's worked with my group, Teresa has become central to much of what we do. Her ability to connect with people on a deep level has made her a tremendous interviewer, even with those with significant mental health problems. Her integrity, patience, and persistence have meant we could hand her even the toughest jobs and know they would be done well and on time. Her intellect and ambition made me leap at the chance when she asked if she could do an original research project for her senior thesis. Teresa's drive and motivation have enabled her to overcome significant economic disadvantages to become a valued student and colleague at one of the nation's top universities.

Teresa embodies the new image of women's strength. She is entirely focused on what she wants to do and how she can do it, not on the facts of her background that have historically held women like her back. When she sees an obstacle, she uses all her mental strengths to march right around it. She is tough as leather, but as sensitive and insightful as the best therapist.

It's not only college-age women who are seeing themselves as powerful, however. Research by psychologists Abigail Stewart and Carol Ryff shows that most middle-age and older women have a deep and abiding confidence in their identity, their values, and their purpose in life.[5] They accept themselves and reject social pressures to think and act in certain ways, instead pursuing their interests and exercising their talents creatively.

The stereotype of women as unsure of themselves and their contributions, unwilling to lead others, and vulnerable under stress is just plain wrong, at least for the vast majority of women. Most women are secure in their beliefs and their goals. Every woman leads in a thousand ways every day, and women's styles of leadership are the most effective style for today's global economy. Women are extraordinarily resilient in even the most dire circumstances, rising above adversity to create powerful networks for change and to bring meaning to their lives and the lives of others.

The Evolution of a Revolution

Ironically, women's strengths have developed not only in spite of but in some ways as a result of the tribulations and challenges they have faced over the millennia. Because women have not had the physical strength or social status in our evolutionary history to demand that their voices be heard or their needs respected, they have had to develop ways to survive and thrive that have not required brute force or social power. Today, women and their children comprise the majority of people in poverty around the world, and across history women have not been in positions to demand basic resources. So they have had to become extremely clever at taking what they have and making it work. As a result, they have developed strengths for seeing many ways around their goals, focusing on getting a job done rather than on accumulating power, and on remaining persistent and optimistic even when things look bleak.

Because women haven't had the physical strength to fight off attackers, they have learned to mobilize friends and family to protect them. Because women have been the primary caregivers to their offspring for thousands of years, they have developed unique emotional and interpersonal skills that have helped ensure their offspring's survival. Women's impressive ability to read and understand others' emotions may have emerged from their need to anticipate possible violence from males and to protect themselves and their children.

If women's psychological strengths have evolutionary roots, this means they have been present for thousands of years. Why then has it taken so long for women's strengths not only to become visible but also to become powerful instruments of social change? There have been, of course, many battles fought, particularly over the last century, to gain women the opportunity to exercise their strengths. Psychologist Wendy Wood of Duke University argues that new technologies also played a critical role in the emergence of women's strength.[6] Washing machines, refrigerators, and microwaves have remarkably reduced the burden of keeping house and feeding a family since our grandmothers' day. Contraceptives have allowed women to avoid pregnancy if they wish. In turn, the freedom and opportunity created by these technological changes have allowed women to develop their many talents more fully. Indeed, technology has allowed women to become much more assertive over the last fifty years as they have entered the labor force, achieved more advanced education, and delayed marriage and childbirth to establish careers, according to research by psychologist Jean Twenge of San Diego State University.[7] In other words, social changes seem to be leading women to be more willing to claim their full rights to status and power, and to see themselves as competent beings. In addition, as it has become more common for girls to grow up with mothers who were working, had advanced education, and were themselves more assertive, girls have become much more assertive and have come to expect gender equality.

In her book *No Turning Back*, Stanford historian Estelle Freedman argues that the political and personal freedoms women have gained over the last century have forever changed women's expectations for themselves and other women. Freedman quotes Gertrude Mongella, secretary general of the Fourth World Conference on Women, held in Beijing in 1995, as saying, "A revolution has begun and there is no going back. There will be no unraveling of commitments—not today's commitments, not last year's commitments, and not the last decade's commitments. This revolution is too just, too important, and too long overdue."[8]

I am not arguing that women are superior to men. To quote the late Israeli prime minister Golda Meir, "Whether women are better than men, I cannot say—but I can say they are certainly no worse." Instead, I want to spotlight women's many gifts, so that society and individual women can embrace and benefit from them, rather than deriding these very talents and qualities as "playing like a girl." It is time to reverse the meaning of "playing like a girl" so that it becomes a compliment rather than an insult. It is time to overturn the cultural stereotype of women as less than men. It is time for society to recognize and make the most of the extraordinary strengths of women for the betterment of everyone. And it is time for women to embrace and employ their talents so that they can reach their full potential.

Of course, some women are stronger than others. As you are reading about the strengths of women, exceptions may come to mind: "Oh my [sister/mother/daughter/friend] is not strong like that!" You may also object that you don't have a particular strength, or many of the strengths. Historically, women have been very hard on themselves, focusing on their weaknesses, ruminating about every flaw in their character, talents, and appearance. The media perpetuates this obsession with flaws by publishing endless articles and books on what's wrong with women and how to fix it. Even when a woman exercises her strengths, she may question whether she has the right to do so, and what other people will think of her for being strong. Advertising executive and author Lois Wyse said, "Men are taught to apologize for their weaknesses, women for their strengths."

When you hear about the amazing strengths of women, you may be inclined to say, "Oh, I could never be that strong." Or you may think that even if you had the strength to fight back from adversity, or you learned to overcome your fears and stand up to be counted, you'd have little to offer—few talents, skills, or opinions that anyone would find valuable. You're wrong.

I challenge you, as you are reading this book, to focus on your strengths, and the strengths of the women you know, rather than on weaknesses. Notice how those strengths play out in small ways and big ways, and notice how much they affect other people. *Become* a woman of strength, build your strengths so that you *can* do anything you want to do with your life, and be brilliant in whatever you do.

Every woman was born with something to give, to her family, her community, and her world. In small ways and in dramatic ways, all women give every day—they give of their love and nurturance, their wisdom, and their abilities. As Audre Lorde said: "When I dare to be powerful, to use my strength in service of my vision, then it becomes less and less important whether I am afraid."[9]

Being as Powerful as You Can Be

As women take up Lorde's challenge and dare to be powerful, they are sparking a revolution in the very concept of what it means to be a woman. Gone are the days when women were defined by what they are *not*: not physically powerful, not mentally tough, not ambitious—not men. Instead, women are now defining themselves in terms of what they *are*: mentally adept, solid and assured, emotionally astute, and interpersonally skilled. They are bringing these strengths to their care of their families, to the marketplace, to community service, and to political leadership. And the world is a better place for it.

Every day, women rise above tired old ways of solving problems and relating to people to create wholly original solutions and relationships that improve their lives and those of people around them. Companies are making more money because women are bringing to the global economy their skills at working with diverse populations and at seeing many pathways to their goals. Communities and nations are recognizing the integrity and transformational leadership style of women and calling upon them to lead them into progressive change.

Women exercise their strengths most often in the context of their families and close relationships. They find creative solutions for their family's problems. They bring enormous patience and empathy to their relationships. They navigate the emotional upheavals of raising children and sustaining marriages, usually with deftness and success. Close relationships thrive because women bring their mental, identity, emotional, and relational strengths to every interaction, building, nourishing, and relishing in love and in growth.

This revolution spotlights women's strengths, not their weaknesses. Rather than focusing on the obstacles to their progress, women of the revolution deftly go over, under, and around these obstacles. They are not concerned with *what* women should or should not be doing. (Have children or not? Join the army? Be national leaders?) Instead, women of the revolution are concerned with *how* women can do anything they want and need to do.

This is the "how to" book of this revolution. I will shine a bright light on the extraordinary strengths women are bringing to bear to change the world in increasingly powerful ways. Women have always had these strengths. But thanks to the liberation our foremothers won for us over the last century, and thanks to freedoms created by technology, women are now flowing through the doors of opportunity and showing up in boardrooms, parliaments and congresses, service organizations, and educational settings. As women exercise their strengths in these venues, the eyes of the world are adjusting to the new vision of women as strong, clever, insightful, and inspiring. It's taking some time for the world to get a clear picture of women of the revolution. But I aim to help by documenting the ways women are redefining themselves and transforming the world through their strengths. In the meantime, I intend to give women the tools to claim their strengths and use them to live their lives to the fullest in whatever venues they choose.

Every woman was born with the capacity to be strong, including you. No matter how beaten down or weak you feel, I can help you build your mental, personal, emotional, and relational strengths so that you have the power to exercise your talents, pursue your interests, and express your opinions—at home, in your community, and in your workplace. This book is chock full of tools to build your strengths, exercises that any woman can do by herself or in the company of friends. Some of them may be difficult, many will be fun. But all will bring you to a place where you feel alive and vibrant and powerful.

Every woman deserves to recognize and claim her many strengths so that she can capitalize on the power that is within her. We need all women at the table of leadership and change, including you. There is too much to do, too many problems to fix, too many wonderful new things to accomplish. You don't have to aspire to have power and influence, but we can't waste what you have to bring to the table.

So join me at this table of strength—strength that will set you free to give all you have and to enjoy life to its fullest. A place is set for you. You are welcome, you are needed, and you will enjoy taking your place there.

ONE

The
Unique Strengths
of Women

2.

Genius Redefined: Understanding Women's Mental Strengths

My grandmother Geneva raised thirteen children during the Great Depression. My grandfather's job on a farm in rural Illinois brought in some cash, but not nearly enough to feed and clothe their large brood. When they were lucky and got a scrawny chicken to slaughter, Grandma Geneva would somehow get three meals for fifteen people out of that chicken. She'd combine a little bit of meat with vegetables from her garden to make casseroles or soups. She'd boil the backs of the chicken for hours to extract every bit of flavor and nutrient from them. In addition to her garden, Grandma Geneva would troll along the railroad tracks near their house to find wild asparagus and black-berries. She'd take some of the kids mushroom-hunting in the local woods. She would make whole meals out of dandelion greens, wild onions, and leftover pork fat. She was a better survivalist than "Bear" Grylls—she did it for fifteen people.

Of Grandma Geneva's thirteen children, nine were girls. Think about this—that means nine weddings to pay for. How in the world did she and my grandfather pay for nine weddings? Grandma Geneva was proud, but she wasn't stupid. She knew there are many things in this life you can't do on your own, and you have to know when to ask for help. She taught her children that families are interdependent and family members must be there for one another, in whatever ways are necessary.

The siblings who were working chipped in for other wedding costs. The daughters also chose the kind of men who would not only help pay for their own weddings but would step up, lend a hand, and do what needed to be done for the family. As the years went on, and Grandma and Grandpa grew more frail, my uncles and aunts stepped up again and again, fixing Grandma and Grandpa's old house, helping to pay their bills when the Social Security checks were spent, and caring for Grandma's and Grandpa's physical needs when they each developed cancer. In the years since Grandma Geneva's death, these uncles and aunts, and the dozens of cousins they produced, have continued to care for one another in a network of interdependence that will go on for many generations. Because my grandmother gave herself and her talents to her children fully, but also instilled the fundamental principle that "you help each other any way you can," she created a huge network of support, first for herself and my grandfather, and then for her hundreds of offspring and the hundreds of other people their lives touched.

The first time I took my husband to a get-together of my Grandma Geneva's family, he pulled me aside and said, "There are so many people here, and there's so much going on, but it's so calm!" At that gathering, there were forty aunts and uncles, fifty-three cousins, forty-five spouses of cousins, and a few dozen children of the cousins. People were cooking food, playing with children, fixing broken toys, and sharing stories. Grandma Geneva's offspring are generally very busy and productive, but they don't call attention to themselves. They get things done, but don't worry about getting credit for it, just like Grandma did.

Often when you see photos of families from the Great Depression era, you see sad, undernourished kids. When I flip through photos of my Grandma Geneva's family, I see happy, vibrant children growing up secure in the fierce love of their parents. My grandmother found ways not only to feed and clothe her children despite abject poverty but also to ensure they got an education and developed identities marked by self-respect, concern for others, and integrity. My mother and her siblings revered their mother for her ingenuity in triumphing over the massive hardships of the Depression through cleverness, creativity, and sheer determination.

I'd say Grandma Geneva was pretty smart. Not the kind of smart that is measured on intelligence tests or the SATs. Indeed, she had little formal schooling, so I'm not even sure she could have read the questions on such tests, let alone answer them. But Grandma Geneva took the hand life dealt her and used all her mental strengths to conquer obstacles and provide for her family. She kept going even when the conditions seemed hopeless, because she wanted—she *had* to ensure that her children were healthy and growing into the best people they could be. She asked for help when she needed it, and created a culture of caring that empowered her and her family to accomplish much more than she could have done on her own. She never asked for thanks or praise for all her efforts, and she raised children who also focused on doing what needed to be done for each other rather than on being noticed for their good works.

Women are smart in the ways that Grandma Geneva was smart. They bring tremendous mental strengths to what they do in each day, effectively fixing problems, serving other people, and building their own lives. Like Geneva, women find novel, creative ways to accomplish their goals given whatever circumstances they find themselves in. They don't get distracted by issues of who gets credit for solving a problem—they just solve the problem and get on with things. They keep going with a potent determination to get the job done no matter what. They make use of other people's talents and skills in a synergistic way that leads to the best possible solutions to problems.

Mental Strength vs. Social Status

Women's mental ingenuity and toughness hasn't been recognized traditionally. If you ask people, particularly middle-aged and older adults, whether men or women are mentally stronger, they will likely reflect on which sex is more established in positions of power and influence, whether serving as government leaders or corporate executives (men); prestigious academic "thought leaders" (men); or strong-minded, clever, and resolute media "personalities" (men). And they will probably conclude that men are mentally stronger. Of course, there are many reasons other than mental capability that men are more likely than women to be in top government, corporate, and academic positions, including vast historical differences between men's and women's access to education, and outright prejudice against women leaders.

But around the globe—if not always in the world of the top-dollar media or the sequestered corporate office or the isolated ivory tower—women steadfastly and adroitly solve problems and lead others into better lives every day. If they can't access positions of official power, they go through the back door to get what they want. As historian Estelle Freedman documents, for centuries women who saw needs for social change but were denied access to elected office or other sources of power organized other women to create change.[1] Women have founded hundreds of non-governmental organizations and social action groups to fight for basic resources, justice, and peace. Let me cite just a few examples.

Women for Women International is a women-led group that helps women around the world who have lost everything to war and conflict.[2] After the women in their programs are provided financial aid for food, water, medicine, and shelter, they are given training in leadership skills and vocational and technical skills. The aim is to help women gain a sustainable, independent life, and to bring women's voices into leadership positions in their communities and countries. In the devastated country of Rwanda, over fifteen thousand women have graduated from Women for Women International's training program, and today 41 percent of Rwandan businesses are owned by women.

Small groups of women often come together in the midst of personal tragedy to fight for change, and when their wisdom and courage catches the media's and public's attention, a larger social movement emerges. When widows of men killed in the 9/11 attacks believed the government wasn't telling the full story of the intelligence failures that led to their husbands' deaths, they organized to fight for an independent commission to investigate how 9/11 happened—the 9/11 Commission was the result of their efforts.

CodePink is a U.S.-based group of women that organized in 2002 to oppose the invasion of Iraq; since then, they have held annual Mother's Day rallies across the street from the White House; sent peace delegations to Iraq, Pakistan, Turkey, and several other nations; and worked to elect officials who will commit to pushing for peace and social justice legislation.

In the 1990s, four Israeli women who had sons serving in Lebanon organized to protest the "silent war" Israel had been waging for over a decade. Founder Rachel Ben Dor asked, "Why should we send our children to die because our leaders can't solve our problems by talking?"[3] Calling themselves simply The Four Mothers Movement, they picketed the Israeli defense ministry and organized a letter-writing campaign that eventually collected over twenty-five thousand signatures. The group grew to include several hundred citizens from all walks of Israeli life, including ex-soldiers, and met weekly with Knesset members and other public officials. The Four Mothers convened intensive discussions with the Israeli prime minister and defense minister, and their persistence helped lead to a shift in public opinion about the occupation of Lebanon. During the subsequent campaign for prime minister, the Labor Party's candidate, Ehud Barak, announced that if elected he would withdraw troops from Lebanon. He won in a landslide, and Israel's troops were fully withdrawn by May 2000. In each of these cases, women ignored arguments that there was nothing they could do to change how their government or communities were behaving. They banded together and recognized one another's talents, came to mutual decisions about what changes they wanted made, and then designed clever, novel means to achieve those changes.

Over the last generation, the world has begun to appreciate women's mental adroitness, and women are literally changing the face of power in business and academia, mobilizing their tremendous mental strengths to do things differently, and better. As we saw earlier, women now hold approximately 46 percent of managerial and administrative business titles in the United States—and while still short of the proportion of women in the country, it's getting closer! Women represent over 40 percent of the academic staff in higher education institutions, with similar figures in the United States. From 2006 to 2008, the percentage of female professors in higher education institutions in the U.K. rose from just below sixteen percent to almost nineteen percent.[4]

We still have barriers to cross and ceilings to crack, however. The face of power at the very top of corporations and government remains, for the most part, a male face. Only fifteen of the Fortune 500 companies are run by women. The U.K. is also behind the U.S. in terms of women-led businesses. In order to match the level of women-led businesses in the United States, the U.K. would have an additional 900,000 business and 150,000 start-ups every year.[5] Despite the gains in Congress and governor's mansions across the nation, the percentage of women running for these top elected positions in the U.S. has gone down compared to the 1990s.[6] Female representation in the U.K. government still has a long way to go: in 2009 under the Labour government there were only 126 female MPs out of a possible 645 seats in the House of Commons.[7]

We need more women wielding power and influence because women bring a distinct set of mental strengths to problem solving, a set of strengths that is redefining what we mean by mental power and intelligence. Moreover, we need more women to recognize and accept their own mental strengths so that they can move forward toward their goals, grow and thrive as individuals, and give their best to those they love.

The New Meaning of Smart

For too long, we have confused intelligence with assertiveness. Boys speak up more in the classroom, and that leads boys and girls (and their teachers!) to infer that boys are smarter. Men come forward with proposals to solve problems faster and more assertively than women, and this makes men appear to be more capable as problem solvers. But just because you are willing to put yourself and your ideas out there doesn't mean you are smart—it just means you have the confidence to promote yourself whether or not you are correct. In 1992, Jane Campbell defined the "male answer syndrome"—the tendency of men to state a confident answer to any question, no matter how much they know about the topic. A friend of mine calls it "being wrong with authority." Confusing assertiveness and confidence with intelligence ignores the real stuff of mental power.

We also confuse intelligence with what intelligence tests measure. Intelligence tests were designed to assess skills that make for success in school, such as the ability to analyze and solve abstract problems (such as math or logic problems), to have a large vocabulary, and to read and understand complex passages of literature. These are clearly important skills, and women and men generally get about the same overall scores on these tests. The bigger issue, though, is in the *definition* of intelligence represented by IQ tests. As useful as abstract reasoning and vocabulary are in some settings, they are not the only ways, or even the best ways, people can be smart.

In recent years, psychologists have been blowing old-fashioned notions of intelligence out of the water. Psychologist Robert Sternberg is one of the champions for a new view of intelligence. He argues that intelligence isn't just what intelligence tests measure and it isn't something you are either born with or not. Instead, he says:

> Intelligence is the ability to achieve success in life, given one's personal standards, within one's sociocultural context. One's ability to achieve success depends on one's capitalizing on one's strengths and correcting or compensating for one's weaknesses through a balance of analytical, creative, and practical abilities to adapt to, shape, and select environments.[8]

That is, being a successful person—making a living, getting along with others, doing things that are important in your community—depends on using whatever you have to deal with the situations you find yourself in, while also living in sync with your personal values. By Sternberg's definition, it's obvious that my Grandma Geneva was a genius in handling the problems of her life, even though she was barely able to read.

Sternberg and his colleagues have conducted studies around the world, tracking successful people in other cultures (who don't score high on American intelligence tests) and documenting the resourceful strategies they have developed to thrive in their natural environment. For example, villagers in Kenya fail miserably on American IQ tests, but they build up an intricate knowledge of herbal medicines, which are critical to their survival. Similarly, Brazilian street children cannot do math problems that children with formal schooling can do, but those same street kids have been observed running successful businesses, selling trinkets and paying bribes to local officials. These businesses require them to do quick computations while negotiating cash transactions, a skill many Americans seem to be losing as they adopt the habit of paying electronically.

Sternberg's examples are about how different cultural contexts require and create different mental strengths and intelligence. Women have developed mental strengths in response to their specific cultural lives, too. In this chapter, we'll explore the specific mental strengths of women. Research has identified at least four such strengths:

- Women are able to see many ways to use existing resources to accomplish their goals. They recognize that there is not just one way to do things, and they value novel, innovative approaches to problem solving.
- Women stay focused on getting a job done rather than being obsessed with getting their way. This keeps their minds open to the opinions and ideas of others, and they are willing to go with others' solutions even if it means others get credit and they don't.
- Women know when to ask for help and aren't afraid to do so. As a result, they don't stay stuck for long, trying to prove they "can do it by myself" and instead capitalize on the combined strengths of everyone around them.
- Women remain optimistic and persistent even when things look bleak. They keep looking for solutions when others give up and implement these solutions with confidence and hope.

Problem-Solving Gymnastics

At the heart of Robert Sternberg's definition of successful intelligence is the ability to use whatever you have at your disposal to do whatever you have to do—feed your children and yourself, make a living, pursue your interests, literally build a life. Intelligence involves being able to see problems differently from others, and to be willing to use your own judgment rather than going along with the crowd. Business gurus have called this "thinking out of the box" or engaging in a "paradigm shift." Evidence shows that women were exercising this mental strength for years before the business gurus gave it a flashy new label.

Women have had to confront seemingly immovable walls and complex obstacles to reaching their personal goals. What do they do? They perform mental handsprings over the walls. They cartwheel around them. They find a pole and vault gracefully over. Most women are able to coordinate and manage their goals, interests, and needs with the circumstances in which they find themselves, even when those circumstances are not optimal.

Women have become mentally flexible, in part, because over history they often have not had their own resources in terms of money, or access to education, power, or even freedom. Instead they have had to rely on whatever resources have been given to them, mostly by the men in their lives, to achieve what they want. Some women have garnered tremendous power and resources through men. Many have had to scrape by with much less than they needed, however, either because their men didn't have resources themselves or because they were abandoned by their husbands, partners, or family members. Thus they had to find a way to survive and help their children survive with less than they needed—as my Grandma Geneva did. They have had to find ways of building fulfilling lives despite being denied access to education and employment.

Getting by with what you have and dealing with the hand life deals you is something women are still doing today. For example, consider the women who become single mothers after divorce, like Jean, a twenty-four-year-old redhead with two small children in suburban

Wisconsin. When she was a senior in high school, Jean had dreams of becoming an elementary school teacher and had earned good enough grades to make it into college. She often imagined herself standing in front of a room of fresh-faced youngsters, patiently explaining the day's math lesson while some kids listened intently and some squirmed in their seats.

But Jean was also infatuated with Tom, a tall, blond point guard on her high school's basketball team. After dating for a couple of months, Jean and Tom became intimate and soon Jean found herself unexpectedly pregnant. Jean didn't know Tom very well, but her small-town upbringing, as well as her desire to believe in Tom, led her to agree to marry him. Their daughter, Julia, was born two months later.

Julia had little wisps of light red hair, blue eyes, and enormous pink cheeks. Although Jean had shelved her dreams of going to college to become a teacher for a while, she was in heaven every time she cradled Julia in her arms. Her relationship with Tom wasn't so heavenly, however. He had taken a job in an auto parts store and hated everything about it. When he came home at night, he was tired, irritable, and ready for a drink. Tom seemed to have little interest in Julia, regarding her as a loud annoyance. The fights between Tom and Jean became more frequent, as did Tom's drinking bouts. Within a year, Tom had gotten fired for drinking on the job and the couple had no money.

Jean realized she had to free herself from Tom, for her own sake and Julia's. One night when Tom was out drinking, she bundled up Julia, packed some clothes and left, for good. She borrowed a few hundred dollars from her parents, who couldn't afford to give her more, and found a tiny apartment for her and Julia. She made the apartment cozy and workable with borrowed furniture and dishes from her parents and friends. It wasn't ideal, but it was a start.

Unfortunately, Jean's high school education meant she could only get a low-paying job. By the time she paid for day care, the rent, and the debt that Tom had amassed on their joint credit cards, Jean's income was gone. This definitely wasn't how Jean had envisioned her life unfolding—she had never imagined being a single mother in difficult financial straits—and she knew that she could do better, for herself and for her daughter. Jean quickly adapted to her new circumstances, identifying every student loan and scholarship that might help her get more education. She found a new job as a transcriptionist that allowed her to stay home with Julia, and scraped and saved every possible penny. When she felt defeated, she would go into Julia's bedroom at night, taking inspiration as she gazed at her baby's beautiful face, saying, "I promise you, my little angel, we are going to be okay. I can do this—I have to do this, for you and for me."

Within a year, Jean was enrolled in a teachers' college on a scholarship and holding down a part-time job as a research assistant for one of her professors. Julia stayed in the co-op day care on the college campus while Jean worked or went to classes, and they had enough money for the two of them to get by. Jean graduated in three years and landed a job as a fourth-grade teacher in her hometown elementary school. Thus, by adapting to unforeseen circumstances without losing her core sense of self, Jean managed to educate herself, find a rewarding job, attain financial stability, and provide a secure life for her young daughter, all in the space of a few years. Rather than fixating on how her life had gone wrong, Jean stayed mentally flexible, ingeniously using the available resources to rebuild her life.

Mental flexibility is a major reason that women are gaining leadership positions as the economy becomes more global. According to a recent survey of business and government leaders, women are better able to ignore rules and traditional ways of doing things.[9] They are more willing to take risks and try innovative ways of dealing with issues. As Connie Jackson, chief executive of St. Bartholomew's and the Royal London Charitable Foundation, said, "As a leader, there are times you need to risk going in a direction that no one else has ever taken before. You have to step out there and follow the path you think is right."

Women business leaders don't tend to be wedded to standard business practices and are able take into account the perspectives of diverse cultures in creating and marketing products. Because women have not been in positions of power for long, few of us have developed a rigid sense of how people are *supposed* to do things. That gives women the freedom to find creative solutions to problems, to buck "the rules" of "how everyone does it."

Take, for example, Indra Nooyi, who was promoted from strategist to CEO of the multibillion-dollar firm PepsiCo. Nooyi, an Indian-born dynamo in her fifties, is positioning PepsiCo for growth in China, the Middle East, and India. Most CEOs approach globalization with the question "How can I sell what I have to these people?" Instead, Nooyi asks the novel question "How can I make what other cultures want to buy?" Rather than trying to find slogans and price points that will sell quintessential American products such as Pepsi and Lay's potato chips to people in very different cultures, Nooyi is learning about the regional tastes for snack foods and creating new products that satisfy and lure those tastes: lentil snacks in India, a white mushroom–flavored version of Lay's in Russia. She has also acquired small companies that understand local tastes and produce foods to fit those tastes, such as juice drinks in Eastern Europe or granola bars in New Zealand. As a result of Nooyi's innovative approaches to global marketing, first as market strategist and now as CEO, PepsiCo's sales have increased an average of 8.4 percent in recent years, compared to 6.5 percent for Coca-Cola.

Mental Strength #1: Women find many pathways to accomplish their goals; they are neither conformist nor rigid. They take whatever resources are at their disposal and use them to solve problems and create a fulfilling life.

Getting It Done, Not Just Doing It My Way

Because most women haven't yet had the opportunity to become accustomed to holding positions of authority, they don't process situations in terms of gaining or maintaining power. Because they are not preoccupied by grabbing influence, women are able to imagine a wider range of solutions to problems, some of which might even require that they relinquish a measure of control. They don't see accepting others' solutions to problems as a threat or a defeat—they see the value in others' opinions and ideas and are willing to go with them if that's what makes the most sense. As a result, solutions can reflect the best option of several, or the collective wisdom of the group, rather than the individual opinion of one person.

Across a variety of educational institutions, businesses, and volunteer or nonprofit organizations, studies show that women are more likely than men to adopt a democratic leadership style, working cooperatively with others to complete projects and goals. They are more likely to see the value in others' opinions, to actively solicit those opinions, and to engage in give-and-take toward an optimal, mutually satisfying outcome. They don't get hung up on being right or getting credit. Instead, they focus on finding the best possible way to solve problems.

Men, on the other hand, are more likely than women to adopt an autocratic leadership style, focused on accumulating and exercising power—the old "command and control" style of leading.[10] People with an autocratic leadership style insist that they know what's best and that everyone else march in line. Dissenters are not only ignored, they may be punished. If the autocratic leader happens to be a genius, this may work out fine, but in most cases the narcissism of autocratic leaders results in defeat, even tragedy, for them and for people around them.

Government may be the place that most needs the leadership style of women. Successful governing requires individuals with different talents and knowledge bases, and who, representing different constituencies, come together to forge solutions for the common good. The common good often loses out, however, to power grabbing and influence peddling. Moreover, even government leaders who intend to serve their public are not as effective if they take an autocratic approach to governing, always assuming that their way is the right way and everyone else has to march in line, because they don't make use of the talent around them to find optimal solutions.

Many women get into government because they are sick of the narcissistic, power-hungry ways of current government leaders. Traci

Wells decided to run for mayor of her medium-sized town in Iowa after a major snowstorm shut down all the roads. Her neighbor, seventy-six-year-old Gus, had a heart condition but insisted on getting out and shoveling his walk. To her horror, Traci looked out her kitchen window to see Gus collapse in his backyard. After quickly calling 911, Traci rushed next door to perform CPR until the ambulance came. The ambulance didn't come, though, and didn't come and didn't come. Finally, after nearly forty-five minutes, it arrived. Twenty minutes earlier, Gus had died in Traci's arms. "What the hell took you so long?" Traci said in a quivering voice through clenched teeth. The ambulance driver explained that many roads, even main roads, had not been plowed yet, and that they had had difficulty getting through five-foot snowdrifts to get to Gus's house.

Traci's sadness over Gus's death turned to fury when she learned later that day that the roads near the mayor's house had been some of the first to be plowed after the snowstorm, even before the main arteries of town. This mayor was well known for taking care of himself and his buddies first, whether it came to plowing roads or appointments to city jobs or contracts for city work. Traci had long thought someone should call this mayor on his influence peddling and nepotism, but most people were too afraid of retribution to do so. Traci didn't run a business and her husband worked in another town, thirty miles away, so she wasn't afraid of the mayor. She organized her friends and family, fellow church members, and Gus's family to start a letter-writing campaign to the local newspaper complaining about cronyism in city government. She went to town board meetings to question the mayor's proposals for new projects, asking why certain businesses seemed always to get the best city contracts.

Then she had the audacity to run for mayor against the incumbent. By the date of the election, most townspeople had heard about the mayor's shady dealings and knew Traci's name from her letters and opinion pieces in the local newspaper. She won the mayoral election by eleven percentage points.

One of Traci's first initiatives as mayor was to review the city's plans for emergency services. She appointed the chief of police, the fire chief, the director of the local hospital, and the director of city maintenance to evaluate the effectiveness of services and make recommendations for change. Within a couple of weeks, word came back to Traci that the meetings of this review panel had devolved into buck-passing on problems, with each member insisting his organization would need more money to improve the effectiveness of its emergency response. She got calls at all hours of the day and night from members of the panel, arguing for more resources and suggesting ways Traci's career might benefit from allying with them over the other department heads.

Traci attended the next meeting of the review panel. "Gentlemen," she began, "I know all of you have the best interests of our city at heart, and many ideas for how emergency services can be improved. As you know, the city does not have a surplus in its budget, and I ran on a platform of no new city taxes. As a result, we are going to have to improve services without spending more money. That means you are going to have to get creative in finding new ways to work more efficiently and effectively with each other. Now I have some ideas, but you all have more experience in your respective positions, so I want to hear your ideas. I will pledge to implement the two or three best plans that you develop to integrate your department's services with services of at least one other department to improve the overall quality of life in this city. I will implement no plans that involve giving just one department more resources."

The members of the review panel sat in stunned silence for a minute, then began to protest. Although Traci had to continuously reiterate her demands for cooperation, she cajoled several useful plans out of the review panel, including one for the integration of the city's services across several departments. Her work with the panel set a tone for all her other initiatives: she insisted everyone work toward shared goals and rewarded cooperation among city employees and contractors.

Of course, there are power-grabbing women as well as men who focus on the common good and not simply on the accumulation of power. And there are still male-dominated businesses in which co-operative, goal-oriented leadership is a disadvantage. Many a woman has had the experience of putting forward an innovative proposal for change in her business or community organization only to have some man claim credit for her idea. Indeed, as women have been fighting their way into positions of leadership and power in the last few decades, they have had to learn how to get credit for their ideas and their work.

Increasingly, however, leadership gurus, such as organizational psychologist Bernard Bass of the Center for Leadership Studies at Binghamton University in New York, are arguing that the modern economy requires leaders who can foster cooperation among employees and peers who come from different backgrounds and bring various types of expertise to the table.[11] Technology is moving too fast and customers are too diverse for any one leader to have everything it takes to succeed. Instead, leaders must bring together all the human capital under their leadership in a spirit of cooperation working toward common goals.

Women also bring an ability to focus on the task at hand rather than on wielding power to their approach to parenting. Raising children involves constant negotiation over independence and autonomy, over whose rules govern the household, and over standards of conduct. This is especially true when children become adolescents and the biological and social forces in their lives push them to defy rules and their parents' authority. Research by psychologist Lawrence Steinberg of Temple University finds that many fathers cope with this battle over authority by clamping down on the rules and getting more rigid in their assertion of authority; they deal with conflict by cutting off the conversation, using language such as "You'll do it because I said so!" Or they walk away and withdraw, avoiding conflict by becoming absent or silent. Mothers, on the other hand, are more likely to engage in give-and-take with adolescents; mothers will assert their authority as needed but are also willing to give their teenagers some room to grow and make their own mistakes, within certain boundaries.[12] One reason mothers are able to do this is because they are focused on helping their children navigate the pressures of adolescence and develop the ability to make good choices on their own rather than establishing who is boss.

This doesn't mean conflict does not exist between mothers and their teenagers. But many mothers are able to resist defining conflicts in terms of who is in charge, who wins, and who loses. This helps them stay more calm, more persistent, and more open to seeing the ways in which they can help their teenagers through the challenges of adolescence.

> **Mental Strength #2:** Women are goal-oriented. They work toward getting a job done, rather than getting their way.

Many Hands Make Light Work

Wendy, a vibrant forty-three-year-old woman, had been married to her husband for twenty-three years when she filed for divorce. The marriage had never been good. For years, he had cheated on her, been neglectful of her and their children, and occasionally had been abusive. Why didn't she leave him earlier? "I didn't want my kids growing up poor," she said. Her husband had a well-paying job and the kids were accustomed to a comfortable life. Wendy had no college education and, she felt, no marketable skills. She couldn't count on her husband supporting the kids if she left him. So she stayed until her oldest was off to college and the youngest was in high school. But after a long, nasty argument one day, she finally filed the divorce papers. "It was time," she said. "The kids were nearly grown, and I'd had enough."

To her surprise, Wendy found that the most difficult thing about being single was taking care of her house. Her husband had been wealthy enough that she had been able to hire others to do anything that needed to be done around the house. She had never unplugged a stopped-up sink, never dealt with a furnace that wouldn't work on a cold night. She no longer had money to hire repairmen, so she was on her own. How did she cope? She did what many women know to do at times like this—she gathered help and expertise from others.

Actually, Wendy had to create a completely new support network. Her husband didn't want their mutual friends and acquaintances to know that they were divorcing, and most of these people didn't know how to unplug a sink anyway, so they weren't an option. "Didn't really like those people," she said. So Wendy started going to Parents Without Partners (PWP) to meet others who were in similar life circumstances. Through PWP Wendy met men and women who were willing to help her learn the basics of taking care of a house, how to find affordable repair services, and the like. She had no problem calling any of these new friends to ask how you use a plunger to unplug a toilet, or what options you have when water is pouring into your basement during a rainstorm.

Wendy also solicited help in watching out for her younger daughter, Rochelle. Wendy had taken a job as a bookkeeper, so for the first time in Rochelle's life, no one was at home when she returned from high school in the afternoon. Neighbors alerted Wendy that Rochelle was bringing other teenagers home with her, and things seemed to be getting pretty wild, with loud music coming from the house and kids' cars screaming away from the house. So Wendy asked one of her neighbors, a woman she had become friends with, if she would pick up Rochelle from school in the afternoon and Rochelle could stay at the friend's house until Wendy could get home from work. In exchange, Wendy babysat her neighbor's two young children while the neighbor worked evenings as a waitress. Both women benefited, and Rochelle's behavior, and grades, soon stabilized.

Now let me be clear: Wendy is a woman with a great deal of personal pride. She has a strong sense of her own self-worth, which saw her through her terrible marriage and messy divorce. But she also knows when she needs help and is not afraid to ask for it. "It's just logic," she says. "I can't do everything myself and I am sure not going to let things fall apart when other people can help me!"

Much of the research on women's help-seeking has focused on battered women and has asked, "Why don't they seek help to get out of abusive relationships?" There are many answers to this question: battered women often fear that their batterers will kill them or their children if they try to leave, or like Wendy they don't want to plunge their children into poverty by leaving, or they don't understand that it is their right not to be battered. But many battered women do seek help to get out, even with these kinds of obstacles. Asking for help— whether in sharing responsibility for tasks or in tracking down expertise from others—is critical in every challenge in life, even those far less stressful and threatening than being in an abusive relationship. Women usually see no shame in asking for the help they need. This is one reason they are good at leading cooperative groups—they don't assume they know everything and empower others to contribute to problem solving.

Women's ability to ask for help has evolved over the millennia from the realities they have faced. Because women have not had the physical strength or social status over evolutionary history to demand that their voices be heard or their needs be respected, they have had to develop ways to survive and thrive that have not required brute force or social power. Because women haven't had the physical strength to fight off attackers, they have learned to mobilize friends and family to protect them, a strategy psychologist Shelley Taylor of the University of California, Los Angeles, calls "tend and befriend." This ability to recruit allies and supporters has evolved into a mental strength that helps women see when others have valuable resources they can draw upon, to form mutually beneficial alliances with these people, and know how and when to draw upon these alliances. This not only saves women's lives in some circumstances, as when women band together in groups to change laws and policies to protect them from violence, it also makes women great leaders in business and politics.

Nowhere is the benefit of women's strengths in cooperating with others for the mutual good better illustrated than in the village savings and loan associations that have emerged in developing countries around the world. These associations usually involve around thirty women from a remote village, who live in abject poverty. The women each chip in a small amount (for example, $2.50 in U.S. dollars) to a community pot, then make short-term loans from this pot to one another at a low interest rate. The women use the money to buy basic household goods and food, and to finance small businesses selling handmade goods and food in local marketplaces. CARE International initiated clusters of these groups in several countries in Africa; they soon became independent of CARE, and are thriving a decade later, with hundreds of thousands of members.[13] Together, the savings and loan associations pool millions of dollars, almost all of which is loaned out to members. The repayment rate is almost 100 percent, and the groups regularly turn a profit, which they pour back into their pot for loans.

Moreover, the quality of living for the women in these groups and their families has improved dramatically. Women who have previously been barely able to put food on the table are now sending their children to school, buying equipment to improve their production of food for their families and their businesses, repairing their houses, and hiring other people to help run their businesses. The rates of domestic violence have also declined in these families as women have gained monetary independence and power. Sarah Nangiro of the Nawokotelei Village Savings Association in Uganda says, "Initially, [my husband and I] used to have frequent quarrels and fights because whenever the child got sick or there was no salt at home, I would confront him to give me the money. He always tells me he lacks it. But now I can care for both the children and my husband."[14]

These groups are not restricted to women, but they are overwhelmingly populated by women. Women find the cooperative nature of the groups, the social cohesion and group support, highly attractive. They are satisfied with the small loans and able to use them creatively to accomplish their goals. Men, however, often get frustrated with the requirement that loan decisions be made by consensus, and believe they need larger loans. So men leave these groups more often than women do, and as a result don't benefit from the financial assistance they offer as much as women do.[15]

Mental Strength #3: Women tend to enlist other people's help, expertise, and ingenuity rather than insisting on doing everything themselves.

Optimism Over Obstacles

If my Grandma Geneva had taken a rational assessment of the chances her family would survive, let alone thrive, given the family's economic resources during the Great Depression, she would have thrown up her hands and given up. But she didn't. If she had simply put a happy spin on things, humming "Happy Days Are Here Again" and waiting for a solution to her problems, she would not have done too well, either. Instead, she remained determined and confident that she would find ways to feed her children and give them what they needed to become successful adults. She kept going into the woods and walking along the ditches beside the train tracks to search for food. She kept boiling that scrawny chicken even when it seemed to be picked clean.

This kind of stubborn optimism in your abilities is one of the strongest predictors of success in many walks of life. Renowned Stanford psychologist Albert Bandura has shown that self-efficacy—the belief that you can do what it takes to accomplish your goals—is critically important to success in school, in work, and in any task you take on. Similarly, thousands of studies have shown that people who believe in themselves even when things look bleak are more success-ful, have better emotional and physical health, and get along better with other people. Determined optimism is grounded in reality: it's the pursuit of a better outcome rather than a blind faith that things will somehow work out.

Given the lack of freedom and outright oppression women have faced over the ages, you may be taken aback to learn that women are highly optimistic and have a strong sense of self-efficacy and agency. Optimism has been key to women's survival when they have faced long odds, just as it was key to my Grandma Geneva's survival. Over the last few generations, women have been getting even more deter-minedly optimistic than they were in my grandmother's day. Psychologist Jean Twenge, the author of *Generation Me*, gathered data on nearly thirty thousand adults using questionnaires that measured "personal agency"—the belief that you can accomplish your goals despite obstacles. She found that women's scores on personal agency have been going up dramatically since the 1970s, and that men's and women's scores on agency were indistinguishable by the 1990s.[16]

Remaining optimistic and hopeful is especially important when you are facing a major tragedy or loss. You may feel as though your whole world has ended, as if there is no reason to go on living. You may have huge problems to overcome; for example, new widows must find ways to support themselves and their children financially, emotionally, and practically without the aid of their husbands. Yet remaining optimistic is critical to putting your life back together—it keeps you motivated and empowers you to make difficult choices and decisions.

A few years ago in California, my colleagues and I conducted a study of people who lost a loved one (a spouse, parent, sibling, or child) to cancer. My interviews with the participants revealed enormous resilience in most people—particularly in the women. Despite that their world had been upended by the death of a loved one, most of these women were confident they could bounce back and rebuild their lives. Rhonda, a forty-eight-year-old woman whose husband died of cancer, epitomized the optimistic women in our study:

> I think that when you lose a loved one, it's a rebirth for yourself. You can't always dwell on the loss of a loved one. You have to look forward to what you are going to do with your life now—who you are as a single person, which is very disturbing. Many people have been married much longer than I was, and they have to find out who they are. And it's a whole new experience, learning who you are as a single person.[17]

Although Rhonda deeply missed her husband, she chose to face her loss as a challenge and use it to grow personally. Like Rhonda, people in our study who were optimistic overcame their symptoms of grief and moved forward in their lives more quickly. This optimism is not just a "keep a happy face on" type of optimism. It's a fundamental belief in yourself and your ability to overcome obstacles that motivates you and broadens your opportunities and options. People who are optimistic literally see more solutions to problems, and see more ways around obstacles, compared to people who are not optimistic. This makes them more effective in overcoming tragedy.

In business and other leadership positions, women's optimism makes them more creative in generating innovative plans and novel approaches that others might dismiss as "impossible." The value of women's forward-looking, can-do attitude is now being recognized in the business world. The survey of international business and government leaders mentioned earlier also found that women tend to be very good at learning from disappointment and rejection and carrying on with an "I'll show you" attitude. As Libby Sartain, senior vice president of human resources at Yahoo, Inc., says, "If I make a mistake, I may be hard on myself initially, but then I quickly shake it off and figure out how to get beyond the situation. I don't let it undermine my confidence. In fact, sometimes when my back is against the wall, the best in me comes out."[18]

One of the most determinedly optimistic people I know is Nancy, the fifty-something chair of an academic department at a major university. Being chair of a department means that your colleagues are always wanting more resources (space, salary, students) and the university administration is always telling you there is no money for more resources. Although the response of many chairs is either to rant and rave at the administration or tell faculty they are being unreasonable, Nancy's unfailing response is, "Well, I think we can make this happen." When it became known that a prominent researcher at another institution was interested in moving to Nancy's department, the administration said "*Absolutely not*," because all the faculty positions were filled. Nancy, however, found a way to redefine the faculty positions so that somehow there was an opening. When the question arose where this researcher's lab space would be located, everyone said it was impossible to find new space. Nancy cajoled some of the most stubborn and intransigent members of the department into reconfiguring their labs and giving up some of their space for their new colleague. In short, Nancy never believes that there isn't *some way* around obstacles.

Nancy's story illustrates the synergy of women's mental strengths. Her optimism keeps her mind open to new opportunities and solutions when other people's minds would be closed. When the standard or usual way of doing things isn't working, Nancy looks for entirely new ways of approaching problems. In turn, her ability to see many pathways to her goals fuels her optimism. It's a lot easier to remain optimistic when you aren't stuck in "the way things are" and instead can redefine situations and take risks on novel solutions. Nancy also doesn't get stuck on doing things her way—she can reach out to others for ideas and assistance, and doesn't worry about getting the credit for having solved a problem. This opens myriad new possibilities for overcoming obstacles, which again makes it easier to stay optimistic.

Women who are optimistic tend to use more effective strategies for coping with difficult circumstances. They are more likely to accept the reality of their circumstances and do what they can to overcome their problems, and to reframe their problems as positively as possible. For example, psychologist Charles Carver and colleagues have found that among women undergoing surgery for breast cancer those who were more optimistic used more humor to cope and were better able to accept the reality of the situation. In turn, they were less distressed about the surgery and over the months following the surgery.[19] Optimists also take better care of themselves, following doctor's orders and engaging in healthy behaviors that fend off disease. In another study of breast cancer survivors, psychologist Vicki Helgeson and colleagues showed that women who retained a sense of optimism and personal control had better physical functioning in the four years after their surgery and chemotherapy treatments.[20]

Six years after she divorced her husband, after she had reestablished a home, gotten a job, and was on her feet financially, Wendy, the woman we met earlier, developed breast cancer. After having surgery, she went through radiation therapy five days a week for months, then months of chemotherapy. Although she had every right to say "Why me?" and fold under the seemingly never-ending stress that life had handed her, she instead said, "What am I going to do? Give up? *Of course not!*" Wendy sought multiple opinions on her treatments and then did what she had to do to defeat the cancer. She got through the treatment, bald and proud, and remained cancer-free for over a decade. Her cancer has returned in the last year, but her spirit and optimism are just as strong. Rather than wallow in frustration and despair that the monster she thought she defeated has returned, she sought out experimental therapies that so far have arrested the growth of her cancer. She and her new husband are maintaining an active life, planning new vacations, and enjoying every day to its fullest.

How can women remain so optimistic? They have a deep sense that their lives have meaning and purpose, and that it's their job to keep pursuing that purpose no matter what. For many women, that purpose is to care for their children. Grandma Geneva persisted because she had to, in order to feed her children. Wendy was determined to escape her abusive marriage and build a more positive life for herself and her children.

Inez McCormack is one woman who maintained a determined optimism through one of the most protracted, bloody, civil strifes in recent history, the conflict between Protestants and Catholics in Northern Ireland. The Troubles, as this conflict is known, took 3,468 lives between 1969 and 1996. The men leading the two sides would not talk with one another, would not even sit in the same room, and instead communicated through threats and violence. McCormack became involved in organizing women's civil rights marches, modeled on the nonviolent U.S. civil rights movement, to push for equality, human rights, and peace in Northern Ireland. She says, "In those days, equality in Northern Ireland was expressed as the need for 'one man, one vote.' It was women, on both sides of the sectarian divide, who finally began to say 'enough.' "[21] McCormack banded with other women to form Women Seen and Heard, to give voice to the stories of women's lives wrecked by the violence, death, and economic ruin caused by the Troubles. The only rule of this group was that anyone, from any background, would be included and treated with respect, regardless of their opinions. Later McCormack helped to form the Equality Coalition, which worked to get language of equality and human rights for all people into the Good Friday Agreement that officially ended the Troubles.

McCormack had every reason to be pessimistic about ending violence in her beloved Northern Ireland—it seemed everyone else in the world was pessimistic. But she rejected that pessimism and kept working with the belief, the hope, the confidence, that peace could be won.

Her determined optimism attracted hundreds of supporters, colleagues, and admirers who came together to make peace happen.

Building on the lessons learned from McCormack and women in Northern Ireland, the international group Vital Voices launched Women Leaders Building Peace and Prosperity to bring women's mental strengths to bear on protracted conflicts throughout the world.[22] One recent initiative is in the Middle East, where the Jewish-Arab conflict seems endless and hopeless to many. Women Leaders Building Peace and Prosperity helps to enhance and elevate the leadership skills of Jewish- and Arab-Israeli women to become agents of change in their communities. These courageous women reject the standoff mentality that has dominated the Jewish-Arab interactions for decades and insist that by employing women's mental strengths of determined optimism, working together for the good of all rather than for self-interest only, and finding novel ways around problems, even this conflict can be resolved.

Marie Curie, who fought discrimination because of her gender, endured the tragic accidental death of her husband, and went on to be the first person to win two Nobel prizes, summed up women's determined optimism well: "Life is not easy for any of us. But what of that? We must have perseverance and above all confidence in ourselves. We must believe that we are gifted for something, and that this thing, at whatever cost, must be attained. Perhaps everything will turn out very well at the moment when we least expect it."[23]

Mental Strength #4: Women never say never—they remain optimistic that obstacles can be overcome.

Women's exceptional mental strengths may or may not show up on IQ tests, but they show up in the tremendous effectiveness of women in all walks of life. Women build their own lives, even out of the ashes of despair or in the midst of deprivation. Women build the lives of others by honoring the talents and brilliance of people around them, and bringing these together to derive optimal solutions to problems. And women build their communities by persistently vaulting around obstacles, pursuing the common good via new and innovative pathways.

3.

Resilient Selves: Understanding Women's Identity Strengths

I was sitting in Salon Bellezza the other day, getting my hair done and flipping through the magazines, and I started getting anxious. The front covers screamed "10 Steps to a More Confident You!" "Modern Power Dressing!" "Avoid These Fashion Blunders!" Suddenly feeling inadequate and in need of help, I turned to the "10 Steps" article and read how insecure women are at work, in their relationships, and in bed. The article offered ten easy tips to conquer your womanly insecurities and be more self-assured. The "Power Dressing" article suggested that successful women still need designer fashions to overcome their self-doubts at work, and the "Fashion Blunders" article was meant to help women avoid horrific blows to their self-esteem caused by silly clothes choices. When I walked into the salon, I had been feeling pretty good about myself, despite my baggy jeans, frumpy T-shirt, and obvious need for a haircut. After flipping through the magazines, I wasn't so sure I was okay.

Women have gotten a bad rap. We constantly hear that women think poorly of themselves, that we have no self-confidence—or that whatever confidence we have comes from finding the perfect haircut or tailored power ensemble. If you Google "women and self-esteem" you'll get over seven million hits, most of them Web sites on the many sources of women's chronically low self-esteem, including poor body image, jealousy, and abuse. Since the so-called sexual revolution, women's identities have supposedly been marked by constant conflict: at work we feel like frauds and at home we feel like negligent mothers and wives. We are ambivalent over whether we want to be feminine or masculine, and ping-pong back and forth between the two gender roles. One day we are all gentleness, caring, and frills; the next day we stride through the world armored with assertiveness, self-promotion, and pantsuits. Women strain to balance their weak, split identities—conjuring up images of Sybil, and perhaps inspiring the character played by Toni Collette in the 2009 television series *The United States of Tara.*

According to the American Association of University Women (AAUW), women's weak identities emerge early in life. In 1991, the association released an influential study that declared that girls "lose their self-esteem on the way to adolescence."[1] Popular books such as Carol Gilligan's *In a Different Voice* and Mary Pipher's *Reviving Ophelia* claim that before adolescence, girls have a range of interests and strong opinions about the world. As they enter dating age, girls lose their "voice" as they confront demands to become subservient and silent in order to be attractive to boys.[2] They stifle their opinions, personalities, and interests and instead pretend to be what they think boys want them to be. In 2002, the Girl Scout Council launched a program to "address the critical nationwide problem of low self-esteem among adolescent and pre-adolescent girls."[3]

Women's True Self-Image

The problem is that none of this is true, at least for the majority of women, and hardly at all for girls of the twenty-first century. The AAUW study was refuted by subsequent research using large samples and better measures of self-esteem. One study involving over 100,000 participants found that girls' self-esteem does *not* fall precipitously at adolescence.[4] Although girls are more anxious about their appearance than boys, there are no differences between girls' and boys' self-esteem in academic matters. Girls have *higher* self-esteem than boys in moral and ethical matters, that is, in how they feel about their own behavior—and well they should. A 2008 survey of American youth by the Josephson Institute found that significantly more girls than boys agreed with the statement "It's not worth it to lie or cheat because it hurts your character."[5] In contrast, significantly fewer girls than boys agreed with the statements "In the real world, successful people do what they have to do to win, even if others consider it cheating" and "A person has to lie and cheat sometimes to succeed."

Claims that girls lose their voice in adolescence were based on Pipher's case studies of girls seeking psychotherapy for mental health problems, and on Gilligan's interviews with a select group of girls (without direct comparisons to interviews with boys). Psychologist Susan Harter of the University of Denver has conducted some of the only rigorous empirical work on "voice" in adolescent girls and boys.[6] She and her colleagues asked several hundred girls and boys, ages twelve to seventeen, to complete a questionnaire measuring confidence and voice. This questionnaire tapped the extent to which teenagers were able to "express their opinions," "share what they are really thinking," "let others know what is important to them," and "say what is on their mind" with peers, parents, and teachers. There were no significant differences in girls' and boys' scores on these measures. Further, the study found increases, instead of declines, in both girls' and boys' ability to express themselves as they got older.

Well, you might say things have changed, and although twenty-first-century girls now have a strong and positive identity, adult women—who grew up in a different cultural and work environment—still struggle with low self-esteem, little sense of mastery in the world, and ambivalence over whether they should act more feminine or more masculine. But the evidence does not support these claims, either. The majority of adult women define themselves as a comfortable mix of feminine and masculine traits.[7] Even most studies dating before 1970, as well as the more recent ones, failed to find substantive differences between women and men in self-esteem or a sense of control or mastery.[8] Anyone can find an individual study that shows men have higher self-esteem and sense of mastery than women, but when you average the dozens and dozens of studies that have been done, you'll find a minuscule difference between men and women, which depends on the measure of self-esteem or mastery you use. The phrase "much ado about nothing" comes to mind.

The mischaracterization of women's and girls' identities as weak and conflicted has many potential negative consequences. As psychologist Jean Twenge notes, the widespread belief that girls and women have low self-esteem and flawed self-concepts can set up negative expectations and self-fulfilling prophecies. When things go wrong—they aren't doing well at school or work, their relationships are going sour, they are distressed and don't know why—women may conclude it's because there is something wrong with their self-esteem and personality rather than because there is something wrong in their environment. This is what happened to me in the hair salon. I began to feel insecure and wondered if I needed psychotherapy or a fashion makeover, when what I really needed was to stop reading those articles.

The perception that women have weak identities and low self-esteem can also discourage the public at large from believing that women are fit for positions of leadership and power. "She'll blink when she stares down the enemy," they think, because women don't have the self-confidence to push their views and fight to the end when they have to. In their research on women in leadership roles, psychologists Alice Eagly and Steven Karau found that stereotypes of women as unassertive and lacking in confidence are particularly likely to keep women out of highly male-stereotyped leadership positions, such as those in the army.[9] Indeed, figures for 2006 show that there were only forty-three high-ranking female officers in the RAF; the Navy and the British Army combined.[10]

In the workplace, women's poor self-esteem is one of the excuses given for the continuing gender gap in wages and promotions. According to government figures published in the *Financial Times* magazine, women's earnings are, on average, about three-quarters of those of their male counterparts. The gap is widest in financial services, where women earn just under half of what men do.[11] Why? According to a 2003 cover story in *Fortune* magazine, it's because women shy away from the high-pressure, power-infused jobs that pay well, opting instead for the "softer" jobs that don't force them to assert themselves—or because they leave the workplace altogether to go raise kids.[12] Wage and promotion discrepancies can't be because of good old-fashioned discrimination, right? That's a thing of the past, right?

Not according to Lilly Ledbetter, who worked for nearly two decades at the Alabama Goodyear Tire and Rubber Company as an overnight supervisor. Ledbetter received a Top Performance Award in 1996 and regular pay raises throughout her career. She also experienced regular sexual harassment and discrimination, including requests for sexual favors from supervisors. Shortly before she was to retire, Ledbetter discovered that men doing the same job were being paid $4,286 to $5,236 per month, while she was being paid $3,727 per month. She filed a complaint with the Equal Employment Opportunity Commission, and was promptly reassigned by Goodyear to a job lifting heavy tires. Ledbetter sued Goodyear, who claimed that she was being paid less because of poor job performance. The jury didn't believe Goodyear, and Ledbetter won a settlement of $3.3 million, which was later reduced to $300,000. Subsequently, the Supreme Court ruled that Ledbetter was not entitled to compensation because she didn't file her complaint within 180 days after receiving her first discriminatory paycheck—which she had probably gotten more than twenty years earlier. In 2009, Congress passed, and President Barack Obama signed, the Lilly Ledbetter Fair Pay Act, allowing a worker to file a complaint up to 180 days after her *most recent* discriminatory paycheck. Sadly, Lilly Ledbetter's retirement benefits are based on the discriminatory pay she received from Goodyear, so she will continue to live paycheck to paycheck. Still, she said, "I told my pastor, when I die, I want him to be able to say at my funeral I made a difference."[13]

Flipping the Image

Given all they are up against, what really amazes me is that most women, like Lilly Ledbetter, are extraordinarily resilient. The truth is that women build identities that are even stronger than the pressures to devalue themselves. These identities then carry them through hard times and make them the exceptional business, community, and family leaders they are. My research reveals that:

- Women exhibit a strong, stable sense of self that isn't dependent on the circumstances in which they find themselves. Instead, women maintain a core sense of self, even when the external circumstances of their lives change drastically.
- Women create identities based on social context rather than social status, connecting to others in ways that bring meaning to their lives, expand their knowledge base and perspectives, and foster a broad network of care in times of need.
- Women build lives made of multiple roles. They recognize the importance of balancing relationships and work. As a result, they find myriad avenues for self-expression and social support, making them less vulnerable when things go wrong in one part of their life.

Bouncing Back (and Forth)—But Always Centered

Picture a rubber band. No matter how much it is stretched, squashed, or bent, it will always return to its original shape. Materials that have elastic properties are less likely to break when they are put under great strain. Women's sense of self is like that—able to incorporate changes or adapt to new circumstances while retaining, or after a time bouncing back to, their original shapes.

Where does this elastic identity come from? Over history, women developed flexibility in how they express their identity out of necessity. Women have often been thrust into circumstances they did not choose for themselves. For generations, and still today in some cultures, many women had no choice about the men they would marry or the places they would live; instead these choices were made for them by their families. Even when they have had complete independence in choosing a partner, more women than men feel they must subjugate their career to their partner's. A recent case in point is Michelle Obama, a graduate of Princeton University and Harvard Law School, and a wildly successful attorney. She resigned a high-paying, prestigious job as vice president for community and external affairs for the University of Chicago Hospitals to campaign for her husband, and then to serve as First Lady and "mom-in-chief" to her two young daughters. As she said in a 2008 interview, "As every working mother understands, there will always be hard choices that must be made to keep our families happy and whole. . . . Someone has to be focusing on the kids, making them feel safe and grounded, and that's me."[14] Granted, the position of First Lady provides Michelle Obama many opportunities to pursue goals that are important to her. But it's not as though it was entirely her idea to change her career path.

The fact that for centuries women have been accommodating the careers of their husbands has forced women to become exceptionally creative and resilient in adapting to new circumstances. Many women are tremendously skillful at fashioning a life wherever they find themselves and with whatever resources are at their disposal. Consider the experience of Marjorie Fairweather.

Marjorie was born in Melbourne, Australia, in 1918. During World War II, while employed as a secretary for the U.S. Air Force, she met a dashing young American officer named Ronald, and the two fell deeply in love. When the war ended, they married and moved to the United States, where Ronald pursued his Ph.D. in political science. In 1953, Ronald won a two-year research grant to study the politics of the Philippines for his dissertation, so off they went to Manila. Marjorie learned how to beat clothes with a wooden club in cold water to get them clean, as hot water and washing machines were not available. She learned to wind strips of linen into bandages while volunteering at the local hospital. She soaked up the culture around her, developing a reverence for how people can be deeply happy while being desperately poor.

In March 1956, Marjorie gave birth to their first child, Richard. Nineteen months later, Marjorie delivered twins, a boy and a girl. They were in the United States at the time, but when the twins were only six weeks old, and Richard was not yet two years old, Ronald took a position with the U.S. State Department and was assigned to Pakistan. He went ahead to begin his new duties, and two weeks later, Marjorie packed a truckload of diapers and formula and hopped on a military transport plane with her three young children for the two-day journey to Lahore.

Over the next fifteen years, Marjorie raised her three children in Lahore, Pakistan; Tehran, Iran; and Bangkok, Thailand, moving every few years with each of Ronald's diplomatic assignments. Each move required transplanting herself and her family to a new home in a new country where she didn't speak the languages or know the customs. Marjorie greeted these changes as adventures, with new people to meet and new cultures to learn. She refused to cloister her children in the American Embassy compounds as did most of the other State Department families. The children learned Pakistani, Farsi, and Thai, as well as English.

Throughout it all, Marjorie adapted her interests and talents to the possibilities and constraints she found in her new homes. In Pakistan, with some tweaking of *The Joy of Cooking*, she taught the wives of politicians, scholars, and doctors how to make American dishes using local ingredients to help them combat homesickness. In Iran, she helped distribute powdered milk to mothers and babies. In Thailand, she worked in a residence for abandoned elderly of Thai, Chinese, and Russian ancestry. She taught English as a second language in a Thai university. Most of these positions were voluntary because the organizations would not hire a woman. But Marjorie knew she had to pursue her own intellectual and personal interests any way she could given the restrictions placed on her, and found ways to do so in every country.

Then, at the close of the Vietnam War in the mid-1970s, Ronald decided to retire from the State Department and return to his roots in western Michigan, where he took up a professorship at his undergraduate alma mater. After more than twenty years in Southeast Asia, western Michigan was as much of a foreign culture to Marjorie as any she had been thrust into previously. Still, she adapted. She noticed that the elderly, particularly the poor elderly, had little in the way of community services, and began to work with not-for-profit agencies and churches. She cajoled wealthy businessmen to donate funds to start up services. Within a decade, largely due to Marjorie's efforts, a new recreational center, designed to meet the needs of the elderly, had been built. Shortly before Marjorie retired in 1998, she was named "Person of the Year" by the local newspaper.

Marjorie is clearly a remarkable woman. Over her lifetime, she has faced many challenging situations but embraced each one. She surveyed what the environment had to offer, evaluated her own talents and interests, and found a match that allowed her to build a life that fit her values and her sense of self. There were hard times—the daily struggle to keep her children healthy and safe in developing countries and the rejection of her talents and skills because of the traditional gender roles of the countries in which she was living. Still, she pressed on, enlisting the aid and friendship of rich and poor, dogged in her confidence that she could construct a life for herself that had meaning and purpose, wherever she was.

I believe most women today share Marjorie's strengths. Women, young and old, are capable of transforming difficult situations, such as having to move to a new town for their husband's job, or being laid off from their own job, into opportunities for growth and for the confident expression of their own talents and interests. Women's stable but adaptable sense of self equips them to make huge changes in their lives in response to their own shifting priorities.

Rachel, thirty-two, was a tax attorney for a major corporation in the Louisville, Kentucky, area when she and her husband, Todd, decided to have a child. Rachel knew it would be tough to manage her career and a newborn, but fortunately she and Todd had enough money to afford good day care, and Todd had some flexibility in his work hours as a professor at the University of Louisville School of Law. Their first child, Kayla, was healthy and good-natured, and Rachel and Todd soon worked out a manageable routine of work and family life. Then two years later Rachel was pregnant again. This pregnancy didn't go as smoothly as the first, but Rachel put it off to the fact she was older. When their son Dylan was born, Rachel and Todd hired a superb nanny to take care of both children, and were confident they could manage with two children as well as they had with one.

By Dylan's first birthday, though, Rachel knew something was wrong. Unlike Kayla, who wanted to be held and cuddled all the time, Dylan was more content to be left alone in his crib, and sometimes screamed when he was picked up. He didn't make eye contact with his parents or the nanny, and he rarely smiled in response to anything they did. Rachel and Todd were stunned when Dylan's pediatrician suggested he had autism. A specialist confirmed the diagnosis, then laid out an intensive behavioral treatment plan that involved multiple sessions per week with a psychologist. Rachel and Todd would need to learn how to carry through with the therapy at home.

When they received Dylan's diagnosis, Rachel had taken a leave of absence from her job, in part to attend all the treatment sessions but also to give herself the time she needed to handle the shock of this change in their lives. A month after they began Dylan's treatment, Rachel knew she couldn't go back full-time to her job at the firm. She just couldn't concentrate on her work. But more important, the psychologist treating Dylan had told her that it would take intensive therapy for several years to give her son the chance to develop as a typical child. Rachel wanted to give Dylan that chance.

Rachel tried being a full-time mother for the first few months. After a while, she knew she'd need more intellectual stimulation as well as activities away from her children if she was going to be self-fulfilled. She looked into the possibility of working part-time as a tax attorney, but she didn't find many options. The legal community is structured around the expectation that attorneys will work unseemly hours per week.

Rachel and Todd had joined a support group for parents of children with autism, organized by Dylan's psychologist. They generally found the group helpful in normalizing their experience and giving them practical tips for dealing with Dylan's behavior, including the temper tantrums that became more frequent as he reached his version of the

Terrible Twos. Many of the parents in the group did not have the financial means that Rachel and Todd did. They could barely afford therapy, and the public schools their children attended did not provide up-to-date care for children with autism.

Contemplating the challenges facing the other parents in their support group, Rachel grew interested in the legal and social issues around having a special needs child; for example, the rights of parents and children to have access to appropriate educational programs, insurance coverage, and social welfare services. Rachel offered research help to one of the other couples, who were waging a battle against their insurance company, which had declined to cover the cost of therapy for their child with autism. For another child in the group, she spent time on the Web determining whether he could be transferred to a school district that had better services for children with autism. Over time, her inquiries on behalf of other parents became her passion.

By Dylan's third birthday, Rachel had developed a real expertise in fighting the system on behalf of parents of children with autism. She decided to formalize her work in this area by starting a consulting business specializing in social and legal advocacy for fellow families. Rachel still did all her work from home, but now that Dylan was showing real progress in his development and was attending a part-time preschool for children with special needs, she had more time to attend meetings and court hearings on behalf of her new clients. Often, once an insurance company, school, or government office heard that parents were bringing a licensed attorney along, they suddenly became much more cooperative with the parents' requests. Rachel charged sliding scale fees, only asking parents to pay what they could. She wasn't in it for the money; she was doing it to fulfill her passion to serve other families of children with autism and because the work gave her the intellectual stimulation she had been missing. Rachel was able to put aside a highly successful career as an attorney to care for Dylan because her sense of self was not dependent on the salary she brought home or the admiration she got at work, but instead on her core set of values which she adapted to the changing situations in her life.

Women's ability to maintain and express their core values despite the shifting sands beneath them—in short, their integrity—is greatly needed in politics and government, where identities and values are often based on today's public opinion polls. Sheila Bair, the chair of the Federal Deposit Insurance Corporation (FDIC), is a woman whose identity and message have been strong and stable despite tremendous pressure to "go along with the program" of the powerful government officials and banking executives with whom she has worked. As early as 2001, in her position an assistant secretary in the U.S. Treasury, Bair began publicly raising concerns that the subprime lending industry was taking advantage of some borrowers and creating a dangerously unstable market. No one wanted to hear that the go-go economy of the 1990s could come to a screeching halt, however, and Bair was advised to "can it." Unable to support policies she thought could eventually topple the economy, Bair left public service to teach at the University of Massachusetts and wrote two children's books about money and finance. She was still striving toward her goals of protecting consumers, but by educating future business leaders and teaching young children and their parents how to handle money. In 2006, she decided to try again to change government policies, and accepted the appointment at the FDIC. By early 2007, she was arguing vigorously in private meetings and in public speeches that aggressive lending policies would eventually be disastrous to both consumers and banks. The government was slow to act and focused on propping up financial institutions rather than on making loans more affordable for borrowers. The Bush administration's $700 billion bailout bill included little help for borrowers at risk of defaulting. "The thrust has still been on the back end, of providing assistance to institutions, and not on fixing the loans themselves," Bair said in October 2008. "And for whatever reason, the borrowers have been viewed as politically unpopular, which has made it difficult to get the political will to fix the mortgages. And that's the core of the problem. That's what needs to be fixed."[15] That November, Bair announced her own ambitious plan to prevent 1.5 million foreclosures. The White House and the Treasury Department portrayed Bair as self-promoting, while ignoring the substance of her arguments.[16] Some banking executives, who wanted the Bush bailout money to continue to flow to them, declared her incompetent. Bair was stalwart, however, and as foreclosures rose and financial institutions began to fail, she could have legitimately said, "I told you so." She refrained and was retained in 2009 as head of the FDIC by the Obama administration to help deal with the financial crisis it had inherited.

For some women, their core sense of self is shaped by religious or humanitarian beliefs. Regardless of the situations they confront, they maintain their integrity and mission to serve. One such woman is Marian Wright Edelman, founder and president of the Children's Defense Fund. Since the 1970s, the CDF has become a leading advocacy group for children, focusing on issues including teenage pregnancy prevention, violence against children, and the effects of poverty on children. Edelman's devotion to children is fierce, trumping political and personal ties. Marian Edelman was a close friend and supporter of Bill and Hillary Clinton for decades before the Clintons entered the White House, campaigning for Bill Clinton, and nurturing Hillary Clinton's image as an advocate of children's causes. The relationship between Edelman and the Clintons steadily frayed as Clinton moved to the center on social policies. When Clinton was poised to sign a Republican bill to reform welfare, ending sixty years of federal guarantees of assistance for poor children, Marian Edelman wrote an opinion piece in the *Washington Post* pleading with the president to resist the legislation. She organized a rally in Washington called Stand for Children. When Clinton signed the bill in August 1996, Marian Edelman denounced Clinton for a "moment of shame" and making a "mockery of his pledge not to hurt children."[17]

Thus women's strong core identity allows them both to resist pressures to compromise their values for political or social expediency and to find ways to express that identity when circumstances change in unexpected ways. This independent core identity also permits women to see ways of exercising their values and interests that someone whose identity is tied to status and position might not see. As Marian Wright Edelman reminds us, our identity and values play out even in our everyday choices: "We must not, in trying to think about how we can make a big difference, ignore the small daily differences we can make which, over time, add up to big differences that we often cannot fore-see."[18] By displaying and demonstrating their core values in a wide variety of situations, women make big differences.

Identity Strength #1: Women have a core sense of self that is stable but adaptable to various circumstances.

Who Are You?

When you ask adults "What do you do?" or "How do you see your-self?" men tend to say "I'm an attorney" or "I'm a construction worker and a member of the union" or "I'm a schoolteacher." They define themselves primarily in terms of what they do and the groups they belong to, and social status plays a large role in how they communi-cate their identity. When women answer this question, they too will mention their profession but in the next breath will add "And I'm Joey's mom" or "I'm married to Tom" or "I'm a Webster." Women's images of themselves are intricately entwined with their relationships with other individuals. Women's identities are made up not only of their individual talents, traits, and interests but also their connections to others.[19] I'm not only a psychologist and a writer, I'm also Michael's mom, Richard's wife, John and Catherine's daughter, Jeff and Steve's sister, and so on. At its most dynamic—as with Rachel's work with families of children with autism—social context trumps social status. This inclination to self-identify by relationships and not just by accomplishments is a source of strength for women. I call this strength having a *social identity*.

Women's social identities build huge, broad networks of acquaint-ances, colleagues, friends, and families, with which women have enduring and manifold connections. These connections expand women's sense of self by filling it with a wide array of perspectives and experiences. Women don't lose their individual selves, but instead, their *me* becomes *me and you, and you, and you, and you.* These are not split identities, but pieces of an intricate quilt, each beautiful in its own right, stitched together in a complex though integrated master-piece.

Women's social identities are one reason they are so mentally flex-ible and adaptive. They can bring fresh eyes and innovative solutions to problems because they have the knowledge and insight gained by their close relationships to others. Olive has a particularly strong social identity. She is interested in, and appreciates, everyone around her, not just her immediate colleagues but the local grocery store clerk, her young rowdy neighbors, and the janitor in her office building. She never misses an opportunity to check in with the people in her life, asking about what's going on in their lives, how their families are doing, and what's on their mind. She knows *what* they do, so she asks *how* they are doing. "What *do* you like about Eminem?" she jokes with the teenager next door, in a nonjudgmental way that leads him to list the redeeming virtues of rap. "How's that ACL?" she asks Jimmy the janitor, checking in on him when he returns from surgery. "How did you get cantaloupe so early?" she asks her grocer as he is setting up a display of melons in March.

Olive's social identity is a large part of her success as a principal of a private/public high school that serves both kids from well-off fam-ilies in the suburbs and kids from poor inner-city families. She sees this school not as an institution but as a diverse family that learns and grows together on a daily basis—and she sees herself as one member of this family. She knows every one of the six hundred students by name, and her ability to connect with their interests and individual personalities garners their respect and trust. She knows all of her staff, from the deans and teachers to the cafeteria workers, on a personal level—their spouses, their children, their concerns. When new con-tracts with the cleaning staff recently had to be negotiated, Olive came to the table not only knowing every one of the individuals she was negotiating with, but understanding and caring about where they were coming from, seeing herself united with them. She was able to invoke a collaborative spirit around the table in which people wanted to work together. When a union official from outside the school came into one of the meetings and insisted on changing the structure of the benefits package, Olive was able to point out to him how such a change would not only be financially unfeasible for the school, it would give an advantage to certain workers over others, damaging the collaborative spirit among the staff. The cleaning person who acted as the local union rep at the school agreed and politely suggested that the outside union guy let them handle the negotiations. Eventually, they collectively came up with a new package that the school could afford and that improved the benefits available to everyone.

Like Olive, many women build complex identities that reflect their relationships with people of many different backgrounds and positions. Rather than closing off discussion of personal matters, they invite it—and gain an expanded, ever-growing, and full knowledge of other people's situations as well as their own.

Women's strength in fostering a social identity also creates a robust network of friends, acquaintances, colleagues, and family on whom they can lean during times of need. Julie discovered the importance of her social identity when her mother, Helen, was diagnosed with lung cancer. At thirty-nine, Julie, a single mom with three kids, had risen to the rank of deputy editor of the largest newspaper in her town of half a million people. At the paper, she was responsible for providing editorial notes on articles, identifying talented reporters, motivating the staff, and helping to set the priorities for news coverage. She absolutely loved her work. Still, it was the sort of job that could lead to resentments if a journalist felt as though her stories weren't getting as much front-page coverage as they deserved or believed he had been consigned to a boring beat that didn't offer room for promotion.

Yet Julie did a great job, developing close personal ties with everyone at the paper while simultaneously taking the time she needed to raise her kids. When she was asked about her work, Julie didn't simply say she was the newspaper's deputy editor; she described her role nurturing young reporters, and, like Olive, indicated that the newspaper was like a family. When the staff would brainstorm article topics for the paper, Julie often suggested topics that would capture the attention of readers ranging from suburban soccer moms to the young professionals living in downtown lofts, as well as merchants and clerks all over the city. She understood what worries people, what interests people, and what people are thinking because she listened deeply to all the people in her life.

Helen's diagnosis put her balancing act into a tumble. Julie's dad was a wreck, so it was up to Julie to go to the medical appointments with her mother to ensure she got the best care and that someone else in the family was able to hear everything the doctors said. The doctors told Helen she only had four months to live, as the cancer had already spread into her liver.

Attending the doctors' appointments with Helen cut into Julie's time at work. She tried mightily to meet all of her obligations, but she wasn't as punctual in giving editorial feedback as usual and missed several meetings. Julie's boss and coworkers insisted that Julie spend whatever time she needed away from the office to care for her mother. Another member of the editorial staff temporarily took over some of Julie's responsibilities. Her boss arranged for her to join editorial meetings on speakerphone when she was sitting in the hospital with her mother. In the meantime, her colleagues sent flowers to Helen and baked casseroles for Julie and her kids.

Julie wanted to spend as much of the time Helen had left with her, but didn't want her kids to have to sit around their grandparents' gloomy house or the hospital while she visited. Thankfully, Julie had developed relationships with a panoply of friends, neighbors, and the parents of her children's friends. From the day they found out about Helen's diagnosis, Julie's neighbors and friends kicked into gear and organized playdates and babysitting for Julie's kids. One neighbor even took it upon herself to set up a schedule for each of Julie's kids, listing when they would be at different friends' houses for a day or evening while Julie was with her mother. These neighbors and friends also brought casseroles, and pies and cookies, until Julie had to ask them to lighten up because she had more food than her family could eat!

The doctors were right, and Helen died four months and six days after receiving her diagnosis. More than two hundred people attended her funeral. Many were friends and family of Helen and her husband, but at least fifty of those who came were Julie's coworkers, neighbors, and friends. They were there to support Julie.

As discussed in the previous chapter, psychologist Shelley Taylor suggests that women's style of social identification and networking developed over evolutionary history as a way of dealing with danger and threat. Because women were relatively small in stature and muscle strength, they couldn't fight off attackers as easily as men could. When predators approached, an individual woman didn't have the option of wrestling the predator to submission. And because women have been the primary caregivers to children, they couldn't run away, either. Instead of developing a "fight or flight" response, women developed a "tend and befriend" approach to defending themselves. They created large networks of social relationships, especially among other women who would come to their aid when a threat approached. So when that saber-toothed tiger crept nearby, groups of women would band together with clubs and spears to create a wall of protection for one another.

In our day, we observe the vestiges of women's ancient tend-and-befriend defense style in situations of threat and tragedy, such as Julie experienced when her mother was ill. Groups of women come together in times of need, often accompanied by men, to give each other material support (e.g., casseroles and babysitting), emotional support, and mutual defense. When times are good, women tend their relationships with others, reciprocating support, building trust and goodwill, and strengthening connections. This is not to say that women are caring for others and connecting with them only so others will come to their aid when they need it. Instead, what started as a way to adapt to threats over evolutionary history has become a fundamental characteristic of how women see themselves and their values. Women don't simply network; they come to identify themselves through the networks in which they are a part.

Women have a solid sense of who they are based on their values, their sense of purpose, their interests and talents, and their personalities. At the same time they see that self as richly interconnected with others in ways that support and enhance their core self while being in mutually satisfying and reciprocal relationships with others. Women's social identity makes them exceptionally good at organizing, teaching, and leading others; at resolving conflicts; at working with others to achieve synergistic solutions to problems; and at building healthy families.

Identity Strength #2: Women define themselves in relation to their social connections with other people.

When Balancing Isn't an Act

When women began entering the workforce in unprecedented numbers in the 1960s and '70s, some sociologists made dire predictions about the costs and consequences of work for women.[20] Because women had a fixed store of energy, they said, women's health would decline greatly under the strain of their new multiple roles. Holding down a job and taking care of a family would overtax them. Moreover, women would find work and family roles inherently conflicting, requiring completely different skills and personalities: a feminine personality to nurture a spouse and children and a masculine personality to fuel career success. The energy needed to flip back and forth would leave women burned out, depressed, sick, and miserable. It sounds eerily like the advice given in the nineteenth century against women exercising because their bodies were too weak to handle the strain (while, of course, being constricted by corsets).

Thankfully, these predictions fell far from the mark—as anyone who had witnessed women such as my Grandma Geneva juggling work and family could have realized. In fact, most studies find that women with multiple roles—in the workplace, taking care of a family, volunteering in their community—are *more* healthy than women with few roles. (By the way, this is true of men, too.) As Michelle Obama told *60 Minutes*, "Women are capable of doing more than one thing well at the same time."

Women who forge multiple roles can draw upon multiple sources of self-esteem and satisfaction. Different roles in life provide you with far-ranging groups of people to enjoy and tap for support in times of need. When one role is creating feelings of stress, you may be able to balance that stress with the benefits of other roles in your life. For example, a study of people who were caregivers to a family member with a disability found they experienced significantly less stress if they were also employed outside the home, compared to caregivers who weren't employed outside the home.[21] Their job roles served as a release from some of the burdens of caregiving, making it easier for them to cope with those burdens.

Women are especially likely to develop multifaceted identities. They are expected to do so—as a mother, as a spouse, as a child of older parents, as a friend, as a coworker, as a citizen. Men, as we have seen, are more likely to define themselves very strongly in terms of their careers—even if they have a family, enjoy hobbies, and participate in community activities. This can be dangerous, because if things start to sour in a man's work life—for example, he is unexpectedly laid off—the foundation of his self-worth and self-image can be completely shattered.

My research has shown that women's multiple identities, like their social identity, offer important protection against traumas in life such as a sudden loss of income or an expected disability. In a one-year study of over 1,300 women and men from the San Francisco Bay Area, my colleagues and I found that those who enjoyed multiple roles— good family lives as well as a job or active volunteer life—experienced less depression and anxiety even when they were faced with major stressors, such as personal illness, a death in the family, or a demotion at work.

Some research suggests that having a work role outside the home is especially important for women's well-being.[22] Women who are employed have their own source of income, not connected to their partner's income, which provides self-esteem and independence and, depending on the situation, a higher quality of life for the family as a whole. Employed work can also increase a woman's sense of mastery, helping her to assert her own needs even at home.

Take, for example, Marci, a thirty-two-year-old marketing manager for a major chain of furniture stores in Denver. After her twin boys were born, Marci agreed with her husband, Pete, that she would stay home. Pete felt strongly that the boys needed a full-time mother, and Marci was somewhat daunted at the prospect of keeping up with her job and caring for two newborns. The boys kept her extremely busy and Marci enjoyed watching them grow into toddlers and giving them opportunities to explore their world. When the boys entered elementary school, however, Marci felt lost. She just couldn't get motivated to clean the house, do errands for the family, sew, cook, or do other things to keep herself busy all day. She tried volunteering in the library at her sons' school, but she didn't find that fulfilling, either. Marci began to feel more and more like a failure, and this, in turn, led her to be irritable with her sons and her husband.

Marci knew she had to do something or her relationships with her family would deteriorate and she would become more depressed. Her main problem was that she considered herself a boring, purposeless woman who was reaching middle age. She made a pact with herself to change. She started to pay attention to her moods and noticed that she felt worst about herself when the boys were at school: she viewed each day as a big black hole, with several hours of nothingness confronting her. When she reviewed her life over the previous months, she realized that the one activity that had felt fun and fulfilling was her work organizing and advertising a charity auction on behalf of her sons' school. So she brainstormed ways she could exercise her skills and experience in marketing during school hours. She decided she would search job listings for part-time marketing positions, find out if there were any volunteer positions that could utilize her business skills, and investigate the possibility of opening her own consulting business. Marci recruited the support of her husband, who was thrilled she was doing something to improve her increasingly sour disposition. She noticed that she got excited as she thought about the marketing jobs she might be able to land.

Marci scoured newspapers and the Web, called local volunteer agencies to see if they needed help, and read how-to books on starting a consulting business. Pete helped her by talking with some attorneys he knew about the legal requirements involved in starting a firm. Within a couple of months, Marci decided that launching her own marketing business would give her the freedom to choose her clients and the power to control her hours, so that she could spend time with the boys after school and in the evenings. Her first client was herself! Launching her business was tough, but within six months she had two companies as clients and was as busy as she wanted to be. Marci successfully expanded her self-image to include being an extroverted, entrepreneurial businesswoman, and in the process overcame her depression and brought new satisfaction to herself and to her family.

Each role that a woman takes on, at home and at work, requires different talents and styles of interacting with other people. As a result, juggling multiple roles stretches a woman's sense of self, sharpens her skills, and broadens her knowledge. She can then bring that diversified knowledge base, skill set, and sense of self to every role she fulfills.

Researchers Elizabeth Vandewater, Joan Ostrove, and Abigail Stewart of the University of Michigan reasoned that having multiple roles should therefore expand and strengthen women's sense of self over time, leading women to form more mature and well-defined identities. They followed two groups of women—one group that had graduated from Radcliffe College in 1964 and the other that had graduated from the University of Michigan in 1967—taking measures of their roles and identity development multiple times until the women were in their forties. Women who had more roles in their twenties— as workers, partners, parents, community volunteers—had more clearly formed identities in their forties. They had clarified their values and standards and could articulate these to the interviewers. They were independent thinkers who could follow their own values when others pressured them to do otherwise. They were secure enough in themselves to be warm and compassionate toward others. Indeed, it appeared that involvement in multiple different roles early in adulthood had pushed these women to develop mature identities characterized by complexity, integrity, and stability.[23]

Of course, not every role is beneficial to a person's well-being. Most studies find *role quality* to be even more important than the number of roles a woman has adopted. Paid employment is great—unless you are not paid enough in one job to meet your bills and have to work two or three jobs; then it becomes a stressor. If you are paid enough but are required to work twelve to fifteen hours per day, or the workplace atmosphere is full of conflict and strain, then it's just as likely to be bad for your health and well-being as it is to add to your self-identity. In our study of 1,300 adults in San Francisco, women who were less satisfied with the nature of their jobs—who felt insecure in them, were working more than they wanted to, or didn't like what they were doing—were more anxious and depressed. Similarly, having a family life is great—unless you and your partner fight all the time, or your children are out of control; then your role as a partner or a mother may be hurting your well-being rather than improving it. In the San Francisco study, women who felt that their relationships with their partners and their children were full of strain were more depressed and anxious, too.

We'd like to think that in these liberated days, male partners, especially the generations that are in their twenties and thirties, would contribute their fair share to the burdens of the home—shopping, cooking, doing dishes, cleaning the house, taking the kids to school and activities, helping the kids do their homework, and so on. There's been a great deal of attention paid to the fact that men have substantially increased the number of hours they spend on housework and caring for children. From the 1960s to the turn of the twenty-first century, men doubled their contributions in hours to housework and tripled their contribution to child care. Yet women still do 70 percent of the housework. Over the last few decades, women also doubled the amount of time they spend with their children, even though they've also entered the workplace in record numbers.[24] So although men are contributing more to child care, women have upped their involvement with their children as well, resulting in little net relief for women. In our study, my colleagues and I found that the more dissatisfied women were with the division of child-care tasks in their family, the more depressed and anxious they were.

Thus it's astonishing to find that the rewards of multiple roles still often trump the stresses associated with these roles. Psychologist Mary Ann Parris Stephens at Kent State University and her colleagues interviewed ninety-five women who were simultaneously occupying the roles of mother, wife, and caregiver to a disabled relative, asking about the strains and rewards associated with their various roles. There certainly were strains: the women talked about "conflicts with children," "lack of companionship with my husband," and "my care recipient criticized me or complained." Not surprisingly, the more strains women reported, the worse their emotional well-being and physical health. But these strains were balanced by the rewards of the individual roles. Reflecting on being a mother, women said they were rewarded because "children brought meaning to my life" and "felt needed by the children." As a wife, they identified rewards such as "husband backed me up" and "felt companionship with my husband." And in the caregiver role, they mentioned "I knew the care recipient was well cared for" and "I saw the care recipient enjoy small things" as benefits. The more rewards they identified, the better their emotional and physical health, even if they were also experiencing strains in their roles.[25]

Any role in life carries risks of strains and stresses, as well as the hope of rewards. On balance, multiple roles tend to be good for women.

Identity Strength #3: Women's identities are multifaceted, based on several roles rather than one fixed role.

Far from being fragile and conflicted, plagued by low self-esteem and high self-doubts, women's identities are solid but adaptable, richly interconnected with others, and complex and multifaceted. Having a strong core identity undergirds women when their circumstances change or pressures against them mount. They can maintain the integrity of their values and goals while being creative and nimble in exercising these values and goals. Having a social identity gives women a complex but integrated sense of self and creates a deep, intimate network of relationships that provide opportunities and safety in unanticipated ways. Having multiple roles broadens women's base of knowledge and experiences, and buffers them when difficulties arise.

Women's identity strengths are intimately connected to their mental strengths of seeing many pathways to their goals, remaining task-oriented instead of worrying about gaining credit, enlisting help to solve problems, and maintaining an optimistic, can-do attitude. Women bring these identities that are enriched and expanded, robust and flexible, to their work as mothers, partners, and leaders at work and in the community. They inspire others to be, like them, people of integrity, broad in vision and appreciative of every individual and opportunity.

4.

Emotions as Tools: Understanding Women's Emotional Strengths

Women's emotional lives—their sensitivity to their own feelings and those of others, and their willingness to express themselves—have driven men crazy for centuries. In the first century BC, philosopher Publilius Syrus wrote, "Woman loves or hates. She knows no middle course." The nineteenth-century French writer Stendhal opined, "Women are always eagerly on the lookout for any emotion."

My sympathies to Publilius Syrus and Stendhal, but being emotionally sensitive and savvy tremendously benefits women—and the men they live with. Women's emotional strengths have allowed them to survive and thrive for centuries. Today, women's ability to understand and manage their own emotions buoys them in the face of adversity and promotes healthier—and longer—lives. Women's emotional strengths are crucial to their effectiveness as partners, parents, and friends, helping them to respond empathically and supportively to their loved ones' needs. Women's emotional strengths also contribute to their success as leaders in their communities and their companies, allowing them to tune in to what others are feeling but not necessarily saying. Women's high-quality emotional radar allows for more productive and mutually satisfying relationships, at work and at home.

Women can tolerate and manage their emotions in ways that

improve how they function day to day. Because women are aware of their own emotions and the emotions of others, they are often able to identify the causes and consequences of emotions. That gives them important information in finding the right time and the right way to communicate and negotiate in emotionally charged situations. And what situation in life comes emotion-free?

Psychologists Peter Salovey and John Mayer, who originated the concept of emotional intelligence, identified its four components: accurately perceiving others' emotions; understanding your own emotions; knowing how to use emotions to get through life; and managing emotions adaptively.[1] These researchers developed a test that measures each of these four components, not simply by asking people whether they think they have these strengths, but by presenting people with scenarios and situations that force them to use emotional intelligence. Here are a few sample questions:[2]

What mood(s) might be helpful to feel when meeting in-laws for the very first time?

	Not Useful				Useful
a) Slight Tension	1	2	3	4	5
b) Surprise	1	2	3	4	5
c) Joy	1	2	3	4	5

Tom felt anxious, and became a bit stressed when he thought about all the work he needed to do. When his supervisor brought him an additional project, he felt ____. (Select the best choice.)

a) overwhelmed

b) depressed

c) ashamed

d) self-conscious

e) jittery

Debbie just came back from vacation. She was feeling peaceful and content. How well would each action preserve her mood?

Action 1: She started to make a list of things at home that she needed to do.

Very Ineffective   1   2   3   4   5   Very Effective

Action 2: She began thinking about where and when she would go on her next vacation.

Very Ineffective   1   2   3   4   5   Very Effective

Action 3: She decided it was best to ignore the feeling since it wouldn't last anyway.

Very Ineffective   1   2   3   4   5   Very Effective

Now, you may be saying to yourself, "How could anyone not know the right answer to these questions?" But people do differ in their ability to discern what would be the most effective, or adaptive, answer to questions like these. More to the point, women significantly outperform men on this test, getting higher scores on emotional intelligence.[3]

When you ask people how they *think* they performed on the emotional intelligence test, men estimate their scores to be much higher than do women. Despite (or because of) relentless stereotypes about women being more in touch with their emotions, women are less ready to embrace their emotional intelligence. It's time that they did.

According to research by Salovey and Mayer, as well as psychologists Marc Brackett, Susan Rivers, and others, emotionally intelligent people are more psychological healthy and are less likely to use illegal drugs. They have better social skills and better-quality relationships. In contrast, people low in emotional intelligence are more aggressive and more likely to create conflict with others. Emotional intelligence is vital to high performance work, especially for supervisors. Managers who are emotionally intelligent have more productive relationships with others and are seen as having more integrity.[4]

I believe women have all of the components that make up emotional intelligence and are great emotion communicators as well:

- Women are excellent readers of others' emotions. They tune in to how others are feeling and respond with care.

- Women understand how they are feeling and what triggers their emotions. They are aware of their moods and how they affect their behaviors and actions.
- Women know how to express their emotions, choosing the right time to approach and assert to others how they are feeling.
- Women are able to "hang in" during times of distress, giving others the room to express their emotions and then finding ways to turn those feelings into productive actions.
- Women are experts at stepping back from upsetting situations, managing their emotional responses in order to pursue the outcome they want.

Let's explore each of the emotional strengths of women in turn.

Emotion Readers

When you look into the eyes of another person, what do you see? Anxiety, sadness, happiness, disgust? If you are a woman, the odds are high that whatever you see is what the other person is actually feeling.

Hundreds of studies have examined people's ability to "read" the emotional expressions in other people's faces. Generally, these studies present participants with photos of people expressing various emotions, such as those on the next page. These are from the research of University of California, San Francisco, psychologist Paul Ekman, who is also an expert at detecting lies through emotional expression (the crime solver in the 2009 TV series *Lie to Me* is based on Ekman). Ekman and other scientists have found that women are consistently more accurate than men in identifying what emotions other people are feeling. Women are also particularly good at reading emotions in others' posture, hand gestures, and tone of voice.[5] So when another person grimaces or groans, raises his eyebrows or shifts nervously, sighs or gets a twinkle in his eye, women notice and decode these expressions better than men.

Even as infants, girls have an advantage over boys in reading the

Figure 1. The Universal Expressions of Emotion

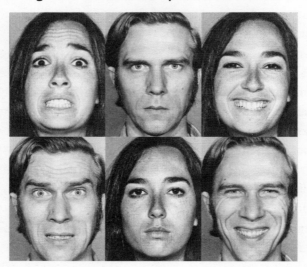

Faces used to test people's ability to perceive others' emotions. Copyright © 1976 by Paul Ekman, Ph.D. Courtesy of the Paul Ekman Group, LLC.

emotions of others.[6] How do researchers determine this? One way is to show an infant a photo of a person displaying a certain emotion on his or her face—the classic downturned mouth and eyes of sadness, the rounded mouth and popped-open eyes of fear, the smiling lips and crinkled eyes of happiness. After a period of time, the infant will stop gazing at the photo, suggesting that he or she has become habituated, or familiar, with it. The researchers then present the infant with another photo of a person displaying a different emotion. If the infant seems uninterested in the new photo, the scientists consider it a sign that he or she doesn't distinguish between the emotion in the previous photo and the new photo. If, on the other hand, the infant gazes attentively at the new photo, they believe the infant perceives a difference. Even before one year of age, girls show more signs of distinguishing emotions than boys do. As children grow older and acquire verbal skills, researchers are able to ask them to label the emotions in photos. In these studies, too, girls outperform boys in correctly identifying emotions.

Psychologist Erin McClure suggests that biological as well as social processes play a role in girls' skills at emotion reading.[7] Certain structures in the brain, such as the temporal cortex, are involved in perceiving others' emotions, and prior to the age of three or four, these structures develop at a faster rate in girls than in boys. Boys' brains catch up to girls' in development by age three or four, but girls have already gained the edge of those early years accurately perceiving emotion in others. In turn, as young as age two, girls show more responsiveness to others' emotions than boys do, perhaps because they perceive emotions more clearly.

Social forces also shape girls' emotion-reading skills from an early age. Adults engage in more emotional interactions with young girls than young boys. Research by British psychologist Judith Dunn has found that mothers are more emotionally expressive to girls than to boys. As children grow older, mothers talk more about emotions with their daughters than with their sons. They are also more likely to draw their daughters' attention to the social causes and implications of emotions. For example, if another child on the playground is upset about something, a mother is more likely to talk with a daughter than with a son about why that child might be upset, and what might help the other child to feel better about the situation.[8] As a result, girls get more practice than boys do in talking about emotions with their mothers and in learning about the causes and consequences of emotions. They enter kindergarten as relative emotion experts.

So girls seem more biologically primed, from infancy, to pay attention to and perceive others' emotions. This jump-starts the social aspect of girls' emotional skill development, eliciting more emotional interactions with adults and more discussions about emotions and their causes. Girls are also encouraged to pay attention to others' emotions, to take others' emotions into account in their social interactions, and to be responsive to others' emotional displays. As a result, adult women are generally better at accurately perceiving what others are feeling. They tend to be more responsive to others' emotions, showing their own emotions in response to other people's emotional displays.

Why is it important to be able to accurately read others' emotions? If you can't read others' emotions, it can get pretty difficult to operate in daily life. This inability is starkly illustrated in research on people with autism, who often lack the ability to perceive and understand others' emotions.[9] This makes it excruciatingly hard for them to understand what's going on in social interactions or even to have everyday social conversations with others. Temple Grandin, a professor of animal sciences at Colorado State University and a person with autism, describes it this way:

Social interactions that come naturally to most people can be daunting for people with autism. As a child, I was like an animal that had no instincts to guide me; I just had to learn by trial and error. I was always observing, trying to work out the best way to behave, but I never fit in. I had to think about every social interaction. When other students swooned over the Beatles, I called their reaction an ISP—interesting sociological phenomenon. I was a scientist trying to figure out the ways of the natives. I wanted to participate but did not know how.[10]

Emotions are signals—signals that are critical to human functioning across all cultures in our evolutionary history. Different emotional expressions signal a person's state of mind and indicate what actions he or she might take in the moment. Sadness indicates that a person has lost something and needs comfort. Fear arises when a person experiences a threat, and can often be a plea for protection. Anger signals that a person has been thwarted and may lash out in retaliation. Paul Ekman discovered that these core emotions, and the facial expressions and actions that accompany them, are universal across cultures.[11]

Being able to read others' emotions allows you to anticipate actions and respond quickly and effectively. Obviously, this is a skill that benefits both men and women who have it. But being able to read others' emotions may have been particularly critical to women's survival over evolutionary history. Psychologist Jean Baker Miller of Wellesley

College theorizes that women's impressive ability to read and under-stand others' emotions emerged from an urgent need to anticipate possible violence from men. Women couldn't fight men physically, so they had to learn how to detect and avoid the threat of violence before it occurred. Women became exquisitely attuned to men's emotional ebbs and flows, able to foresee triggers for outbursts, and skilled at soothing rising rage. In relationships that are not plagued by violence, being able to read a mate's emotions helps women to recognize prob-lems in the relationship early on, so that they can respond before problems grow larger. The emotional strengths that evolved to avoid danger now give women tremendous insight into other people's desires, intentions, and weaknesses—insight that women use to moti-vate, lead, and love.

Women's roles as the primary caregivers to children have also honed their skills at reading others' emotions over the centuries. Especially when they are very young, children cannot articulate their needs and concerns fully or accurately. Instead, when children want or need something, they emote—they cry, they show fear, they withdraw and become sad, they smile and seem delighted. Being able to accurately read their children's emotions gives women a window into a child's deepest concerns and joys, even when he or she may be trying to hide them. This allows mothers to anticipate when a child is troubled and respond earlier and more effectively. It also allows mothers to appre-ciate when a child is happy and savor that happiness.

Becky and her family lived in a suburb of Phoenix. Her two girls, Casey and Tina, seemed to be thriving in the local elementary school, and Becky kept busy with her part-time job as a store manager. When her youngest child, Casey, was in fifth grade, Becky began to notice that Casey had become less talkative and vibrant on the drive to school. Previously, Casey had sung along with the radio, or would excitedly tell her mother what was scheduled at school that day. Then Casey would smack a big kiss on Becky's cheek and bound out of the car into the front entrance of the school. For the past couple weeks, however, Casey had become nearly silent, basically sitting still in the backseat, looking at her lap for much of the ride. She seemed hesitant to get out of the car, and Becky had to ask for a good-bye kiss. Disturbed, Becky had asked Casey a few times if everything was okay, and Casey just nodded or offered a weak "uh-huh" in response. Casey's older sister was clueless as to what was going on when Becky asked her.

So one Friday evening Becky arranged for her older daughter to go over to a friend's house for dinner. Then Becky took Casey to her favorite ice-cream place for an after-school treat. They talked a bit about the events of the day while they ate their ice cream, and then Becky suggested they walk through the park across the street. Casey was reluctant, but Becky insisted. After a while, Becky said, "Sweetheart, I know something is wrong. It's written all over your face and your body. I really want to help, and it's important that you let me know what's going on." Casey remained silent for a long while, but finally tears streamed down her cheeks. "I feel so stupid, Mom, and so ugly." It turned out that Casey held a secret crush on a boy in her grade named Luke. She had told one of her girlfriends, who told other kids, and Casey's secret was all over the school. Luke, who was a bit of a jerk, had approached Casey in the hall a few weeks earlier, in front of other kids. Casey was nervous and thrilled, hoping he might ask her to "go out," fifth-grade style (which amounted to telling other kids they were a "couple"). Instead, Luke announced, in an unnecessarily loud voice, "Listen, Casey, I'm sorry but you just aren't hot enough for me. So get over it." Casey ran away in tears as some of the kids in the hall broke out in laughter. Since then, going to school had been torture for her. Most of the other kids had forgotten the incident, but Casey was sure everyone was still talking about her and laughing at her behind her back.

Becky hugged Casey as she sobbed. She told her that something very similar had happened to her when she was in middle school. Casey looked up at her mother with bloodshot eyes and said, "Really?" Becky and Casey talked for the next hour about how mean other kids can be, and how it's possible to hold your head up high, even when you've been embarrassed. By the time they went home for dinner, Casey felt relieved. The following Monday morning, Casey sang to the radio on the way to school. She got out of the car with her old energy and told her mother, "I've decided I'm not going to let those kids ruin my day today!" She gave Becky a kiss and skipped off to the school entrance. Becky's keen perception of Casey's feelings alerted her to the trouble in Casey's life, and gave her the opportunity to help Casey deal with her fifth-grade tragedy. Because mothers are able to tune in to their children's feelings, they can head off disaster, repair broken hearts, and forge bonds of trust and intimacy that serve their children every day of their lives and enrich women's lives immeasurably.

In business, accurately reading others' emotions is key to building productive relationships with fellow employees, including those who report to you. Managers who can read their subordinates' emotions are clued in to dissatisfactions, even when the subordinates don't feel comfortable voicing them, which gives the manager a chance to address dissatisfactions, and their causes, before employees leave. For example, a manager who is able to see stifled frustration on an employee's face when she's repeatedly interrupted by a colleague during meetings can take the annoyed employee aside to build her assertiveness in speaking up in meetings—and structure the meetings so that her colleague is discouraged from taking over the discussion. Being able to perceive others' feelings also enables women to be more effective in negotiations, by helping them discern what is most important to potential clients or to opponents, regardless of the issues they put on the table. In one study of managers working in a variety of businesses, researcher Kristin Byron administered a test of emotion perception that required managers to indicate the emotions depicted in photographs of other people's faces and bodily postures, and in the vocal tone of audio recordings. Byron found that women managers who performed better on this measure of emotion perception were also rated by their subordinates as more supportive and by their supervisors as more effective on the job.[12]

Perceiving others' emotions gives women tremendous advantages in social interactions. Other people telegraph their thoughts and intentions in the emotions on their faces, and women read these messages expertly. They can then use this information to respond more effectively to others in the workplace, at home, and in their communities.

Emotional Strength #1: Women are expert at perceiving and tuning in to other people's feelings.

What Am I Feeling?

Women are just as good at perceiving and understanding their own emotions as they are at perceiving and understanding others' emotions, and positive emotional self-awareness develops early in girls. In a study of ten- to eleven-year-olds, psychologist Jane Bajgar and her colleagues presented girls and boys with hypothetical scenarios and asked them to talk about how they and the other person in the scenario would feel.[13] For example, one scenario was: "The dentist tells you that you have some problems with your teeth that need to be fixed immediately. The dentist makes an appointment for you to come back the next day. How would you feel? How would the dentist feel?" Girls consistently were better than boys at understanding and articulating how they and the other person in the scenario would feel. In the dentist scenario, the girls were more likely to give responses such as, "I would feel scared and worried. The dentist would probably feel worried and happy to fix me." Boys were considerably more clueless, saying things such as, "I would feel it would hurt. I don't know how the dentist would feel."

Being able to recognize your various emotions—and the sources behind them—is a hallmark of good mental health. You need to be aware of your emotions and understand their causes if you are going to be effective in managing these emotions. Research by psychologist Doug Mennin of Yale University has found that people with significant problems such as depression, chronic severe anxiety, and eating disorders are often unable to distinguish between different emotions in themselves, let alone understand their causes. Understanding your own emotions is important from an early age. Psychologist Katie

McLaughlin measured emotional understanding in 1,065 low-income, middle-school children from a diverse community. She found that those who seemed to have trouble understanding their emotions had higher levels of depression, anxiety, and disordered eating behaviors, and were more likely to be aggressive.[14] Understanding your emotions can help you respond appropriately and effectively, even in stressful times.

Tuning in to what her emotions were telling her possibly saved Carolyn's life. At forty-three, Carolyn thought she might have met a man with whom she could spend the rest of her life. Keith was a thirty-nine-year-old research scientist in a large oil company based in Dallas, Texas. Because she had never felt very pretty in her five-foot-two-inch rounded body, Carolyn was pleased that Keith, who was tall and fit, with a handsome angular face, seemed to find her attractive. Their romance started with intense conversations, about Keith's work as a scientist and Carolyn's work as a magazine editor, conducted over languorous but adventurous dinners at ethnic restaurants around the city. Their physical relationship was just as intense, with Keith proving to be a demanding but satisfying lover. Five months into their romance, Keith suggested they live together to save rent. Carolyn had felt a bit wary, wondering if their relationship had advanced sufficiently. There were also niggling questions in Carolyn's mind: Why didn't Keith ever talk about his previous relationships? She tried to tell him about her previous marriage, but Keith clearly wasn't interested and quickly changed the subject. Why had he remained single, particularly given how handsome and professionally successful he was? Did Carolyn really want to live full-time with Keith's intense personality? But Keith was persuasive, and the prospect of having found a life partner was enticing.

A few weeks after Keith moved into Carolyn's apartment, she received a phone call from Keith's former landlord asking when he was going to pay his back rent. Carolyn was stunned to hear that Keith not only owed three months' rent, but also owed money for damages to the wall in his living room, which the landlord said Keith had apparently punched in with his fist. When Keith got home from work that evening, Carolyn gave him the message from the landlord, expecting he would have some good explanation, or at least would be apologetic. Instead, Keith flew into a rage, screaming that Carolyn had no right to be prying into his business. She tried to explain that the landlord had simply offered information without her asking any questions, but Keith threw his coat and briefcase across the room at her, then stomped into the bedroom, slamming and locking the door behind him. Carolyn stood motionless, worrying he might come back out and continue screaming, but also growing angry he had reacted so unreasonably.

Carolyn left the apartment and walked the short distance to her friend Pam's apartment. When she described the incident with Keith, Pam said, "There's something wrong with this guy. There's something really wrong." Carolyn downplayed Pam's concerns, wanting terribly to believe that Keith was just embarrassed or didn't understand that Carolyn had not pried into his affairs. When Carolyn returned to her apartment the next morning, Keith had gone to work but had left a message apologizing for his outburst and promising to explain the landlord situation later. He never did, though, offering some lame excuses about having gotten too busy at work to remember to pay his rent, and having accidentally punched a small hole in the wall when he was hanging a picture.

A couple of months passed without incident, when one Sunday morning, as Carolyn and Keith were reading the paper after breakfast, the phone rang. Keith answered the call in the living room, and though he was trying to speak quietly, Carolyn could hear the anger in his voice. She walked to the doorway of the living room and overheard him saying, "How did you get this number, you f—ing bitch? I don't care what your f—ing lawyer says, I don't owe you anything! You deserved what you got for lying to me! Don't ever call me again or I'll finish what I started!"

Carolyn slunk away from the doorway, trembling. What was he talking about, that this person got what she deserved? What had he started with this woman that he was threatening to finish? Carolyn startled sharply when Keith yelled, "I gotta go out!" then left, slamming the door. She eased herself back into the kitchen chair, wracking her brain for benign answers to her questions about Keith. But she could find none. Every alarm bell in her psyche was screeching, "Danger! Get out of here!"

Carolyn did leave, but before she did she got the phone number of the last call from the caller ID on the phone. She went over to Pam's again, worrying she would hear "I told you so." Pam just opened her arms to her, offering a big hug and telling Carolyn that she was right to listen to the emotional alarms in her head. At Pam's, Carolyn dialed the number from the caller ID. A woman answered. Carolyn told the woman that she was living with Keith and had overheard their phone call earlier that morning. The woman, named Marissa, initially started cursing Keith, but then settled down and began telling Carolyn the harrowing story of her relationship to Keith.

Marissa and Keith had lived together for over a year—Keith had moved into Marissa's apartment, supposedly to save rent, just as he had moved into Carolyn's apartment. About six months after they began living together, Keith started getting rough with Marissa, first as part of sex play, and then whenever he was angry with her. When they were arguing, he would grab her and shake her, and he had slapped her in the face on a couple occasions. One day, Keith confronted Marissa about a man he had seen her talking with. She said he was just an acquaintance at work, but Keith exploded, accusing her of cheating on him. She denied it, but this only angered him more, and he punched her in the face. She fell to the floor, her nose broken and bleeding. After he stormed out of the apartment, Marissa went to the emergency room for treatment, and never returned to the apartment, despite having left all of her possessions behind. She went to live with her parents in Fort Worth, commuting to her job in Dallas until she could save enough money to buy new clothes and rent a new apartment.

In the three months that followed, Keith apparently did not pay the rent for the apartment he had shared with Marissa, and eventually he abandoned it to live with some friends until he moved in with Carolyn. When the landlord was unable to get the rent out of Keith, he hired a collection agency to harass Marissa. She paid the rent to get rid of the collection agency's calls, but then hired an attorney to go after Keith for the money.

After her phone call with Marissa, Carolyn was reeling, and had an overwhelming feeling she had dodged a bullet by listening to her feelings and walking out on Keith. A few days later, Keith called Carolyn at work. He began the conversation with "Where the hell have you been?" Carolyn told him she knew about Marissa and her broken nose. Keith bellowed, "You bitch! How dare you call Marissa! She's a f—ing liar! You come home right now!" Carolyn took a deep breath and said there was no way she was coming back to the apartment. Keith replied, "You'd better come back, you slut, or I'll do some damage to your precious things! Listen to this!" Carolyn heard a loud crash. "There, your lovely big-screen TV is history! You come back right now or I'll break everything in the house and then come find you!"

Carolyn hung up and immediately called the police. It took her four months and the ordeal of pressing charges, but she extricated Keith from her apartment and got most of her things back. Carolyn had to apply for a court order to stop Keith from calling her or showing up outside her work to harass her. She wished she had listened to her initial doubts about Keith, though she was deeply thankful that she had heeded her feelings early enough to avoid the violence Marissa had suffered.

Understanding your own emotions also helps you make important decisions even when you aren't faced with a crisis. Although economists try to tell us that decisions should be made on wholly rational criteria, weighing costs and benefits, emotions play a big role in every decision we make. Emotions are a clue as to what we value and what our goals are. The things we get passionate about should influence our decisions; we should go after the things about which we hold strongly positive feelings and avoid the things for which we hold strongly negative ones.

At a more subtle level, we sometimes experience gut feelings about the various options in our lives, and these gut feelings can be insightful, as was Blair's gut feeling about which job she should take. Blair had just gotten her Ph.D. in sociology from a prestigious Ivy League school.

Her dissertation research had been published, and she was one of the hottest young academics on the job market that year. Blair interviewed for faculty positions at six universities, ranging from other Ivy League schools—one a top-ranked sociology department in the country—to large research universities out on the West Coast, to a state university in the Midwest. Blair had grown up in Wisconsin, and although she had spent the past six years getting her graduate degree on the East Coast, she had longed for the slower, more friendly lifestyle she had grown up with. Still, she had come to appreciate the intellectual and cultural vibrancy of New York City and Boston. The status of landing a job in the highest-ranked department in the country was definitely attractive. After a hectic two months of interviews and negotiations, she received job offers from the Ivy League college in New England, the midwestern state school, and two universities on the West Coast.

All her peers and her thesis advisor assumed she'd take the Ivy League job—it was the obvious choice from a rational perspective. Blair wasn't at all sure that's what she should do, however. When she thought about the job, she felt a combination of exhilaration and dread. The exhilaration came from thinking about the wonderful students and colleagues she would have, the pride of being recognized as the one person in the country who landed this job, and the prospect that her career would have a swift trajectory if launched from this department. The dread came from the knowledge that she'd be working in a pressure-cooker atmosphere of fierce competition and high expectations. Also, she'd continue to be 1,500 miles from her family, whom she missed terribly.

When Blair thought about the job in the Midwest, she felt a combination of pleasant tranquility and worry. The pleasant tranquility came from imagining a lifestyle of reasonable work hours with friendly colleagues who had lives outside of work. She imagined herself buying a nice home and a nicer car, which would be possible with the lower cost of living in the Midwest. The worry came from the prospect that she might find the pace of life too slow, the cultural scene deficient, and the quality of her work atmosphere less than she was accustomed to.

Blair decided she needed to gather more information to back up her imagined versions of life at the two jobs. She made trips back to the midwestern department and to the Ivy League department to talk with her prospective colleagues and some of the students. She also spent a day in each of the towns, driving around neighborhoods and through shopping districts. She made a point to go into coffee shops and grocery stores in each town and just observe people. She spent a couple of hours with a real estate agent in each town. All the while, she stayed keenly aware of her emotional reactions to the places, the people, the "feel" of everything she encountered.

When she returned from her trips, Blair knew that her heart was in the Midwest. The tranquility she had imagined when she thought about moving to the Midwest had become a deep sense of "rightness" about being there, in terms of the department and its people, the town and its atmosphere. In contrast, when she revisited the Ivy League department, she felt she was contemplating "someone else's job." During the trip, she felt weary, a sensation she thought she might have the entire time she lived there. Blair had a difficult time explaining her decision to her advisor and graduate school friends, but she was totally sure she was making the correct decision for herself.

Five years later, Blair had tenure at her midwestern university, owned a lovely home within walking distance of the campus, and was engaged to a professor in the history department. She never regretted giving up the more prestigious job, and because she had been so happy in the department she chose, the quality and quantity of her work over that five years had been tremendous, gaining her two national awards.

Women's understanding of their own emotions gives them a window into their own soul. They look to their emotions to clarify their values and goals, to make choices for their lives, and to understand the world around them.

Emotional Strength #2: Women understand their own emotions and the sources of these emotions.

I'll Tell You What I'm Feeling

A few years ago, my colleague Cheryl Rusting and I reviewed dozens of studies comparing women's and men's tendencies to express various emotions.[15] You won't be surprised to hear that women are considerably more likely to express a wide range of emotions than men are. They laugh, they cry, they wrinkle their noses in disgust, they frown with disapproval.

Being able to express feelings toward others in appropriate ways is an essential skill in building good relationships. It breaks down barriers, clears up misunderstandings, and promotes trust between people. Often, women are able to do this when they are vulnerable, such as at a crossroads in a romantic relationship.

Ellen and Connor, for example, were both in a post-baccalaureate teacher training program, after graduating college in Baltimore. They were on track to finish their program in May, and by early spring Ellen became increasingly worried about where their relationship was heading. She had a job lined up teaching math at a private high school in Providence, Rhode Island, for the fall, while Connor was planning on remaining in Baltimore. Although Ellen had tried to approach the topic delicately, Connor had only given her noncommittal answers, stating that it was "too soon" to talk about the future. Ellen decided not to push the issue, worried that she would come off sounding clingy or demanding. She understood Connor's reluctance to discuss a long-distance relationship but grew increasingly frustrated and anxious about their impending separation. She worried that Connor didn't value her enough to factor her into his long-term plans, and wondered if she was more serious about the relationship than he was.

Finally, in mid-April Ellen decided that rather than simply asking Connor what he thought, she would express her feelings on the subject, explaining exactly why the discussion was important to her. Strolling together toward her apartment after a pleasant evening at a local French bistro, Ellen told Connor that though it did seem a little soon to talk about the fall, she realized they were planning everything else that far in advance, including jobs and housing. Although she enjoyed the time she spent with him, the uncertainty regarding the future of their relationship was gnawing at her. Connor could tell that Ellen was upset, but she maintained composure and clarity as she expressed her feelings. They discussed at length how their relationship might work over the distance of four hundred miles. They examined their likely budgets and schedules and discovered they would be able to see each other more often than either of them had thought—enough that they both reinvested themselves in their relationship.

In his interactions with Ellen, Connor displayed the classic tactic known as "stonewalling," which was identified by researchers John Gottman and Robert Levenson at the University of California, Berkeley. Gottman and Levenson found that when men and women in close relationships talk about subjects over which they are in conflict, men often stonewall—their faces become frozen, bereft of any emotion, unreactive to their partners. Men also refuse to talk about the emotional subject, often becoming silent or walking away as women try to work through their differences. It's not that men aren't feeling any emotion. They just refuse to show any emotion, because they can't deal with their own feelings or the feelings of their partner.[16]

In this situation, Ellen knew that she had to express her emotions or she would remain unhappy, and possibly lose her relationship with Connor in the process. On the other hand, part of knowing when and how to express emotions includes knowing when it is inappropriate to do so; once she had made her point, Ellen realized she also needed to discuss the situation analytically, instead of emotionally, since feelings weren't going to close the distance between Providence and Baltimore. It was also likely that Connor would just walk away again if he got too uncomfortable with her emotional expression. By using her emotional strength to figure out how and when to express her feelings to Connor, Ellen managed to diffuse her anxiety and encourage both honesty and openness in their relationship.

Being able to express emotions benefits women's mental and physical health. UCLA psychologist Annette Stanton and her colleagues followed a group of women in treatment for breast cancer for three months. Women who were able to express their worries and distress to others at the beginning of the study needed fewer medical appointments for cancer-related pain and experienced less distress over the three months compared to women who did not express their emotions to others.[17] Most likely, this is because holding in your emotions takes physical work, labor that is taxing on the body. James Gross of Stanford University has studied people who are watching emotionally evocative films, such as movies of gory surgeries. While they view the movie, he tells some of the participants to suppress expression of any emotion they are feeling, while others are allowed to express any emotions they feel. Those who are told to suppress their emotions show greater physiological arousal while watching the film than those who express their emotions.[18] Similarly, men who stonewall in difficult conversations with their wives and partners show greater physiological arousal than when they don't stonewall. A lifetime of suppressing your emotions appears to raise blood pressure, damage the heart, and tear holes in the stomach, leading to cardiac problems, ulcers, and other diseases.

Expressing your emotions can also signal to others that you need help. You need other people to validate and comfort you. You need others to provide you with practical assistance—money, job connections, babysitting, heavy lifting, and so on. When you stifle your emotions, other people may not clue in to what you need, particularly if they aren't really good at reading the signs of your emotions on your face and in your posture.

Other people aren't always supportive of your expression of emotions, however. In Stanton's studies, women whose partners or friends didn't want to hear about their emotions, in some cases even criticizing them for expressing their emotions, didn't benefit as much as other women from emotional expression. Men may not benefit from emotional expression as much as women because such expression is socially unacceptable for men. Men who do express their emotions risk being criticized or ostracized by others.[19]

What should a person do if his or her world doesn't support the expression of emotions? James Pennebaker of the University of Texas at Austin has found that emotionally expressive writing can be a useful substitute, or complement, for expressing emotions to others. In twenty years of important research, Pennebaker discovered that people who write down their deepest thoughts and feelings about tragedies they have experienced, including the suicide of a spouse, violence they have endured, and unemployment, show improvements in mental and physical health compared to people who simply write about non-emotional topics.[20] People who write about the emotional events in their lives experience a release of tension that comes by way of "letting out" their memories and concerns. Pennebaker believes that the process of translating your emotions into language—into a story that helps you understand and integrate your experience with the whole story of your life, goals, and values—is what makes such journal writing beneficial. Experiencing a tragedy without being able to express emotions about it is usually psychologically distracting; it leaves a big elephant in the room of your conscious, distracting you from everyday activities, niggling at you when you least need it. Keeping an emotional "secret" isolates you from the social world, even though others don't know it; it can sometimes even cause a person to feel ashamed. Constructing a story around an emotional event by writing about it integrates it into your life narrative and frees you to interact more authentically with others and attend to the life that is going on right now.

Wait, you may say, what about expressing anger? Aren't women really bad at expressing anger? In our research, Cheryl Rusting and I have indeed found that women are less likely than men to express anger. And it's not that women don't experience anger as much as men do. When you ask them privately, women are just as likely as men to say they would get angry in situations that should make them angry, such as other people cutting in line at an ATM, and women report experiencing just as much anger in their daily lives as men do. When you observe men and women, however, men are considerably more likely than women to actually *express* their anger.

Yet it appears that expressing anger may not be as adaptive as expressing other emotions. Many studies show that men and women who frequently experience and express their anger are more likely to be chronically hostile and prone to heart attacks and cardiovascular disease.[21] Expressing anger can also damage relationships and invite retaliation from others, and women are especially likely to get hurt when others retaliate. On the other hand, contrary to popular notions, suppressing your anger doesn't tend to make you depressed, lead you to drink alcohol or binge on food, or give you a heart attack.[22] So it seems that women are particularly emotionally intelligent when it comes to expressing their emotions. Women know which emotions are healthy to express and when to do so, and even which emotions are better to keep under a lid.

Emotional Strength #3: Women know how and when to express their emotions.

Hanging In There

Knowing what you're feeling and having an outlet to express those feelings makes it easier to tolerate the feelings while they're happening. On the other hand, if you don't know what you're feeling, and don't believe you can show your feelings to others, the feelings and the physiological arousal that goes along with them can press and jab at your insides, becoming increasingly painful mentally and physically, to the point where they become intolerable.

Women are not only better at tolerating their own emotions than men, they are better at tolerating other people's emotions. Women can hang in there with a friend who is tearfully recounting a recent tragedy in her life, or with a child who is sobbing but can't articulate why, or an employee who is anxious about a presentation. They patiently wait as the emotional person calms down at his or her own pace. Then they slowly draw out the person, asking about his or her feelings and accepting the emotions on display. Slowly, as the other person is able to pull down the heat of the emotional experience, it becomes possible to discuss the root of the emotion and how best to address it.

Because men don't know what to do with their emotions, they have difficulty tolerating emotional distress—in themselves and in others. Men experience difficulty "being" with others' emotions. They get overwhelmed when their partners, children, and coworkers get emotional. They tend to jump immediately into advice-giving mode, offering solutions for fixing a problem before they really know what the problem is, or if there is a problem at all. As a result, the emotional person can often end up feeling misunderstood, invalidated, patronized, and incompetent.

Often these differences between women's and men's ability to tolerate distress result in thorny arguments between couples. Women frequently accuse their husbands of not caring enough to talk about their problems, and men frequently accuse their wives of seeing problems that don't exist. Kay's husband, Thomas, had a really hard time dealing with being upset. Rather than negotiating conflicts with Kay, Thomas would either stonewall, stubbornly and silently insisting on his point of view, or withdraw, often leaving the house so he didn't have to talk with Kay any further. Fortunately, Kay had an intuitive understanding of how difficult it was for Thomas to talk about emotional topics, and she loved him and their relationship enough to find creative ways to help him be more emotionally expressive. She didn't push him or get frustrated when he was clearly getting overwhelmed. Instead, she gently declared a "time-out" in their conversation, making it clear she didn't think their issues were resolved but suggesting that they both needed to "cool down" for a while (although she could have kept on talking). Then later she would raise the issue again, but only after thinking of ways to frame it in a non-threatening and non-accusatory way. Finally, she would propose some simple steps they could begin to take to overcome the situation. Over time, Thomas began to trust that when Kay returned to conflict-ridden issues after a "time-out" period, it would be in a way he could handle, and with good ideas for how to address their problems.

Women's ability to tolerate their own and others' distress comes in handy outside of the family as well. In the work world, there are many opportunities for employees to become emotional, and many times when a manager must navigate employees' emotions and their own.

Take, for example, a subordinate who is underperforming at his job and is staring down a job review in just a few weeks' time. The work environment feels like a pressure cooker to him. Despite repeated instructions, he seems unmotivated or even negligent, making mistake after mistake. Or take a colleague who believes she should be given special privileges over other employees because of her long tenure at the company, even though her peers are bringing in 50 percent more business. When she does land a new client, she seems to gloat, asking her teammates to congratulate her on her success, though she does not do the same for them. As a manager, you may just want to explode in exasperation and frustration at these employees. But exploding seldom has good outcomes for getting the job done or for your own perform-ance ratings as a manager. Managers who can tolerate this frustration without exploding or shutting down remain in the game long enough and effectively enough to get the job done. They can also calm down enough to think of assertive and effective ways of communicating with these employees.

Employees may at times bring their personal problems, along with the resulting emotions, to the office. They may have problems with their partner, parents, or children that are affecting their ability to focus on work. They may have emotionally charged issues with other employees. And when you, as a manager, have to give a negative per-formance evaluation to an employee, or even have to lay off or fire an employee, you'll be the recipient of a lot of emotion from that employee. If you can tolerate your employees' emotional displays and the emotions that these displays arouse in you, it's much easier to keep a cool head and respond appropriately to the situation.

Nora, a fifty-seven-year-old mid-level manager at a major invest-ment firm on Wall Street, got plenty of exposure to her employees' emotions in the recent economic downturn. For weeks there were rumors that there would be massive lay-offs. This created anxiety, anger, and jealousy in the office, as employees ruminated on whether they would be laid off and the injustice of being laid off if others, whom they considered weak performers, were not. Whereas Alan, a manager in a different branch of the firm, handled these emotions by

ignoring them, sometimes barking orders to stop being distracted and
get back to work, Nora made a point of reaching out to each of the
people who worked under her. She approached them in a quiet place
or invited them for a cup of coffee to talk about the difficulties of
working with so much uncertainty. Nora wanted to know what they
were facing if they were laid off, and although she couldn't promise
them anything about whether they would be saved or cut, she tried to
help them focus on living each day as it came and not chewing themselves up with anxiety.

When the lay-off notices came from the central office, Nora took
the list of those who were laid off and went to each person individu-
ally to express her sadness and offer a letter of recommendation for the
job hunt. Her employees expressed deep appreciation to her for her
compassion. Due to her efforts before and after the lay-offs were
announced, Nora's employees were in better emotional shape to
handle the news. Compared to the laid-off employees who reported to
Alan, a greater percentage of Nora's employees were able to find new
jobs in the first few months. Alan's employees reported that they felt
abandoned and battered by him.

Women's ability to tolerate distress allows them to hang in there,
dealing with difficult situations with a cool head and a clear purpose.
Since distressing emotions arise in every role in life—in dealing with
children and spouses, in the workplace, in interactions with people in
your community—women have many opportunities to put this emotional strength to use.

Emotional Strength #4: Women can tolerate distress and are thus
better equipped to alleviate it.

Emotion Managers

Accepting that you have negative feelings—that you are angry or
sad or afraid—is the first step to managing emotions so that they do
not spiral out of control or undermine your ability to function. If

you don't accept that you are feeling angry, sad, worried, and so on, you may ignore important signals your emotions are trying to give you—that a threatening situation is looming, or that you are about to be cheated. If you don't accept your feelings, they stay bottled up, under pressure, and later can explode. Because women are not afraid or ashamed to have emotions, they are able to accept their negative feelings, try to understand them, and then respond to them appropriately.

At this point, I have a confession to make. I have focused much of my career to date on the *problems* women have in managing emotions. In particular, my research has shown that some women get too involved in analyzing their emotions, to the point that they overthink and ruminate about them, and spiral down into depression and despair.[23] Overthinking can also lead women to binge on food or drink excessive alcohol in an attempt to drown out their worries and concerns. So overthinking is indeed a problem for some women. But the majority of women don't get stuck in overthinking, and the vast majority of women do not suffer from depression, binge-eating, or alcohol abuse.

Instead, most women find ways of balancing their negative emotional experiences with more positive emotional experiences. Psychologists Frank Fujita, Ed Diener, and Ed Sandvik found that women experience both negative and positive emotions more intensely than men do.[24] So even when women experience more negative emotions than men, their propensity to experience positive emotions more intensely tends to balance their negative emotions.

Positive emotions can literally undo the damaging effects of negative emotions. Negative emotions narrow your thoughts to themes of loss and lack of control. They motivate you to hunker down and withdraw to protect yourself. Positive emotions, according to research by psychologist Barbara Fredrickson, open your mind, allowing you to be more creative in finding ways around obstacles you face. Fredrickson finds that when people can recruit positive emotions in the midst of experiencing negative emotions, the broadening effects of positive emotions undo the narrowing effects of negative emotions, loosening the grip that negative emotions have on thinking and making it easier to find solutions to your problems.[25]

Fredrickson found that positive emotions also undo the harmful physiological effects of negative emotions. She first asked people to watch a short film that aroused negative emotions and cardiovascular activity. Then these people were randomly assigned to subsequently watch film clips that were mildly positive, neutral, or sad in tone. People who watched the positive film clips showed faster cardiovascular recovery from their previous negative emotions than the people who watched the sad or neutral film clips. So women's tendency to balance negative emotions with positive emotions may not only undo the effects of the negative emotions on their thinking and problem solving, it may also prevent these negative emotions from damaging their health.

Women have lots of other ways of managing their moods. In a study of adults who were caregivers for a family member with end-stage cancer, I asked men and women what they do to cope with their distressing feelings. Women reported using significantly more positive strategies than men did, including expressing their emotions, reaching out to others for social support, trying to find a different perspective on their problems, and engaging in active problem solving. In fact, it was hard to determine what the men in this study were doing to cope, except stoically living with their situation.

When you are faced with a huge stressor such as the loss of a loved one, managing your emotions effectively requires you to move flexibly among a variety of coping strategies. Bereavement expert Margaret Stroebe of the University of Utrecht in the Netherlands believes that people who have recently faced a loss must spend time coming to terms with it by recounting memories of the deceased, thinking about the meaning of the loss and their relationship to the deceased, and thinking about their own self-definition. But they cannot become chronically mired in thoughts of their loss or they will be in danger of never moving on with their lives. Thus bereaved people need to balance processing their loss with rebuilding their lives in concrete ways—for example, by simply cooking meals for their families or going back to work.

Esther, a thirty-five-year-old woman who participated in the bereavement study, had recently lost her sixty-nine-year-old mother to lung cancer. She beautifully described this back-and-forth coping strategy:

> Sometimes I question myself as to whether I'm being very unemotional about things, and then I realize I understand what it is that's happened, and I don't try to make it more than it is. When I wake up in the morning, I still have children to feed and things to do. The old life-goes-on saying is true, so there's the reality of it all. You can't just get caught in one thing and dwell on it. I've tried to run away from things, but that's not going to work either. You have to face it sometime.

Esther knew she couldn't shut out her feelings of grief and emptiness all the time, so she gave herself room to experience these feelings and express them in conversations with her friends and eventually through poetry. She also knew she had to take breaks from these feelings and deal with the reality of her continuing responsibilities to her family and work. For this reason, Esther fared very well over time. Her grief subsided and her memories of her mother grew sweeter, enriching her relationships with her own children. By managing her feelings in the wake of her mother's death, Esther not only came to terms with a difficult situation but also grew as a person.

Learning to turn negative emotions into positive ones is also beneficial to women in the business world. One frustrating stereotype of women is that they are overly emotional and can't handle the pressures of the workplace. Women who display emotions, or handle them inappropriately, are sometimes branded as unfit for leadership. However, much of this prejudice derives from the standard male behavior of completely suppressing emotions. As researchers Alice Eagly and Steven Karau suggest, the problem is not that women may cry more often in the workplace than men, it's that crying doesn't fit into the typical work culture, which has for decades been defined by an extreme version of men's gender-role expectations.[26]

As work cultures have become more diverse and less dominated by men, the norms for displaying emotions in the office are loosening up. At the same time, being able to turn frustration, rage, and disappointment at work into something more productive and creative gives women an advantage. Studies of emotion regulation in the workplace find that people who manage annoyances in positive ways—by trying to take a positive perspective on their frustrations or finding ways to infuse some positive emotions into their day—perform better in the workplace and are more psychologically healthy.[27] For example, workers in a bank's customer service call center earned better performance ratings if they tended to respond to their customers' annoying questions ("How do I operate the ATM machine?") by taking a genuinely positive perspective. In contrast, if they simply faked being nice to the customer, they were more emotionally exhausted and numb at the end of the day.[28]

Women's ability to manage their emotions through a variety of strategies, instead of shutting them out or faking them, is finally contributing to their rise to professional leadership roles. Nora, the supervisor in the Wall Street firm that laid off many workers, had exceptional skills at managing emotions. Instead of denying her feelings and stonewalling her employees, she acknowledged and accepted that the job uncertainty everyone was facing was frightening—and a good reason for employees to resent the company. She helped her employees air these emotions and then shifted their focus to dealing with the demands of their jobs (or their job hunts) as best they could. In contrast, her colleague Alan refused to talk with employees who approached him for information. His work group showed sharp declines in productivity, and some employees were caught stealing materials from the workplace in retribution for their frustrations.

Nora also managed her own feelings about the impending lay-offs well. She couldn't be sure that she wouldn't also get the ax, so she decided to look at the situation as an opportunity to evaluate whether she was really in the job she wanted. Nora made discreet inquiries about similar jobs with other firms—what the pay structure was, what the chances for advancement might be. She also thought about other goals she had for her life—to pursue her interest in painting, to travel more, perhaps to teach English as a second language. Using her contacts at her synagogue and Web-based career services, she discovered two nonprofit organizations through which she might be able to travel to developing countries to teach English to schoolchildren for a couple of years. The position only offered her a subsistence income, but she had saved for years and had a cushion of money that could see her through a two-year assignment.

Nora also reached out to family members and friends for support during the uncertainty at work. She made regular dinner dates with one of her oldest friends, Alicia, and as the two of them ate sushi at their favorite restaurant, Nora recounted some of the conversations she had with employees, or ran ideas past Alicia for what she might do if she were laid off. They laughed a lot and cried a bit, and Nora always went home feeling cleansed and reenergized to deal with the situation at work the next day.

Nora's willingness to deal with her emotions, her ability to take an efficacious perspective on her work situation, to focus on problem solving, and to use her emotional support network to cope enabled her to emerge from the lay-offs feeling proud of how she handled them and optimistic for the future. As it turned out, Nora wasn't laid off. Indeed, she had managed her group so effectively during the period before the lay-offs that her bosses gave her new responsibilities and a moderate raise. But Nora's explorations of how she might pursue other life goals led her to make a five-year plan: she would stay at this firm for another three years and save money like crazy, then she would take a two-year post teaching English overseas with a nonprofit organization. Nora returned to her new position after the lay-offs appreciating her own performance as a manager and enjoying the praise she got from her superiors, but also with a wider sense of purpose for her life and a plan for fulfilling that purpose.

Emotional Strength #5: Women excel at managing their feelings.

A 2001 Gallup Poll found that 90 percent of Americans think that women are more emotional than men. This is often seen as a liability for women, something that holds them back from achieving their goals and makes them more vulnerable. Some of women's greatest strengths, however, emerge in the emotional realm. Women are able to perceive others' emotions, which increases their effectiveness in the workplace, in parenting, and in building bonds with others. Women understand their own emotions, the first step to making decisions that a person can live with and to managing adaptively. Women can express their emotions appropriately, enhancing communication with others and garnering the support they need. Women can tolerate distress, which allows them to stay in the game in crisis situations, even when emotions are running high. And women have a variety of strategies they use flexibly for managing their emotions, making them resilient in times of stress. It's a good thing women are "emotional."

5.

Valuable Links: Understanding Women's Relational Strengths

"I'm a real people person," a woman friend of mine recently said. But what does that mean? I believe there are at least two categories of "people persons." One comprises outgoing, gregarious people who love to socialize and be the life of the party. Some women fall into this category. The other includes people who want to *know* other people, to get inside their heads and see the world from their different point of view. This kind of "people person" has great empathy for how other people feel, and wants to do what it takes to make others feel better. More women have personalities aligned with this second category than the first.

Women's tendency to empathize with others, their willingness to listen and be patient and forgiving, and the sacrifices they make for others, are often seen as liabilities. "Stand up for yourself!" women are told. "Don't listen to them! Don't always give in to others!" These prescriptions have indeed been important for some women to hear. Our culture has long assumed that women are the caring sex, that they are built to nurture others, and it is their natural responsibility to do so, no matter what the cost. Women who violate this assumption are often punished, either outright or through character assassination. By contrast, men who are empathic toward others, or who are willing to forgo their own needs for others, are held up as heroes.

Take, for example, how women and men who are in the army, and
who have small children, are viewed. If the mother of young children
joins the army and gets deployed overseas for a year-long tour of duty,
it's not unusual to hear people suggest she must be more devoted to
her career than to her children, that she is shirking her responsibilities
as a mother. If the father of young children is deployed overseas, he is
a hero, sacrificing the joys of fatherhood for service to his country. The
same has long been true of politicians running for office. As a recent
example, when Sarah Palin, the governor of Alaska and the mother of
five children, was nominated by the Republican Party to run for vice
president in 2008, a frequent question was "Who is going to take care
of her kids?" No one asked the same question of Barack Obama, the
father of two.

The cultural assumptions that women will always be patient and
tolerant, will "stand by their man" no matter what he does, that
women are inherently the caring sex, have led some women to make
choices that are unhealthy for them and for those around them. Most
women, however, find a sustainable balance between exercising their
relational strengths and standing up for their personal rights. Most
women know where that line lies, beyond which they will not go to
help others, because it would not be good for them or good for the
other. Mothers go to great lengths to give their children what they need
and want, yet also recognize that indulging their children's desires, or
letting them get away with bad behavior, will not serve their children
in the end. There's a point at which they know they must always say
"no more."

Many women are good at listening to others and empathizing with
them—this is what draws many women to the helping professions,
and makes them so proficient as therapists and social workers. But
they recognize that listening and connecting to others can be emotionally taxing, and that they need to take time for themselves, let go
of others' cares, and regroup. Women in business find ways of integrating the goals of individual employees with the goals of the
company. They listen to the desires of employees and respect them, but
know that they must also watch the bottom line for the company.

Women's roles as caregivers, especially to children, have honed their relational skills. Over evolutionary history, relational strengths may have literally been built into women's genes.[1] Women who in ancient times were able to understand and respond to their children's physical, social, and emotional needs had children who were more healthy, safer, and more likely to survive and bear their own children. Women who didn't have many relational strengths did not care for their children as effectively, so their children were less likely to survive and bear children. Thus the genes of women who had better relational strengths were more likely to be passed down over the centuries.

These days, women bring their tremendous relational strengths to their parenting, their friendships, their marriages and partnerships; their workplaces, and into the communities. Because women are able to know people at a deep level, they draw out others' best qualities, navigate around others' weaknesses, and successfully encourage and motivate other people. They find common ground and work to develop mutually satisfactory solutions to problems. Women operate well in the midst of diverse opinions and people, because they are willing and able to hear and understand different points of view. Women are "there" when they are needed, ready to take on a leadership role or a supportive role, as the situation demands.

Women's social identities—self-concepts that are intimately integrated with relationships with others—along with their emotional awareness are the foundation for incredibly robust relational strengths:

- Women are able to deeply understand the perspective of others, their viewpoints, concerns, and feelings. As a result, they are able to respond empathically to others, anticipate their needs and desires, and reveal a forgiving attitude toward those who have wronged them.
- Women listen to others, letting them express their point of view, trying to hear and understand them instead of drowning out others with their own opinions.

- Women are patient and tolerant, able to wait while others find a way to get where they want to be (or should be).
- Women know when to put others' needs first, and are altruistic in understated as well as daring ways.

Put It in Perspective

Exquisitely attuned to the feelings of their friends, colleagues, and neighbors, women often have keen insight into other people's experiences, no matter how removed these experiences are from their own daily struggles. Some of this ability comes from women's more developed ability to accurately perceive others' emotions (by looking at their faces, watching their posture and hand gestures, and listening to their tone of voice). Since emotions are a reflection of people's deepest thoughts and concerns, being able to read emotions gives women a window into other people's souls. Women go far beyond this, however, recognizing the pressures besetting people that lead them to behave in certain ways, and delving into others' beliefs and backgrounds to understand how their personalities have been shaped.

In order to understand what another person might be thinking and feeling, you first have to accept that the other person has a different point of view from you. Psychologists call this possessing a *theory of mind*. This may seem a fundamental skill that every human must have, but people differ in the degree to which they understand that other people can—and do—hold perspectives different from their own. For instance, very young children don't seem to get this idea at all. To study theory of mind in young children, developmental psychologists present children with tasks that pinpoint the age at which they are able to distinguish what they know from what others know. Consider the following: a researcher shows a child a candy box with pictures of candy on it and then asks her what she thinks is in it. "Candy," she'll reply. Then the child gets to look inside, and to her surprise there are crayons inside the box. The researcher asks her what another child, who hasn't yet looked into the box, will think is in the box. If a child is at least five years old, most of the time she'll say, "The other child will think there is candy in the box, but it's really crayons." This five-year-old has developed a theory of mind—an understanding that another child can have a different perspective than she does. But when a three-year-old is asked what another child will think is in the box, she's likely to say, "Crayons." Three-year-olds haven't yet developed a theory of mind, so they assume that whatever they think or believe is what others will think or believe. In tasks such as these, girls tend to display a theory of mind earlier than boys do.[2]

Further, when children are older, girls tend to be able to understand others' thoughts, motives, and feelings better than boys. For example, psychologist Sandra Leanne Bosacki presented a group of eleven and twelve-year-old boys and girls with the following story:

> Kenny and Mark are co-captains of the football team. They have one person left to choose for the team. Without saying anything, Mark winks at Kenny and looks at Tom who is one of the remaining children left to be chosen for the team. Mark looks back at Kenny and smiles. Kenny nods and chooses Tom to be on their team. Tom sees Mark and Kenny winking and smiling at each other. Tom, who is usually one of the last to be picked for team sports, wonders why Kenny wants him to be on his team. [Note: girls' names were used when the story was told to girls.][3]

Then Bosacki asked the children questions about the story, including: "Why did Mark smile at Kenny?" "Why did Kenny nod?" "Why did Kenny choose Tom to be on the team? How do you know this?" "Do you think that Tom has any idea why Kenny chose him to be on the team? How do you know this?" "How do you think Tom feels? Why?" In answering these questions, the sixth-grade girls described the possible thoughts and feelings of the characters in the story, their possible motivations and intentions, and the moral judgments driving their behavior. The sixth-grade boys were less likely to talk as if they understood or cared about what might be going through the minds of the characters in the story.

When you take the perspective of another person, you literally use the same parts of your brain that are used when thinking about yourself. In an experiment conducted at Harvard University, researchers used an fMRI machine to record brain activity while people were thinking about themselves or about others. While they were in the scanner, half of the people in the study were told to think about themselves, whereas the other half of the participants in the study were shown a photograph of an unfamiliar person's face (the target) and instructed: "Imagine for a moment that you are this person, walking through the world in their shoes and seeing the world through their eyes. Think about how you, as this person, would experience this event."[4] The same areas of the brain were active in both the participants who thought about themselves and the participants who thought about the target while "seeing the world in their eyes."

Seeing the world through another's eyes can be particularly challenging if you are the parent of an adolescent. Adolescents long for autonomy and independence; they constantly test how far they can stretch the rules of authority. One minute they may seem to be the rational, reasonable children you've known for fifteen or sixteen years, and the next minute they are an incomprehensible muddle of emotions, desires, and bizarre opinions. As the primary caregiver in many families, women have developed skills at applying a theory of mind to their adolescent children's behavior. Researchers have found that when mothers strive to take their adolescents' point of view during conflicts, adolescents become less focused on winning the argument and more focused on maintaining a positive relationship with the mother. In turn, there is less open hostility between the adolescent and his or her mother, and they are better able to work toward a mutually agreeable solution to the conflict.[5] Mothers who try to inhabit an adolescent's perspective may be more generous in their interpretations of teenagers' behavior, better understanding the effects of peer pressure and the anxious desire to fit in. Mothers who are able to take their teenagers' perspectives are also less likely to become angry, to escalate conflict, and to break down the channels of communication.

Ashley's thirteen-year-old daughter, Jenna, was definitely in that phase of adolescence where every discussion with her parents provided grounds for conflict. Ashley's husband, Sean, usually took the position of rule enforcer, holding a strict line on Jenna's curfew hours, the length of her skirts, and the expectations for her academic performance at school. When Sean and Jenna would disagree over one of these subjects, it usually ended with Sean raising his voice and Jenna yelling, crying, and running to her room.

Yet Ashley could understand Jenna's yearning to fit in with other girls and to socialize with her friends. Ashley didn't want to give in to all of Jenna's pleas to enjoy the same late nights, heavy makeup, short skirts, and Facebook time as her friends. But she also thought Sean's regimented approach only goaded Jenna to push the rules even further.

After another screaming match between Jenna and Sean, Ashley went into Jenna's room and sat next to her as Jenna buried her head under her pillow. "Honey," Ashley began, "we have to find a better way to work out these disagreements."

"Daddy is so unfair and unreasonable!" Jenna cried. "You guys are in the Dark Ages with your rules! None of the other kids have parents as strict as you!"

"That may be true, but we believe in our rules and believe that they are best for you," Ashley said. "I know it's important to you to spend time with your friends, and to do things like the other kids do. Your dad and I want you to have fun and enjoy your time with your friends. I believe you can do that and still follow the spirit of our family rules."

Ashley and Jenna proceeded to talk about which of the family rules were most important, and what activities were most important to Jenna in her interactions with her friends. Jenna confirmed Ashley's suspicion that she sometimes wore really short skirts and a lot of makeup to provoke a reaction from her father. She conceded this might not be a great way to get him to cooperate on the things that really mattered to her. Jenna's main concern was that she wasn't allowed to stay out past ten o'clock at night, which meant she had to leave early from school dances and sometimes couldn't join her group of friends at the local multiplex, because many movies ended after her curfew. Ashley offered that now that Jenna was thirteen, the 10 p.m. rule could be made more flexible, to accommodate special social occasions. That didn't mean Jenna could stay out until ten o'clock every weekend night, rather that when circumstances called for it, the rule could be bent.

Because Ashley was willing to see things from Jenna's point of view, Jenna was willing to calm down and work with her to find compromises between the family rules and Jenna's demands for more independence. Instead of open warfare, Ashley and Jenna's relationship was marked by trust, cooperation, and good humor—essential ingredients for helping any teen (and their parents) make it through adolescence successfully.

Similarly, in business and politics, the ability to get inside the heads of other people is essential to devising solutions to problems that others—even competitors—can accept and implement with enthusiasm. This is particularly useful when settling business deals, legislation, and other agreements. Studies of business people find that those with better perspective-taking skills are more successful at negotiating deals that satisfy both parties. For example, in one study, MBA students were asked to play the roles of a candidate for a job or a recruiter from a company. The candidate and the recruiter were given competing goals to work for—the candidate was to work for a higher salary and the recruiter was to offer a lower salary; the candidate was to ask for more vacation and the recruiter was to offer less vacation; and so on. The candidate and recruiter earned certain numbers of points for achieving each goal. Half of the time, the recruiter was instructed to take the perspective of the candidate as he or she was making offers and proposals:

> In preparing for the negotiation and during the negotiation, take the perspective of the candidate. Try to understand what they are thinking in their situation. After reading your role, try to visualize yourself on the other side of the table, in that role, thinking as the candidate.[6]

The other half of the time, the recruiter was not told to take the perspective of the candidate. The negotiations in which the recruiter took the perspective of the candidate resulted in more give-and-take between the two individuals: the recruiter might compromise on one goal in exchange for the candidate compromising on another goal. At the end, perspective-taking resulted in greater gain for both the recruiter and the candidate: they each earned more points, indicating they had achieved more of their goals overall.

Negotiating was Kate's specialty. She had been trained in labor law at the University of Chicago Law School, and when she was hired by a Cleveland machine tool manufacturer her employers initially expected her to take the strict company line in all negotiations with the union. Kate took that position for the first couple years but was wholly dissatisfied with the results, which usually involved bitter meetings, hurled accusations, expensive strikes, and week after week without progress.

By her third year on the job, Kate decided to do things her way. Instead of convening meetings that included several people on each side—which set up a situation wherein lower-level attendees spent the whole time posturing to impress the group with how tough they were—she insisted on sitting down with the union president one-on-one. Before the first meeting, she learned as much as she could about the current president of the union—about his job history with the tool company, his family, his hobbies, his religion. When they got together, she chatted with him about the Cleveland Indians, since she had learned that he, too, was a big fan of the team. Then, as the talk turned to business, Kate started not by stating the company's position, but by asking the president to tell her what the issues and concerns of the union were. She already knew what they were, but she wanted to hear them from the president, to notice what he emphasized, to hear which issues got him the most emotional, and to see if there were any things he wouldn't, or couldn't, state while looking her in the eye. Then, to the president's astonishment, rather than coming back with the company's demands, Kate repeated back to the president his union's top issues and concerns, asking to be corrected if she misunderstood or misstated anything. As the meeting progressed, Kate did her best to repeatedly identify areas of common ground between the union and the company. When she had to insist on a particular position that the

company couldn't concede, she balanced that with an offer to compromise on some issue that she perceived the union felt strongly
about. In the four years after Kate switched to this perspective-taking
style of negotiation, the union had called no strikes, the company had
cut costs and increased profits, and the relations between the company
and the union had improved markedly.

Women's strong skills at perspective-taking also enhance their ability to teach and mentor others. Women can often see the obstacles that
are preventing people from achieving their goals, whether those obstacles are logistical or psychological, and then offer solutions tailored
to an individual's needs. Anne Mulcahy, former chief executive of Xerox
Corporation, is well known for using her perspective-taking skills to
nurture employees and bring them up through the ranks. She herself
was a Xerox veteran, with twenty-four years in sales and as head of
human resources before she was named CEO. As CEO, Mulcahy regu-
larly reviewed the thirty top executive positions in the company,
ensuring that there were at least two internal candidates being groomed
for these positions. "She is a superb motivator who can push people to
step up their game without demoralizing them in the process," according to Ursula M. Burns, then the company's president.[7] When Mulcahy
took the helm in August 2001, the company was on the verge of bank-
ruptcy, with $273 million in losses. Mulcahy led a turnaround of the
company and focused efforts on innovation, even in the troubled sales
environment immediately following 9/11. Upon her retirement in
2009, the company was strategically sound, with over $1 billion in prof-
its, and Burns rose to chief executive. In 2008, Mulcahy was named
Chief Executive of the Year by *Chief Executive* magazine and one of
America's Best Leaders by *U.S. News and World Report.*

As we will see, women's ability to take others' perspectives is intricately tied to their other relational strengths—their ability to listen to
others, to be patient, and to put others first appropriately.

Relational Strength #1: Women are able to take others' perspectives.

The Active Listener

One reason women are so good at taking perspective is because they listen to others. It's much easier to know what another person is thinking if you're listening to her as she speaks rather than focusing on what *you* want to say as soon as she pauses, or even jumping in and interrupting when that pause doesn't come soon enough. In general, women listen—on a deep level—to what their family, friends, and colleagues are trying to communicate. This doesn't mean that women are incapable of expressing their own needs and desires—far from it—but instead that women are willing and able to hear what other people have to say and integrate it into how they express their own point of view.

For instance, when Anne Mulcahy was asked how she knew what direction to lead Xerox Corporation, she said:

> There are plenty of avenues for getting feedback, but there's nothing that substitutes for the dialogue that you can have with people on the ground, with your customers in terms of how they view the company. I think it is really powerful, and it's something that I expect our entire management team to do as well. This is not an arm's-length exercise. You've got to get up close and personal. You've got to give people permission to give you tough news, not shoot the messenger, thank people for identifying problems early and giving you the opportunity to solve them. So I think part of it is the way you handle candid feedback, but the other part is being present. . . . Nothing replaces sitting around a table and really asking people what's working, what's not working, what's getting in their way, how do we help? I do a lot of that and I think it is the most important thing I do.[8]

Women don't just sit stone silent, preoccupied with their own thoughts, as another person spills out his or her concerns. Instead, they lean forward, bonding with the other person, showing with their eyes, their face, and every muscle of their body that they are listening. When listening to another person, a woman will express empathy, making it clear she understands what the other is saying and feeling, and that she cares. She will ask questions, making sure that she knows the full situation and how the other person perceives it. She will legitimize what the other person says, letting him or her know that these feelings and thoughts are normal and reasonable. She may commiserate with the other person, talking about similar experiences she has had. She may rant and rave with the other person, saying things such as, "I can't believe he did that to you! What a jerk!" For women, listening is an active state.

Nowhere is active listening more important than in women's roles as mothers. When children have difficulty in school or with their peers, they usually seek understanding and help from their parents, as well as affirmation that they are good people in spite of their problems. But even when children desperately want their parents' help, they usually aren't very good at coming right out and asking for it. Their revelations usually seep through the cracks in conversations about other topics. You have to be listening very carefully, not holding any agenda except to hear and understand your child, in order to detect the admission of many problems.

A recent conversation between Judi and her son Ben illustrates the point. Ben is a pretty typical twelve-year-old boy in terms of his communicativeness. He usually only talks when spoken to and provides monosyllabic answers to many questions:

JUDI: How did things go at school today?
BEN: Good. (*Long silence*)
JUDI: How about that Spanish quiz? Did you feel like you'd studied enough last night?
BEN: Yeah. (*Long silence*) Except for the irregular conjugations.
JUDI: The conjugations?
BEN: I think I failed them.

Now at this point, what Judi really wanted to say was "You never even studied the irregulars last night—you said they weren't going to be on the test!" But she knew that would make him clam up immediately, so she took a deep breath and said:

JUDI: Took you by surprise, huh?

What followed was a calm discussion in which Judi tried to impress upon Ben the importance of knowing which subjects were going to be tested—and then studying the appropriate material. Ben agreed to pay more attention when the teacher spoke about upcoming exams, but he also mentioned that when he was text messaging his friend Mike on his cell phone the previous night, Mike had told him not to worry about the irregular conjugations. Judi was surprised to learn that Ben had been text messaging during his designated study time and probed further. It turned out that Ben was constantly being distracted by text messages from his friends during study time, which accounted for his less than stellar academic performance of late. This was a revelation to Judi, and she and Ben proceeded to brainstorm how they could limit his distractions during study time.

If Judi had immediately responded with the accusatory thoughts that were whirling in her head, she probably would not have detected the larger problem with Ben's study habits. But by slowing down and actively listening to Ben, Judi gained insight into why her son wasn't performing better in school—and was able to work with him to come up with a mutually agreeable solution.

One professional setting in which active listening is particularly important is the doctor-patient exchange. It's not easy for doctors to listen—they are rushed and overbooked, with a new patient to see every ten minutes. Often patients bring a laundry list of problems into this ridiculously brief encounter, ranging from minor ailments such as a cold to major health challenges such as diabetes. Patients bring their own agendas to office visits, and sometimes the problems they are worried about are not the problems the doctor thinks they should be worried about. Sometimes physical problems are masks for emotional problems, as when a patient complains about insomnia when the real problem is depression.

So to be an effective listener, a doctor must concentrate and focus on these scarce moments with the patient. The doctor must catch everything the patient says and consider what issues might lurk beneath what he or she is saying; validate the patient's concerns while steering the conversation to the issues the doctor thinks are more important; and then communicate an assessment and treatment to the patient in a way that makes the patient feel heard and taken care of. It appears that active listening may come easier to doctors who are women. Observations of the conversations between doctors and patients in medical settings have found that female doctors are more likely than male doctors to listen attentively, to give patients the time and space to present problems, to ask patients questions to explore their concerns, to avoid getting distracted during the conversation, and to express their understanding and interest in the patient through their facial expressions and body posture.[9] In turn, patients are more satisfied with their doctor's care if the doctor is an active listener, and may be more likely to follow the doctor's orders in taking care of themselves if they believe the doctor was really listening to them.

One of the best doctors and best listeners I know is Carolyn Rochester, M.D. Carly is a specialist in pulmonary medicine, with responsibilities in at least three clinics around Connecticut. When she's not the attending physician in the critical care unit of a local hospital, she's taking care of patients at the Veterans Affairs hospital in a town several miles away, or running a clinic in another town forty-five minutes away. In the meantime, she is the very active and involved mother of two, and an avid biker and hiker. Despite how busy Carly is, and how much she is always needed in multiple places, whenever she is with you, she is 100 percent with you. She leans forward and listens, wants to know what's going on with you, wants to really connect with you. I have to laugh when I watch her teenage son, Nick, try to wriggle out of his mother's listening grip, attempting to keep his mother from knowing quite so much about what he's thinking and doing. Even her son has to admit, however, that he's glad that Carly listens to what he is saying—and what he is not saying—and the bond between the two of them is extremely strong. I haven't seen Carly in private conversations with her patients, of course, but I know they appreciate her listening and her competence—Carly has been named one of the best doctors in the New York area by *New York* magazine.

In our hectic, busy world, people often don't feel listened to. Women's skills at listening, and their desire to listen, are critical to all of their relationships, opening channels of communication and engendering deep trust.

Relational Strength #2: Women actively listen to others.

The Rewards of Patience

Women have a tremendous ability to wait—until their child's tantrum has run its course, until their husband calms down enough to talk, until their colleague finishes a long-winded monologue. It's not that women don't feel annoyed and angry just as often as men do. To the contrary, studies show that men and women are just as likely to experience anger in response to an irritating situation. The difference is that women tend to be better at coping with their anger. They work hard to prevent their feelings from spiraling out of control, which allows them to more calmly choose how to respond.

In a study that my colleague Cheryl Rusting and I conducted at the University of Michigan, we observed that men nursed their anger whereas women soothed their anger.[10] We asked men and women to recall an event that had made them feel very angry, to relive it as best they could:

> During the next ten minutes, try to reexperience the memory you've retrieved as vividly as you can. Picture the event happening to you all over again. Picture in your "mind's eye" the surroundings as clearly as possible. See the people or objects; hear the sounds; experience the events happening to you. Think the thoughts you actually thought in that situation. Feel the same feelings you felt in that situation. Let yourself react as if you were actually right there now. As

you're reimagining the event, write about what is happening, what you are thinking, and how you are feeling.[11]

  Both men and women felt quite angry in recounting this memory and had angry thoughts about the perpetrator of the incident and the unfairness of it all. Then we gave all the participants in the study the option of continuing to think about their feelings of anger and their memories of the angry situation, or doing something completely different that would get their minds off their moods—writing a description of their living room. Two-thirds of the men chose to nurse their angry thoughts, which just made them get angrier and angrier, while one-third chose to distract themselves by writing about their living rooms. By contrast, only one-quarter of the women chose to continue thinking about their angry thoughts and feelings, while three-quarters chose not to dwell on their anger and instead to think about the layout of their living room. Thus angry men tend to nurse their angry thoughts, which leads to increased rage, while women are more likely to choose not to dwell on their negative feelings, which prevents their anger from escalating.

  I believe that millennia of taking care of children have fostered these important qualities of tolerance and patience in women. Children, as wonderful as they are, also tend to be slow, inefficient little creatures, who wander through life at their own pace and on their own terms. If mothers were quick to be frustrated, our species would probably no longer exist—children would never survive into adulthood!

  Being able to take others' perspectives can help you be more patient and tolerant. If you understand where another person is coming from—the pressures they are under, the limitations they face—it's easier to remain patient with them. At age forty-four, Natasha found herself in the position of unexpectedly taking care of an older family member. Natasha's own parents had died when she was in her twenties, and her husband David's parents had lived across the country from them for the past fifteen years. But when her father-in-law died suddenly of a heart attack, David wanted to bring his mother, Iris, to live with them. They had plenty of room. Iris was a lovely person, and

Natasha and the children had always felt close to her. And it was clear Iris couldn't live on her own. She was in the early stages of Alzheimer's disease and could no longer cook or care for herself safely. So although Natasha was worried about how Iris's arrival and her illness would change the dynamics in the house, she agreed that Iris should move in.

The first year proceeded without any problems, and it was actually nice for the children to get a chance to know their grandmother better. But as Iris's Alzheimer's disease progressed, being with her grew more challenging. Iris would ask a simple question, such as "When is David coming home from work?" The children or Natasha would answer, then ten minutes later, she'd ask again, "When is David coming home from work?" And she'd ask again, and again, and again, until David showed up. She would decide that she had to find something, such as an old photograph, and would obsessively search for it for an hour, asking everyone repeatedly if they had seen it. If Iris had a doctor's appointment, Natasha would remind her about it several times on the preceding day, and again on the morning of the appointment. As the time neared to leave for the doctor's office, Natasha would urge Iris to get ready, but Iris would become distracted. Natasha would find Iris half dressed, looking through her closet, when they needed to leave immediately to make the appointment in time. Iris would get irritated with Natasha, complaining later to David that Natasha hadn't told her about the appointment.

Years later when Natasha looked back, she realized this was the most difficult time in caring for Iris—when she still could function in the family with some normalcy, and didn't really seem sick most of the time, but would ask questions with mind-numbing repetition, or accuse you of being the one who had forgotten something important, or do something innocent but very dangerous, such as put a kettle of water on for tea and completely forget about it until the kettle was melting on the stove burner. It was so hard not to get frustrated and annoyed with Iris, to expect her to behave like a healthy adult. But Natasha drew on her ability to take Iris's perspective, to fully appreciate that Iris didn't do any of these annoying things purposely, which allowed Natasha to remain patient in the most trying moments. When she began to get frustrated with Iris, Natasha would stop herself, take a deep breath, and say, "If I were a person with Alzheimer's, if I were Iris, could I do any better?" She knew the answer was likely "no" and this helped her relax, either to answer Iris's question yet again or to redirect Iris's attention away from her latest item of obsession.

Impatience with others often arises when we feel they are impeding our own progress toward some goal. You want to get to work and the person in front of you is driving ten miles below the speed limit, so you get impatient with her. I want to get this chapter written, but my son wants to go to Dunkin' Donuts for a hot chocolate, and I am impatient with his request. Being more patient comes when you recognize that you have multiple goals and priorities, and at times you have to let one go to serve another. I do have the goal of finishing this chapter, but an even more important goal is nurturing my relationship with my son. Taking him to Dunkin' Donuts for a hot chocolate won't get my chapter written, but it will give me a chance to spend some fun, relaxed time with him and talk. That helps me be a bit more patient.

Being patient with others often means forgiving their behavior, and women are especially good at forgiving others because of their perspective-taking skills.[12] When you can understand what is driving the other person's behavior, it is easier not to blame that person but to forgive him or her. Now, forgiveness doesn't necessarily mean excusing, justifying, or forgetting another's behavior. It does mean that you choose to understand the other's behavior as best you can, and to restore your relationship with that other person despite the behavior.

Being able to forgive others clearly has positive effects on relationships. Forgiving your partner or spouse for a transgression allows your relationship to be restored. Forgiving your children for misbehavior can bring your family back together. Forgiving a coworker for acting like a jerk allows the two of you to continue working together productively.

Forgiveness tends to be good for women's health. People who are able to forgive have fewer psychological problems, including depression and alcohol abuse.[13] Forgiveness may also improve physical health. In a study conducted by psychologist Charlotte Witvliet and her colleagues, participants were instructed to think about someone who had offended them, in either unforgiving ways (mentally rehearsing the hurtful offense, or nursing their grudge) or in forgiving ways (empathizing with the offender, forgiving them). When participants were thinking about their offender in forgiving ways, their heart rate and blood pressure went down compared to when they were thinking about the offender in unforgiving ways. Thinking about the offender in forgiving ways also led to more positive emotion and a greater sense of control.[14]

In another study, psychologist Michael McCullough and his colleagues found that when people were ruminating about an interpersonal transgression such as the betrayal of a secret, a boyfriend or girlfriend cheating on them, or being rejected by another person, they experienced higher levels of the stress hormone cortisol.[15] Chronically high levels of cortisol can impair the body's reactions to stress and disease and damage areas of the brain. In contrast, people who forgive others are able to let go of their ruminations about the wrongs they have suffered, thus allowing their body and mind to unwind and be more healthy.[16]

Forgiveness may not be possible, or reasonable, in some circumstances. Still, people often choose to forgive others because they no longer want to carry the anger and hurt they feel. Women's ability to take others' perspectives, to recognize they may have multiple goals in their relationships to others, and to be patient, often make it possible for them to forgive and move on in their lives.

Relational Strength #3: Women are tolerant and patient.

Putting Others First—When Appropriate

Women are able to recognize when others' needs should come before their own. Women's ability to put others first generates tremendous trust and inspires others to sacrifice their own needs for the sake of the group. This is crucial in the professional sphere, because when people work together toward the common good—instead of fighting to maximize their own individual gains—they often find innovative solutions to difficult workplace problems.

Consider, for example, Harriet Stockman, a businesswoman from Springfield, Missouri. When she was in her twenties, Harriet started a small bakery that specialized in making Italian pastries. Back then, the business consisted of Harriet and one other woman she hired to run the front of the store while she baked. The quality of Harriet's products was superb, and within a few years the bakery was a huge hit. Harriet opened a second store in another part of town, then a third. By her forty-eighth birthday, she owned seven stores across the city. She spent most of her time running the business, hiring employees, and dealing with financial accounting and advertising, but she still loved to get back into the kitchen and concoct new products to sell.

Springfield was going through hard economic times, however, with downturns in the farm economy and the departure of most of the manufacturing business from the area. People just couldn't afford fancy Italian pastries, and Harriet's business bottom line began to suffer. She knew she was going to have to lay off some employees, and maybe even close one or two of her stores. She also knew that many of her employees were dependent on their salaries to feed their children and keep their homes, and that they had few skills they could tap to land other jobs.

When she looked at the economic prospects from her employees' perspectives, Harriet decided it did not make sense to announce a unilateral decision as the owner of the company. So she called a meeting of employees to discuss their options—as a group. She closed all of her stores for a few hours one night and asked all of the employees to join her at the ballroom of the local Marriott hotel. As the employees got coffee and cake and took their seats, they were expecting that Harriet would tell them what stores would be closing and who would be receiving pink slips. Instead, she opened the meeting by saying, "I know we are all worried about the strength of our business. I brought us all here tonight to come up with some solutions that will save the business but protect each of you and your jobs as much as possible. If we work together, I know we can get through this difficult time.

"To start things off, I want to make an announcement. I will forgo my own salary from the business for the next six months so that this money can be used to keep the business afloat. It will mean cutting back for my husband and me, but we can live on his salary alone. I am hoping that this move will help to prevent closing any of the stores for the foreseeable future."

Her employees sat with their mouths agape. They all knew that Harriet was a generous, kind person who had helped out each of them in small and big ways over the years. But for her to give up her own salary so that all the stores could remain open and people could keep their jobs was a huge gift.

"Now," Harriet said, "I want to hear your ideas for reducing costs in the business and increasing revenues. You are all on the front lines and can see things I can't see from my office. How can we cut back? What can we do to bring in more money?"

After a few moments, hands shot up and ideas began flying. There was a line of pastries that were very expensive to make and that people weren't buying as much anymore. Those could be discontinued. One of the stores, located in the business district, seldom got any business after 5 p.m. That store could close at that hour and the employees who would usually work there in the evening could shift over to another store that was thriving in a residential area. A few employees even volunteered to cut back on their hours, saying that they had been feeling they were working too much and would like to be home when their children got out of school each day. By the end of the evening, substantial changes affecting all of Harriet's stores had been suggested, many of which Harriet would never have thought of herself.

Harriet could have acted entirely in her self-interest, keeping her full salary, closing underproducing stores, and laying off employees. This probably would have resulted in low morale among remaining employees, who then would be less motivated to save costs at the stores or to perform their job well. By putting the needs of her employees ahead of her own, Harriet inspired them to be creative and cooperative in devising ways to keep the business running.

Women may be prone to put others first because, from a very early age, they are able to see the world from others' perspectives, and are inclined by that understanding to help others. Sue Walker, a professor at Queensland University of Technology in Australia, found that pre-school girls scored better than preschool boys on two standard measures of perspective-taking ability.[17] Then she asked the children's teachers to rate them on levels of positive social behavior (such as cooperating with others) and their levels of aggressive behaviors (such as fighting with others). Girls who performed well on perspective-taking tasks exhibited higher levels of positive social behavior: they were more cooperative and more willing to help others. In contrast, boys who performed well on the perspective-taking tasks had higher levels of aggressive behavior. It appeared that the boys who were good at taking others' perspectives used this skill to take advantage of others by knowing the best way to "get at" them. Walker suggests that girls are socialized not only to take others' perspectives, but to use that under-standing to help and cooperate with others. The culture of boys, however, is more focused on dominance, so the boys who had an advantage in terms of being able to read others' minds use it to rule over other boys.

Some women, and men, go to heroic means to help other people. Researchers Selwyn Becker of the University of Chicago and Alice Eagly of Northwestern University conducted an ingenious study to examine the different ways women and men put their lives on the line to help others. They surveyed records of people who performed heroic feats, including people who rescued others from dangerous situ-ations, gentiles who risked their lives to help Jews during the Holocaust, living people who offered to be kidney donors, and volunteers for the Peace Corps and Doctors of the World. Becker and Eagly discovered that men were more likely than women to be the kind of heroes we see in action movies—people who engage in extremely risky and physically demanding behaviors, such as fighting off attackers or rescuing people from burning buildings. But when they investi-gated other less physically heroic acts, they found that women were just as likely as men—and in some cases *more* likely—to act with courage and valor. For example, gentile women in wartime Poland and the Netherlands were equally or more likely than gentile men to risk their lives in order to help Jewish citizens escape Nazi persecution. Women today are disproportionately likely to volunteer for the Peace Corps or Doctors of the World, both of which entail traveling to needy countries and administering health and medical services in potentially dangerous circumstances. They are also far more likely than men to register as organ donors. So women are heroes in ways that may not be flashy and headline-grabbing but are just as life-giving and powerful.

Finally, putting others' needs before your own is a critical component of good parenting. When parents don't put their children's needs before their own, their children are more likely to develop a wide range of psychological problems, including eating disorders and alcohol abuse, by the time they reach adulthood. In most families, women frequently put the needs of their family before their own personal needs. They put their careers on hold to care for small children or ailing family members. Women make compromises in how they pursue job opportunities and where they live in order to accommodate a mate's ascendance on the career ladder.

Women's willingness to make these types of sacrifices is sometimes judged to be a weakness, evidence of the continued sexism of society. Yet many women have a range of goals and priorities for their lives that include self-serving goals such as promoting their career, but also relational goals such as spending time with their children or assuring that an elderly family member gets good care. Women who have put aside self-serving goals to care for others will often tell you that they don't feel they are sacrificing—they have multiple priorities, and there are times when priorities that involve serving others have to be placed above priorities that involve only themselves. This, according to psychologist Robert Sternberg, displays women's wisdom. Sternberg argues that wisdom requires a balancing of one's own goals and needs with the goals and needs of others. "In wisdom," Sternberg says, "one seeks a common good, realizing that this common good may be better for some than for others. A person who uses his [or her] mental powers to become an evil genius may be academically or practically intelligent, but the person cannot be wise."[18]

> **Relational Strength #4:** Women are able to put others' needs before their own.

The relational strengths of women build others' lives and grow families, friendships, teams, and communities that are marked by open communication, cooperation, and mutual respect. Developing and promoting these relational strengths could have far-reaching effects on the health and prosperity of individuals and our society.

At the outset of this chapter, I noted that women's relational strengths are often counted as liabilities. We have to question, however, if women really are too caring or if the problem is that our society values the pursuit of self-interest over an ethic of caring. Women's perspective-taking and caring are assets when it comes to negotiating deals, nurturing talent, and motivating others—and as we have seen, that is true in a range of settings, from the family kitchen table to the corporate board room. Women's relational strengths primarily become a liability when others try to take an advantage. What if everyone was as empathic, as good at listening, as patient and forgiving, and as willing to put others first, as many women are?

TWO

Discover
and Develop
Your Strengths

6.

Building Your Personal Fitness Program

Now that you have a good sense of the tremendous strengths that women possess, you may be saying to yourself, "I want to be stronger!" You may feel moderately strong in one area but you want to increase that strength and make it more reliable. For example, you may feel you are generally sensitive to others' needs, but you know you occasionally are inconsiderate and want to overcome this weakness. Or you may feel there are strengths you absolutely lack, such as the ability to appropriately express your feelings to others. Or you may have the sense that there is some area of your life that is not going as well as you would like, perhaps your job or your marriage, and you believe that you could use your strengths more effectively to improve that area.

Just as you might begin a personal fitness program to build your physical strengths, you can engage in a personal fitness program to build your psychological strengths. Whether you are looking to pump up in some areas to meet a challenge in your life or you're a bit weak or downright limp in others, you can develop your strengths through regular exercise and become toned and fit.

I'm going to give you a variety of specific exercises to build your mental, identity, emotional, and relational strengths, but your overall strength-building program will be guided by three simple questions you can ask yourself anytime you are not feeling strong:

1. When and where do I run into trouble?
2. What is my positive image for change?
3. What small steps can I take toward that change?

In the following chapters, you will design a fitness program that maximizes your current strengths and rehabilitates those psychological muscles that are feeble. First, let me explain the thinking behind each of these questions.

"When and Where Do I Run into Trouble?"

If you went to a personal trainer to begin a physical fitness program, she would first put you through a series of drills or exercises to determine your strengths and weaknesses. You would do sit-ups, push-ups, sprints, and lift weights, and she would see how well you can perform compared to some established norms. Then your personal trainer would know what muscle groups you need to work on, what your endurance is, or whether you need speed training, and would design a program to enhance your strengths and overcome your weaknesses.

Similarly, before you begin to build your psychological strengths, you need to ask yourself in what situations—when and where—you are having trouble using your strengths. I've designed a series of activities that will reveal your psychological strengths and weaknesses and determine how badly you need to work on a particular strength. Some of these activities require you to use a strength in an interaction with others or to solve a problem. Other activities are "thought experiments" in which you imagine yourself in a situation that requires you to exercise a strength.

Each of the following chapters focuses on one group of strengths. You can skip to the set of strengths you think are the most important for you to work on. If you don't know what set of strengths to start with, you can use the Quick: How Am I Doing? Worksheet on the next page. This five-item questionnaire allows you to do a quick global

---

Quick: How Am I Doing? Worksheet

Use the following scales to rate each area of your life in terms of your global sense of how it is going. If some area is not relevant to you (e.g., you don't have children so you aren't a mother), skip that rating.

---

1. How is your marriage, partnership, or close romantic relationship going?

almost perfectly		just okay		not well at all
1	2	3	4	5

---

2. How is your relationship with your children going?

almost perfectly		just okay		not well at all
1	2	3	4	5

---

3. How is your job or career going?

almost perfectly		just okay		not well at all
1	2	3	4	5

---

4. If you have hobbies or interests other than your job or family, how are they going?

almost perfectly		just okay		not well at all
1	2	3	4	5

---

5. List any other areas of your life that are important to you (such as school, community work, religious activities).

How are things going in those areas?

almost perfectly		just okay		not well at all
1	2	3	4	5

For downloadable versions of the worksheets in the book, visit iamapowerful woman.com.

assessment of how things are going in important areas of your life, and how boosting your strengths might improve your overall quality of life.

If you've answered with a #1 ("almost perfectly") or #2 on all five questions, you should reward yourself in some special way! Clearly, you are exercising many strengths across a wide range of roles in your life. Even if you are near the "almost perfectly" end of the scale in only a couple of areas, you should praise yourself for your successes. Take stock of the strengths that have made that area of your life such a success. Is it your mental flexibility? Your skills at relating to others? Your emotional perceptions? Your integrity and sense of identity and purpose?

Realizing what makes for success in each area of your life that is going well will help you call upon that strength when it is needed and use it in new ways to make your life and others' lives even better. As I said earlier, women tend to be very hard on themselves, focusing on what is wrong with themselves rather than on what they do well. Think about the amazing benefits that come from your psychological strengths—the positive ways your strengths affect your well-being, your career success, your relationships, and your life goals.

Next, look back at the Quick: How Am I Doing? Worksheet. The areas that you've rated as going "just okay" or "not well at all" are where improving or exercising your strengths are likely to do the most good. To determine which strength area to work on, use the Global Strengths Assessment Worksheet on page 129. For each strength area, you will answer one critical question that zeroes in on whether and how you are using that set of strengths in the areas of your life that aren't "almost perfect."

When Anita answered the questions on the Quick: How Am I Doing? Worksheet, she rated her job and her hobbies as "almost perfect." Anita owns a small jewelry boutique in Santa Monica, California, and it is thriving. Searching for unique jewelry made by third world artisans allows her to travel all over the world, and travel is a passion for her. She also makes some of the jewelry she sells, and this gives her the opportunity to express her creativity, as well as to make the business a success. So her career and her pursuit of her hobbies and interests—including the promotion of artists in developing countries, which was politically meaningful to her—are going smashingly.

Anita's evaluation of how her relationship with her boyfriend, Tim, was going, however, was "not well at all." There were good times: when they got away for the weekend, or spent a relaxing evening at the apartment they shared. Much of the time, however, they were cross with each other, sometimes arguing but often just silent. Tim owns a

Global Strengths Assessment Worksheet

For each of the roles listed in the columns, ask yourself the critical questions to make a global assessment of your strengths.

Critical Question	Marriage, partnership, or other close relationship	Relationship with children	Job or career	Interests, hobbies, or community service and leadership	Other areas that are important to you
Mental Strengths: How would being better at overcoming obstacles and working with others improve this area of my life?					
Identity Strengths: How would having a better sense of who I want to be improve this area of my life?					
Emotional Strengths: How could better understanding and managing my own emotions and others' emotions improve this area of my life?					
Relational Strengths: How could relating to others more compassionately and appropriately improve this area of my life?					

landscaping company and works long hours, particularly during the summer. There were weeks when they hardly saw each other, but Anita had to admit she sometimes liked it that way. Still, there is much about Tim she loves. He is funny and creative, and he exudes a passion for his work and business that matches her own. She wants to make their relationship work, but knows a lot has to change or it is going to fizzle out.

Anita answered each of the critical questions in the Global Strengths Assessment Worksheet, focusing on her relationship to Tim (see next page). Anita was surprised when she realized that she wasn't applying her mental strengths to improve her relationship with Tim. After all, she uses them in spades at her business. With Tim, though, she has been focusing on getting her way—that is, getting Tim to change—rather than on getting the job done—that is, improving the relationship. In any relationship, you can never change another person, you can only change yourself. Anita needs to believe that the relationship can be saved.

In terms of her identity strengths, Anita's singular focus on her business makes her very vulnerable if that business should fold. She needs to realize that she can express her creativity and love for travel-ing in many ways, even if the business doesn't succeed. That will relax her a bit and allow her to open some space for Tim. She's right that she needs to decide what this relationship means to her. Otherwise, the relationship will continue to drift and not be particularly satisfying for either her or Tim.

When it comes to emotions, Anita clearly has difficulty appropri-ately expressing herself and managing her angry feelings. She feels as though she has to avoid Tim to avoid arguments. She needs to find ways to tolerate her frustrations with him so she doesn't avoid him, and express her negative feelings in healthy ways.

Finally, Anita should work on developing her relational strengths. She needs to listen to Tim and try to understand his perspective on their relationship. This will take more patience than she has shown before but if she wants this relationship to work, this is a strength she will have to develop.

| Anita's Global Strengths Assessment Worksheet ||
Critical Question	Marriage, partnership, or other close relationship
Mental Strengths: How would being better at overcoming obstacles and working with others improve this area of my life?	When I'm working on my business, nothing stops me from accomplishing what I want to do. I'll fly to the ends of the earth to see a particular jewelry maker. I'll work with my employees for hours to display the jewelry in a way that sells it. But with Tim, I've been assuming that things can't change—or maybe I just can't see how they can change. I guess I want him to change but I haven't been willing to make my own changes.
Identity Strengths: How would having a better sense of who I want to be improve this area of my life?	My whole sense of myself is wrapped up in my business. I guess that doesn't leave much space for Tim. I definitely don't define myself in terms of my relationship to Tim—in fact, I'm not even sure what I want in this relationship for the long term.
Emotional Strengths: How could better understanding and managing my own emotions and others' emotions improve this area of my life?	When Tim and I argue, I get so angry and upset that I just rage against him. I get focused on winning the argument, at all costs—I'll say anything, even really hurtful things. Because I know I lose it with him, I avoid him a lot, trying to avoid getting into an argument. I think I really need to work on this.
Relational Strengths: How could relating to others more compassionately and appropriately improve this area of my life?	I have no idea what Tim thinks about our relationship. I know he doesn't like the fighting either.

So Anita has work to do in each of her strengths area. She will concentrate on enhancing these strengths in her relationship to Tim. But you can see ways that her work on her relationship to Tim is likely to trickle down to other areas of her life. For example, exploring what her relationship with Tim means to her sense of self and identity, and balancing that relationship with her career, will help Anita develop a healthier perspective on her business so that she is not so vulnerable if it doesn't succeed. As you begin to work on specific strengths in specific areas of your life, you'll find that the benefits often transfer to other strengths and other areas of your life as well.

"What Is My Positive Image for Change?"

One of the motivational tools that trainers use to help athletes achieve their goals is to have them imagine themselves performing their sport at a much higher level. For example, a sprinter might imagine herself running a technically perfect race, with her body moving with the efficiency and lightness she wishes to achieve. She imagines every movement of her body, the tautness of her leg muscles, the ease in her back, the swing of her arms. She feels the oxygen coming in through her lungs and racing through her body to energize her muscles. She is smooth, flowing, weightless.

Imagery is also a key tool for psychological change, and many of the exercises in my strength-building program ask you to use your imagination. Imagining yourself using a strength in a way you've never been able to before, then imagining the positive benefits that come from that strength, is a great motivational tool. It can also help you identify the steps you need to take to begin making change.

Let me illustrate how useful imagery can be. Carol, a fifty-year-old elementary school teacher, needed to have a difficult talk with her husband, Doug. He wanted to sell their three-bedroom ranch and downsize to a condo closer to his work in order to reduce their mortgage payments and save on gas. Carol loved the home she had raised her children in, and the lush garden she had built in the backyard. She didn't want to move to a small "apartment," as she called it, in a complex where she couldn't do her gardening. She also didn't like the towns near Doug's job, and preferred the small town where their current house was, with its family-owned stores and light traffic. She had tried to express these preferences to her husband, but he kept pushing his arguments about the cost savings that would come from moving to the condo. Carol was getting increasingly frustrated, and panicked that she would give in and go along with this miserable move.

Carol made use of imagery to prepare for the conversation she committed to having with him. While Doug was at work and Carol was home alone, she sat down at the kitchen table and closed her eyes. She imagined herself telling Doug how much she wanted to remain in their home. At first it was a fuzzy image, but then she tried to imagine exactly what she would say. It was difficult for Carol to keep focused on what she would say and not immediately begin to worry about her husband's reaction—he would probably cut her off, start in with the same arguments about the money they would save with the move, generally just wear her down. But Carol persisted in her imagined scenario, repeating to Doug that she did not want to move, and she believed he should take her wishes seriously. She could see him saying harrumph and launching right back into his arguments, but she forced herself to say, in her imagination, that she understood his points, but her quality of life was just as important as saving some money. She was especially proud of herself for this last line. Then she saw him harrumphing again and giving up for the moment. Although Carol knew this would not be the end of the negotiations, she felt triumphant for standing her ground and expressing her desires. When she opened her eyes, she felt emboldened and determined to carry out her side of this discussion with her husband later that day.

Notice that the image Carol conjured was a specific situation during which she was expressing important feelings to her husband. Having a concrete image of how we want to change is critical to making that change: it points to the specific steps you need to take to get to your goal. If Carol had settled for a vague thought of herself expressing her emotions to Doug, without fully formed sentences flowing into her head, it would have been much harder for her to take advantage of this visualization exercise. By imagining a realistic back-and-forth with Doug, Carol was able to take herself through the experience of exactly what she wanted to say to him.

Having this concrete image allowed Carol to anticipate problems she might have in carrying through with what she wanted to say and to plan for these problems. When sports psychologists work with elite athletes, they train them not only to visualize the perfect race or pole vault or game. They encourage the athletes to imagine all possible scenarios, including ones in which they fall during the race, or hit the bar during a vault, or flub the ball during the game. This obviously is not a pleasant image for the athletes to focus on—the trick is to help them not get stuck with the image of themselves as a failure, but continue playing through the scenario, assessing why they might have failed, and imagining themselves recovering from their mistake. By confronting and working through worst possible scenarios, athletes become less afraid of these situations and less panicked when they actually do happen. They may discover, through their imaginations, ways they can prevent or stop these situations from happening. And they develop strategies for coping with failures when they do occur.

In one version of her imaginary conversation with Doug, Carol saw herself expressing her desires, then Doug cutting her off and pressing his own arguments. Carol recognized that she usually folded at this point, but was able to rewind the tape of her image and replay it, this time with her persisting in expressing her wishes to her husband despite his objections.

In the upcoming chapters as we go through each exercise to increase specific strengths, I'll talk about how to overcome the obstacles that tend to arise as we make changes in that strength area. Although recognizing obstacles to change can be a painful part of forming an image of how we would like to change, these obstacles won't go away if we just avoid imagining how we want to change. Instead, the key to defeating these obstacles is to anticipate them and make plans for overcoming them.

A final feature I want to point out about Carol's image of herself expressing emotions is that she specifically imagined a positive, albeit modest, outcome of her imagined scenario. After Carol persisted in expressing her desire not to move, Doug eventually "harrumphed" and stopped barraging her with his arguments. Bells didn't toll and fireworks didn't go off, but getting him to relent even a bit made Carol feel triumphant. Imagining a positive outcome to the change you want to make is a great motivator. It's also important to make that positive outcome realistic. Carol didn't imagine her husband completely capitulating, agreeing never to move, and apologizing for his selfishness in not previously considering her opinions. She imagined him giving in, a bit, and this was more than she'd gotten in any previous conversation with him about moving. So as you are creating your images of yourself increasing your strengths, cap them off with a reasonable positive outcome you could envision happening.

"What Small Steps Can I Take Toward Change?"

The old-fashioned notion of how psychological change happens is that you explore your past for the events and people that shaped your character and analyze your deepest thoughts and feelings for your true motivations. If you achieve insight into the roots of your personality, voila!—change comes suddenly and magically.

I'm afraid that's not true. Improvement in psychological strength comes just like improvement in physical strength does—by the slow, somewhat laborious process of practicing new skills until they become easy, then ratcheting up the workload on your muscles with more difficult exercises and practicing those until they become easy.

Each step along the pathway to change needs to be a small step. To build strength, you need systematic, gradual increases in how much you work a muscle group, spread out over time. So if you wanted to go from a flabby tummy to six-pack abs, you wouldn't do a thousand sit-ups in one day. All you would get would be a very sore flabby tummy. Instead, you would start with a reasonable (for you) number of sit-ups per day, say twenty, and continue at that pace for a few days, then increase your daily sit-ups to thirty for a few days, then to forty for a few days, and so on. You would gradually see more muscle definition and less flab in your abs, and you would be less likely to injure yourself (for example, by straining your back) in the process.

The same principles apply to building psychological strengths. Just as you wouldn't want to begin a program to build six-pack abs with a thousand sit-ups, you wouldn't want to begin a program to express your emotions more openly by walking into your boss's office and telling him he's a jerk (well, maybe you would *want* to, but it's not advisable). It takes gradual, systematic increases in what you demand of yourself to build your strengths in an area. You have to start small, with changes that are doable and reasonable for you. You practice these changes every day, then gradually ramp up to more challenging changes in your behaviors and thoughts. At every step, you will see improvement in your strength and eventually it will feel healthy and robust.

Now, let's begin working on your individual strengths!

7.

Cultivating Genius: Building Your Mental Strengths

To improve the mental strengths we discussed in chapter 2, you don't need to go back to school or do mind-twisting puzzles to exercise your brain cells. The strengths we are going to work on involve how you look at the world and the challenges life hands you.

For each individual strength, I will first give you activities to assess whether you need to build this strength or are doing fine. These exercises will help you answer the question *When and where do I run into trouble?* Then I suggest ways to boost this strength, by using positive images and taking small steps, so that you can fully capitalize on this strength.

Learn to See Many Pathways to Your Goal

Mental Strength #1: Women find many pathways to accomplishing their goals; they are neither conformist nor rigid. They take whatever resources are at their disposal and use them to solve problems and create a fulfilling life.

Think about a current situation actually happening in your life, one that has stymied you and that you thought might be hopeless to solve even though pursuing the goal is very important to you. It might be finishing college or getting a job you really want. Or it might be something you want for another person—for your child to do better in school or for your parent to get better medical care for his or her high blood pressure. You can also imagine a past situation or a future one that you are anticipating, or invent a problem, something that will give you some emotional space to explore your problem-solving potential.

Imagine bringing together the other people involved—your teacher, boss, colleagues, children, spouse, parent—at a critical moment. Play out the scene in your head in as much detail as you can create. As you "see" events unfold, imagine things not going the way you wish: you don't get the courses you need to finish school, you don't do well on the job interview, your child brings home another D grade, or your parent refuses to take blood pressure medication. All sorts of people are telling you things aren't going to work out: there just isn't a way. What are the obstacles you're facing?

Using the Possible Solutions Worksheet on the next page, generate at least three possible solutions to get around the obstacles that have arisen. For example, you might find other ways of getting the courses you need to finish college, or a way to overcome your bad job interview, or ways to help your child improve her grades, or ways to help your parent get better medical care.

Now on the bottom of the worksheet, rank the relative accessibility of your possible solutions—whether you have the tools and the energy to carry out each solution, and whether you would be comfortable carrying them out—from "1" for definitely no to "7" for definitely yes. If you came up with more than seven solutions, rank the top seven.

Look again. Of your possible solutions, circle those you've already tried. If you've imagined a situation, think about similar real-world situations you've been in and the sorts of things you did to get around the problem. Of your possible solutions, which of these, in loose terms, did not occur to you back then? Circle them.

ideas if you had to and focus on getting the project done using only others'
ideas? If what goes through your mind is "I'm right. Why can't they see
that?!" then Mental Strength #2 needs toning—even if you *are* right!
You are likely to get more done in projects with others if you can put
aside your indignation and make others see that their ideas are
included and appreciated.

If you don't have a current project to track, think back to projects
you've done in the past that have required cooperation with others. Try
to think of a situation in which your way of pursuing the project was
not the one the group adopted in the end. For example, you redeco-
rated a room in your house and the final color scheme or furniture
was your partner's or roommate's choice, or you were part of a group
to identify niche markets for one of your company's products and the
sales director decided to focus on a colleague's suggestion. *How easy
or difficult was it for you to cooperate with others? How easy was it to
accept that your idea didn't get chosen? How much conflict was there
between you and the other people involved?* Use these questions to evaluate whether you are good at focusing on getting the job done even if
you don't get your way, or you get stuck wanting people to see that
your way is clearly best.

Exercises to Build Your Ability to Focus on Getting the Job Done

If you see a little of Bella in yourself—in your job, in your community
activities, or in your home life—you need to step back and ask yourself if getting your way is the most important goal in every situation.
For example, if you are in constant conflict with your children or your
partner over how things are done around the house—how meals are
prepared, how rooms are cleaned, how your kids do their homework—stop and ask yourself what your most important goals are in
these situations. Is it really most important that the spaghetti be
cooked exactly the way you would do it, or is it just as important to
encourage your spouse to help with the cooking, even if dinner isn't
the best it could possibly be? Is it really so important that your kids'
rooms be as tidy and spotless as when you clean the house, or is it just

as important to teach them to take responsibility by cleaning their own room, even if it still looks untidy when they are done?

Imagining a Cooperative You Exercise

To begin building Mental Strength #2, you must commit yourself to being a person who builds other people's skills and builds cooperative teams rather than a person focused on getting her own way. Now, it's difficult to tell yourself to stop insisting on doing it your way. This tendency is usually ingrained in those of us who have it. But positive imagery can help change this habit. Imagine yourself in a situation in which you usually try to push your way of doing things, whether it is on some project at work, or getting the cooking or housework at home done. Then imagine yourself, rather than arguing or nagging to get your way, focusing on the people involved in the situation—your coworker, your spouse, or your children. Rather than focusing on your frustration that they can't see that your way is best, focus on what they can contribute and learn in this situation. If it's a work situation, think about the aspects of your coworker's opinion or approach to a problem that are interesting or potentially useful. Imagine yourself praising your coworker for his ideas and talking about how his ideas could be capitalized on, or possibly integrated with your ideas, to solve this problem. If you are imagining a situation at home, think about what skills or habits your spouse or child might develop by doing a job his or her way instead of yours. Imagine your child beaming with joy at her newly cleaned room (no matter what the room looks like). Imagine your spouse proudly serving his new pasta dish to the family. Imagine yourself enjoying the positive relationships that are growing in your family, and the relief from the burden of having to do everything yourself.

Imagining a Secure You Exercise

Sometimes, wanting to get your way comes not from excessive confidence in yourself, but from deep insecurity. You need to prove to yourself, as much as to others, that you are smart, respected, superior.

So you push and push your own point of view rather than stepping back and risking that someone else gets the glory.

Focusing on getting the job done rather than on promoting yourself takes real peace of mind about your abilities and how others see you. You have to stand by, assured that you and your opinions are valued, while someone else's opinions win the day. If you find yourself worrying what others think of you, or doubt your own abilities when your point of view is disregarded or overruled by others, make a firm choice to value your own opinions and skills even if others don't recognize their merit. You can declare that you choose not to step on others' backs to get respect, but that instead you will stand up and focus on getting the job done even if others don't recognize your contributions to it. Use your powers of positive imagery to see yourself serenely getting on with business rather than obsessing over the fact that you are not getting credit for your good ideas. This can be empowering and freeing. If you let go of concerns about what others think about your role in a project and just focus on getting the project done, you release brainpower and are likely to generate more creative and novel solutions to problems. Ironically, by refusing to worry about what others think of you, you may earn greater respect from them.

Imagining an Assertive You Exercise

If your weakness is not that you insist on doing things your way or on getting credit for your ideas, but that you cave in and don't promote yourself enough, then you can use both positive imagery and small steps to develop the right balance for Mental Strength #2. Imagine a situation in which you find it difficult to express your opinion, or take credit for something. You may hear yourself saying, "Maybe my idea isn't so good." Or you feel tongue-tied when a coworker claims credit for work you did or an idea you had first. Now rewind that scenario and form a positive image of yourself, straightforwardly and confidently expressing your opinion or claiming ownership of your good work or idea. See your positive self being calm and assured, not timid or angry.

Now take out a piece of paper and write down one situation you expect to come up in the next week in which your typical pattern would be to give in to others' ideas when you know yours are much better or allow someone else to take credit for your work. Imagine that likely situation as vividly as you can, but insert the positive you for your typical self. Imagine what the positive you will say to express your point of view or let others know that you deserve credit. Now make a pact with yourself that you will be that positive you this week when this situation arises. You might even want to write a little contract with yourself, such as:

When _____ situation arises this week, I hearby commit to expressing my point of view or taking credit for my ideas or work, just as my positive self would do.

Then, later in the week, after that situation has occurred and you've dealt with it, assess how you did. If you were able to act out your positive image of yourself, reward yourself! Buy yourself something simple but nice—an ice-cream cone, a bouquet of flowers, whatever appeals to you. Relish the sense of empowerment that carrying through with the positive you provides. Realize that you didn't get shot down for expressing your opinions or claiming credit. Make a pact with yourself to enact your positive you *two* times in the next week.

If you weren't able to carry out what the positive you wanted to say, assess what held you back. Was it self-defeating thoughts that your ideas aren't good, or that you don't have a right to claim your credit? Was it an aggressively self-promoting coworker who shouted down your ideas or swooped in and claimed your work as his own? Replay that situation in your mind, but insert the positive you into it. What would she have done with those self-defeating thoughts? She probably would have scolded those thoughts and told them to get lost. Or she might have simply focused on what she wanted to say instead of giving any of her attention to her negative thoughts. What would your positive self have done with the aggressive coworker? Perhaps she would have made sure your boss knew of her work before her coworker had a chance to claim it as his own. Or perhaps she would have interrupted the coworker as he was claiming credit, saying something like, "Thanks, Tom, for letting Bill know about my idea. But I think I should be the one giving him the details." Play through these images of the positive you dealing with the situation you actually faced this week. Then make a new contract to be that positive you when a similar situation arises in the next week.

Learn to Enlist Help When Needed

Mental Strength #3: Women tend to enlist other people's help, expertise, and ingenuity rather than insisting on doing everything themselves.

Most women feel quite comfortable asking for others' help in some areas of their lives. When I'm boarding an airplane, I know I can't hoist my suitcase above my head into the overhead bin, so I'm happy to ask someone nearby who appears stronger to help me. I know I have no clue how to fix a broken computer, so I'm happy to ask the IT person at work to do that.

There are two situations, however, in which women often have trouble asking for help they need. The first is when they don't want to bother other people or impose on them. This often arises in the workplace. For example, my friend Maggie is head of a department but often does tasks she should ask secretaries to do because the secretaries feel overworked and she doesn't want to add to their workloads. This is a case in which women's tremendous empathy for others leads us to take on too much ourselves, rather than insisting we get the help we need.

The second area we sometimes have difficulty asking for help in is in our caregiving roles. Women are supposed to be naturally fit to be mothers or caregivers to other family members. Sometimes, despite our best efforts, we can't take care of a loved one completely on our own. For example, if your son can't control his anger and aggression toward other children despite how hard you've worked to help him, it is a good idea to seek counseling that will help your son gain control and you to learn new parenting skills. If you have a parent with Alzheimer's disease, there is likely to come a time when you can't physically or emotionally handle the demands of caregiving on your own, and your parent will need to go into assisted living.

Some women just aren't cut out for caregiving roles at all, and they suffer great guilt and condemnation by others for not doing what people assume comes naturally to women. Kara desperately wanted a child after she had made it to a high level in her career. She convinced her husband, Rick, that she should get pregnant, even though Rick wasn't enthusiastic about the idea and felt their child-free lifestyle suited them perfectly. Kara did get pregnant, and gave birth to a healthy little boy she named Peter. Kara and Rick both adored Peter, but soon felt they were in over their heads. Peter was not a good sleeper, waking frequently during the night even when he wasn't hungry, and not cooperating with naps during the day. Rick went back to work after just a week off, but Kara stayed home for an extended maternity leave. In addition to her constant sleep deprivation, Kara was just plain bored with being a stay-at-home mom. She longed for the intellectual and social stimulation of her job. She just couldn't get interested in the conversations with other mothers in play groups or with the daily activities of taking care of Peter. She very much needed help—specifically a nanny or day care so that she could return to work. But she felt terribly guilty that she didn't find the mother role intrinsically fulfilling and that stopped her from seeking out child care.

To evaluate your strength at enlisting needed help, you can use the Enlisting Help Worksheet to do the following exercise: go through each of your major roles in life (spouse or partner, parent, caregiver, worker, volunteer) and ask yourself: *Is there anything I could ask someone else to do or to help me with that would make things easier in this role?* If the answer is an honest "no" in each area of your life, then good for you! Take note of the help you are getting from others and pat yourself on the back for enlisting that help. You might also want to make plans to show your appreciation to your helpers and acknowledge how important they are to your life.

If there are any "yes" answers to the question of whether help could make your life easier in some domain, listen to the "but . . ." that may follow your "yes." What obstacles do you see in asking for the help you need? Sometimes there are financial obstacles—you can't afford day care for your child or your elderly parent, for example. *Or is it just that you are reluctant to ask for help because you don't want to impose on others or make them think you can't do everything yourself?* Note the obstacles you see for help that could lift your load. We'll tackle them in the exercises in the next section.

Exercises to Build Your Ability to Enlist Help

For those of you who don't ask for the help you need because you don't want to impose on others, my advice for you is "do it anyway." You need to force yourself to ask for help, first in small ways, then in

---

Enlisting Help Worksheet

Go through each of the following roles you have in your life. *Is there anything you could ask someone else to do or help you with that would make things easier in this role?* Make a brief note of what that would be.

Role	Anything I could use help with?	What kind of help?
Spouse/partner		
Parent		
Caregiver		
Job or career role		
Volunteer		
Other:_____		

increasingly large ways. By doing so, you will discover that the consequences are not as terrible as you imagined. People won't scream at
you. Even if they get annoyed with you, you won't fall apart or melt
into a puddle. And you will discover that the benefits of getting the
help you need can be great. Things you can't accomplish on your own
get done. You feel a tremendous sense of relief. You create relationships
with others that are mutually helpful.

My friend Maggie, the department head who didn't want to
impose on her own staff even to do clerical tasks and thus overworked herself, finally was forced to begin asking for help. The
department was being evaluated by her company's central office, and
the outcome of the evaluation would determine if the department
was given new resources to expand, or perhaps get phased out altogether. Lengthy and detailed reports had to be assembled describing
the department's functioning and productivity, and Maggie simply
could not gather all the necessary information on her own. She ten-
tatively approached the business administrator in her department,
Tammy, concerned that Tammy might say there was no way she and
the staff had time to gather the information Maggie needed. Instead,
Tammy expressed relief that Maggie didn't want to do the report on
her own, since Tammy's future, and the staff's future, depended on
the outcome of this evaluation. Tammy and Maggie worked together
to determine which of the secretaries' usual duties could be curtailed
until the report was finished so that they could help put the information for the report together. Over the course of working together
on the report, Tammy and Maggie came up with a streamlined redis-
tribution of work among the staff that reduced everyone's workload.
They also established how staff could take on some of the tasks
Maggie had done so that she could devote her energies to tasks that
only she could do.

Asking for Help Exercise

If you completed the Enlisting Help Worksheet on page 153 and identified ways others could help you, try the following exercise. Pick out

which type of help would be the least threatening for you to ask for, then make a contract with yourself to ask for that help this week. For example, if you determined that getting someone else to pick up your child from school on Tuesdays, when you usually have a staff meeting that runs late, would be a huge help to you, think about who would be the least scary person to ask to do this for you—your spouse, your mom or dad, maybe a neighbor with a child at the same school. Then make a contract with yourself to ask this person. In your datebook write something like:

Saturday, September 4, ask Linda next door to pick Katie up at school next Tuesday when she picks up her own son.

Then carry through with your contract with yourself. Regardless of how it works out, reward yourself for having carried through. Buy yourself a lobster roll sandwich. Take a long shower. Do something to congratulate yourself for having asked.

Chances are your asking for help had a positive outcome. Linda was happy to pick up Katie on this Tuesday and said she could do it any Tuesday. Revel in how much relief you feel as a result of this. Focus on the fact that it wasn't really that hard to ask, once you did it. Notice that Linda didn't seem to feel imposed on after all.

If asking for help did *not* have a positive outcome (perhaps Linda was annoyed and said she didn't have time to pick up Katie), reward yourself anyway for having asked. And notice that you didn't crumble into a ball when Linda said no. But most important, determine who is the next-least-scary person to ask, and contract with yourself to do the asking. That is, don't back down and tell yourself that you really are imposing on people to ask for help. Instead, tell yourself you need the help and it's reasonable to ask, then make a pact with yourself to carry through.

You can gradually move through all the types of needed help you identified on your Enlisting Help Worksheet using these same steps. Pick one type of help, starting with the least threatening. Determine who would be the best person to ask and exactly what you want to ask him or her. Contract with yourself to do the asking at a specific time and place. Reward yourself for asking, and relish the positive consequences when they come.

Learn to Be Optimistic

Mental Strength #4: Women never say never—they remain optimistic that obstacles can be overcome.

Return for a moment to the important goal you were thinking about when you did the exercises to assess your ability to find paths to your goals, on page 139. Again, play out the scene in your head in as much detail as you can create, imagining things not going as you wish. You feel discouraged and people are telling you this isn't going to work out well. *Do you give in to that discouragement, to the point where you feel all is hopeless? Or do you put that discouragement aside and remain optimistic despite the setbacks?* Women who are strong in optimism continue to pursue their goals and keep hope alive regardless of how difficult the situation is or despite other people's pessimism. Women who are low in optimism are overwhelmed by the obstacles in their way and give up a goal even when others are encouraging them on.

Exercises to Build Optimism

Optimism is a personality trait—some people are probably born more optimistic than others—*but optimism is also a choice.* You've heard the stories about the prisoners in Nazi concentration camps during the Holocaust who remained optimistic that they would survive and be freed, despite all evidence to the contrary. Whether or not they actually did escape the camps, their fierce drive to keep hope alive was a life-giving force to themselves and many other prisoners. Viktor Frankl, who was tortured and starved in a Nazi concentration camp, and lost his father, mother, brother, and wife, wrote: "Everything can be taken from a man but . . . the last of the human freedoms—to choose one's attitude in any given set of circumstances, to choose one's own way."[1]

Recognizing Negative Thoughts Exercise

The most potent enemy of optimism is the negative thoughts that often run through our minds like a radio playing in the background. We hardly notice they are there but they exert powerful influences on our feelings and behaviors. These thoughts may be self-demeaning: "I can't do this" or "Nothing good ever happens to me." They can be negative thoughts about others: "He'll never change his ways" or "The system is rigged against me." Whatever their specific content, they drain us of hope, energy, and the creativity to see a way around problems.

To assess your level of optimism, I asked you to imagine a situation in which you felt very discouraged or hopeless. As you watch the events unfold in your imagination, tune in to the thoughts that are playing through your mind, much as you would pay attention to a radio playing in the background. What do you hear? Are they self-defeating thoughts like "You don't deserve this," or "This will never work out"? Write down the thoughts you are hearing in your mind, each separately, on an index card. Use as many cards as you need, and try to capture all of those thoughts.

Remember Corinne, the flight attendant who lost her job? When Corinne tuned in to the thoughts going through her head, she heard herself saying, "It's hopeless—there are no open jobs for flight attendants and people are still getting laid off." "I'm forty-two and all I've ever done is be a flight attendant. I don't have any other skills." "My husband's salary can't cover the mortgage. We're going to lose our house." She wrote each of these thoughts and several other negative ones down on separate cards. She had quite a stack when she was done.

Defeating Negative Thoughts Exercise

Once you have your own stack of negative thought cards, there are several things you can do with them. The first thing is to *destroy them.*

Burn them. Put them through a paper shredder. Let your dog chew on them. However you choose to destroy them, as you are doing it, tell yourself you are destroying these thoughts. They will no longer exist. They will not have any power over your feelings and actions. As you are destroying the cards, you are destroying their negative content.

An alternative is to lock them away. Put a paper clip or rubber band around them, then put them away in a drawer or cabinet where you won't see them during a typical day. As you do this, say to yourself, "I know these thoughts still exist, but I have banished them to a place where they can't continue to influence me." An advantage of putting these thoughts away someplace instead of destroying them is that you retain the option of pulling them out and reviewing them someday. If you've been able to operate for a while without them influencing you, reviewing them can confirm to you how important it was to banish them.

A third action is to take the cards, one at a time, and come up with a counter-statement to the negative thought written on the card. This counter-statement can dispute the truth of your negative thought. For example, one of Corinne's negative thoughts was that she had no skills other than being a flight attendant. Her counter-statements to this were: "I do too have skills—I play the piano, and I could teach piano lessons for a while." And "That's ridiculous—being a flight attendant means I have lots of marketable skills that are useful in other jobs."

Notice that several of Corinne's negative thoughts had an element of truth to them. It was true that the airline industry was shrinking and there were not many flight attendant jobs to be had. It was true that her husband's salary couldn't cover their mortgage. You can't argue against the truth of real facts. But you can argue against their meaning. When Corinne told herself "It's hopeless—there are no open jobs for flight attendants and people are still getting laid off," this was factually true. But the meaning Corinne read into this fact was "and if I can't get a job as a flight attendant then I can't get any job." This clearly was not true. Corinne could search for jobs outside the airline industry and have much more hope for landing one. Similarly, it was factually true that her husband's job couldn't cover the mortgage, but the meaning she read into it was "We're going to lose our house," and that wasn't necessarily so. There were a number of steps they could take to avoid this—refinancing their mortgage, her husband taking a second job for a while, Corinne taking a sub-optimal job to help pay the mortgage until she found a more satisfying job.

Corinne took her cards and wrote these counter-statements to her negative statements:

> *My statement:* It's hopeless—there are no open jobs for flight attendants and people are still getting laid off.
>
> *Counter-Statement:* That's true, but there are jobs outside the airline industry to be had.

> *My statement:* I'm 42 and all I've ever done is be a flight attendant. I don't have any other skills.
>
> *Counter-Statement:* So what if I'm 42. That means I have experience and maturity. Yes, I've only been a flight attendant. Losing my job gives me chance to try a different career for a while. And it's absurd to say I don't have skills. Flight attendants have leadership skills, teamwork skills, communication skills, management skills, and we know a great deal about how to keep people safe. Those are skills that many employers value.

> *My statement:* My husband's salary can't cover the mortgage. We're going to lose our house.
>
> *Counter-Statement:* No, his salary can't cover the mortgage. But we can refinance, or find other employment while I search for a new career. My parents can loan us some money for a short time, also.

If it's difficult to come up with counter-statements to your negative thoughts, you can enlist the help of someone you trust who tends to be optimistic. Once you have counter-statements to each of the negative thoughts, put the cards someplace where you can pull them out easily—your nightstand, the glove compartment of your car, a drawer in your desk—and review them when you are feeling discouraged.

Imagining an Optimistic You Exercise

If the index cards exercises don't appeal to you, or you just want to try another exercise, here's a good one. Go back to the discouraging situation you've been imagining. This time, however, imagine how you would respond to this situation *if you were optimistic.* That is, use your imagination to turn yourself into an optimistic person as you watch yourself behave, have conversations with others, and react to events. Don't just imagine the problem disappearing—for example, a job suddenly landing in your lap. Imagine that you are facing all the discouraging obstacles you currently face, but instead of seeing yourself behaving pessimistically, suspend reality and imagine what you would look like if you were optimistic. Now write down how you look on the An Image of the Optimistic You Worksheet. How would you act, what choices would you make, whom would you talk to, whom would you avoid talking to, what would you tell yourself? And how do you feel? Probably relieved, energized, and empowered.

This image of the optimistic you can be a great motivator. You can pull out your description of the optimistic you and read it over whenever you are feeling discouraged. Conjuring up the optimistic you can also give you ideas for what counter-statements to use against the negative thoughts that feed your pessimism. Finally, seeing the optimistic you in action can give you concrete ideas of what you can do to begin to overcome your discouraging situation.

An Image of the Optimistic You Worksheet

As you think about a discouraging situation you face, imagine yourself behaving as if you are optimistic about the outcome. Play through the scenario in as much detail as possible. When you have a picture of yourself as the "optimistic you," answer the following questions.

---

1. How would you act? What would you do first, then next, and so on? Be as specific as possible.

---

2. What choices would you make?

---

3. Whom would you choose to interact with? Is there anyone in your life you would avoid, perhaps because he or she is a source of discouragement?

---

4. What would you tell yourself to remain optimistic?

Building Self-Efficacy by Breaking Down Obstacles Exercise

Recall that I said in chapter 2 that self-efficacy—the belief that you can do what it takes to accomplish your goals—is the backbone of optimism. Albert Bandura, the Stanford psychologist who developed the self-efficacy theory, argued that the best way to build self-efficacy is to give people the skills to solve their problems. In turn, the best way for people to solve their problems is to learn to break down obstacles to solutions so that they can take small steps to overcome these obstacles.

So if you need to build your own self-efficacy and optimism, a great way to do it is through the Breaking Down Obstacles exercises earlier in this chapter. By taking an intransigent, seemingly hopeless problem you are facing, breaking down the obstacles to solving this problem into smaller parts that aren't so overwhelming, and then finding small steps you can take to overcome each small part, you will begin to feel more optimistic and confident in your ability to handle difficult situations.

Your Quick Reference Guide

In the table below, I've summarized all of the assessment activities and exercises to build your mental strengths. You can use this table to remind yourself how you are doing and how to boost your strength from time to time.

Building Mental Strengths

Specific Strength	Assessment Activities	Building Exercises
Mental Strength #1: Seeing many pathways to your goals	Generate several possible solutions or ways around the obstacles to the goals you are discouraged about. How easy or hard is this?	**Breaking Down Obstacles Exercise** (page 141) Break down obstacles into their smaller parts, then generate small actions you could take to overcome those small components of the obstacle. **Defining Goals Exercise** (page 143) Make sure your goal reflects what's really important to you.
Mental Strength #2: Focusing on getting the job done rather than on getting your way	Start a new project that requires cooperation with others. How easy or difficult is it to concede to others' ideas in accomplishing the project? Think back to previous projects you've done with	**Imagining a Cooperative You Exercise** (page 148) Focus on a situation in which you are frustrated because things aren't going your way. Generate ideas for ways to focus on team-building or building others' skills instead of being focused on getting your way.

Specific Strength	Assessment Activities	Building Exercises
	others. How easy or difficult was it for you to cooperate with them and concede to their way of doing things?	**Imagining a Secure You Exercise** (page 148) Make a conscious choice not to worry about what others think and just focus on getting the job done. **Imagining an Assertive You Exercise** (page 149) If you don't take enough credit for your work or ideas, imagine the positive you doing so in a difficult situation, then make a pact with yourself to carry through with that positive way of doing things.
Mental Strength #3: Enlisting help when needed	Go through each of your major roles and ask, "Is there anything I could ask someone else to do or help me with that would make things easier in this role?" Note obstacles you see to asking for help.	**Asking for Help Exercise** (page 154) Pick out one type of help that would be the least threatening to ask for, then make a contract with yourself to ask for that help this week. Carry through with your contract with yourself. Regardless of how it works out, reward yourself for having carried through. Then do it all again, asking for another type of help you need, working your way from the least threatening request to the most threatening.
Mental Strength #4: Being optimistic	Imagine you are pursuing an important goal, but hitting obstacles. How optimistic versus discouraged would you be?	**Recognizing Negative Thoughts Exercise** (page 157) As you imagine yourself dealing with a difficult goal, tune in to negative thoughts feeding your discouragement and write them down on index cards. **Defeating Negative Thoughts Exercise** (page 157) Take the negative thoughts cards and (a) destroy them; (b) lock them away; or (c) generate counter-statements to each of them.

(Continued)

Specific Strength	Assessment Activities	Building Exercises
		Imagining an Optimistic You Exercise (page 160) Imagine how you would respond to the discouraging situation if you were an optimistic person. Write down in detail what you would look like. **Building Self-Efficacy by Breaking Down Obstacles Exercise** (page 161) Use the Breaking Down Obstacles Exercise on page 141 to begin to solve a hopeless problem and build your self-efficacy.

8.

Multiplying Adaptability: Building Your Identity Strengths

Your identity strengths involve the way you see yourself in the world and what you value about yourself. If your sense of self is already strong, then the assessment activities in this chapter will help you to more fully utilize your values and fully inhabit your roles. You will focus on forming a clear picture of who you are and what you want to do in your life. If your sense of self needs to be further developed, these assessments will point out the areas in which you can build strength. I won't lie: pointing out your identity weaknesses can be painful. But each assessment is followed by exercises that will allow you to build these strengths, so that you will stand tall with a firm, positive, core sense of yourself that can adapt to changing roles and circumstances in your life.

Learn to Build a Stable but Adaptable Sense of Self

Identify Strength #1: Women have a core sense of self that is stable but adaptable to various circumstances.

Defining Your Core Worksheet

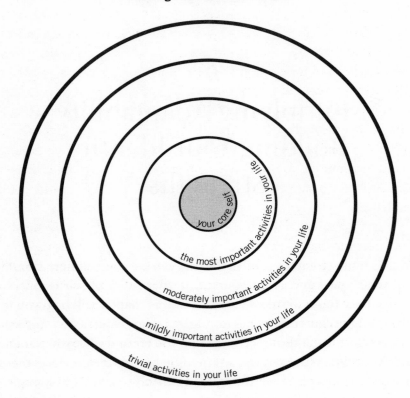

Our talents and interests are a big part of our identity, and if we are lucky, our work, volunteer activities, and hobbies reflect those talents and interests. I like to do research, write, and teach, so my identity includes being a scientist, a writer, and a professor.

Think about your job or, if you don't work outside the home, think about work you do as a community volunteer, in your church or synagogue, or even hobbies or sports that are important to you. Brainstorm your talents and interests and then place them on the diagram in the Defining Your Core Worksheet above, closer to "your core self" if you think the activity is essential to how you identify yourself and farther away if you think the activity is less important. (It's best to use a pencil for this assessment.)

Keep in mind that the talents and interests you consider part of your identity change over time. Are there any activities that used to be a big part of your identity but no longer are—but you wish they were? Are there some that have only recently emerged but seem to be taking over? Draw arrows indicating where you'd like these activities to be versus where they actually are in your life.

Next, think about the activity that is most important to you, that is, the activity closest to your core self. Look at the Defining Your Core Worksheet and remove everything except that activity from the central band surrounding your core self. Remember a few moments when you felt especially proud of your accomplishments and your talents in this activity.

Now imagine that activity disappearing from your life. If it is your job, imagine that you get fired or the company folds. If the activity is organizing the logistics for your kids' soccer team, imagine that you move to a new city and the parents involved in your kids' new team don't make room for you to volunteer. If the activity is your volunteer work for the church auction, imagine that your schedule doesn't allow you to meet with the other church leaders, and so you have to drop out of the group. Whatever the activity, think of some reason why you would no longer be able to do this meaningful work. *How would you feel about yourself if you were no longer doing this work? How would you define what you do in life? What would give you self-esteem? Could you imagine moving on to a different position, even one with less status, as long as you were able to exercise your talents and explore your interests? Or would you feel lost and adrift, empty, even ashamed?*

If you have difficulty imagining how you would express yourself if this activity suddenly disappeared, then Identity Strength #1 needs development. If you feel that your sense of self would fall apart if you lost your job, if you had to move to another city, and so on, then you need to work to disentangle your core self-image and self-worth from specific jobs or places. Who you are resides deep within you, not in some workplace, and not in a certain geographic location. You need to uncover this independent, core sense of self so that your identity is not left to the whims of external circumstances.

Exercises to Build a Strong and Adaptable Core Identity

To begin building Identity Strength #1, return to the Defining Your Core Worksheet. What place, activity, or role is most closely related to your core self? If it is your job, write "job" at the top of the Sense of Self Worksheet on the next page. If it is living in your current town, write that down, and so on. Now write down which of your core values and interests are expressed or served in this place, activity, or role in life. What talents are you exercising, what interests are you pursuing, and what values are being expressed through your job, involvement in your community, etc.?

Imagine Your Adaptable Self Exercise

Spend a moment using your imagination to generate at least one idea for how you could express your talents, interests, and values in some other way. It might be a different career or different community activity. It might be in a completely different role, such as in your role as a parent or child. You should try to think as broadly and creatively as possible. The goal is not to think about a similar job or situation that uses your skills in the same way; rather, you are looking for opportunities to express who you are and what you love that are quite different from what you are doing now.

Betty had always loved the theater, so landing a job as the director of the local community theater was the dream of a lifetime. The position didn't pay well, but Betty was happy to work the seventy to eighty hours a week necessary to teach acting to aspiring actors and community volunteers, oversee rehearsals, help build sets, design advertising campaigns, and raise money for the operation. Economic times were tough, however. There was a real chance that her beloved theater would not survive the drop in donations and attendance at plays. When Betty contemplated the idea of the theater being shuttered—and losing her job—she felt panic run through her entire body. She heard Scarlett's immortal line from *Gone with the Wind*: "Where will I go, what will I do?" And she did not have a ready answer to that question.

Sense of Self Worksheet	
What role or place is your sense of self most closely tied to?	
List the talents, interests, or core values that you express and exercise in this role.	Generate at least one idea for how you might express each of these talents, interests, and core values in another role or position.
1.	
2.	
3.	
4.	
5.	

After agonizing over how she could ever begin a process of "disconnecting" from her dream job, Betty forced herself to fill out the Sense of Self Worksheet to figure out how she could expand her sense of self to include many other roles in life.

When Betty turned to the process of generating at least one other situation in which she could express these personal characteristics, it was tough. The most obvious alternative was to find a new job in a different theater. But all of the theaters in her area, both community organizations and professional venues, were struggling. Jobs were hard to come by. Betty closed her eyes and imagined herself working with actors in a different setting. She slowly realized she didn't *need* to make money doing theater work, which expanded her range of options. As she contemplated the contacts she had made in the community over the years, it occurred to her that she could volunteer to teach acting courses at the community centre or through her church; the community theater wasn't the only place putting up plays in her town. Further, getting teenagers interested in acting would be a good way to keep them off the streets and teach them how to work together. In her role as a mother, she could help

Betty's Sense of Self Worksheet	
What role or place is your sense of self most closely tied to? *Job at the Theater*	
List the talents, interests, or core values that you express and exercise in this role.	Generate at least one idea for how you might express each of these talents, interests, and core values in another role or position.
1. *Love acting*	*Start an improvisational group*
2. *Enjoy teaching acting*	*Help out with Heather's school play*
3. *Love the creative process*	*Write that screenplay!!*
4.	
5.	

out at her daughter's school with the annual play. That really got Betty thinking: She could even start an improvisational group herself. And if she wasn't working seventy to eighty hours a week at the theater, but instead spent thirty-five to forty hours at a job less tied to her sense of self, she would finally have the time to work on the screenplay she had always wanted to write. That would allow her to exercise her creative talents much more than the fund-raising she spent so much of her time on these days. As these possibilities began to flow through Betty's mind (and onto her worksheet), her whole body relaxed. She was *not* defined by her position as director of the community theater but by her love for acting, her creativity, and her ability to draw others into acting. She could express those characteristics in many other ways.

Like Betty, you can find different ways to use your talents and grow your interests, in addition to the ways you currently do. Recognizing that you can adapt to new circumstances without losing your core self can be very reassuring—you don't have to fear change as much. It can also empower you to set reasonable limits on what you will do to stay in your current position, and to have the courage to make difficult changes in your life. When Betty recognized that she could pursue her love of acting and teaching in ways other than being a theater director, it motivated her to cut back on how many hours a week she worked so that she could write her screenplay. You may find that by defining yourself in terms of your core values and interests rather than any specific position or place, you are freed to make substantial changes in your life that better express your core self.

Learn to See Yourself in Relation to Others

Identity Strength #2: Women define themselves in relation to their social connections with other people.

Women's problems with Identity Strength #2 tend to come not from exercising this strength too little, but from exercising it too much. That is, some women define themselves so much in relation to others that they don't have a separate identity outside those relationships. They are literally lost without their identity as a wife, a mother, or a daughter. But in order to realize their full worth—and power—as women, they need to be able to nurture a social identity without putting their own self into eclipse.

Research by Columbia University psychologist Geraldine Downey and Carnegie Mellon psychologist Vicki Helgeson shows that this excessively social identity causes some women to be hypervigilant for signs of trouble in their relationships, to overinterpret conflict with others as a sure sign they are about to be abandoned, and to neglect their own needs for the sake of their relationships.[1] In my own research, I've found that women with an excessively social identity fall into obsessive rumination over every little aspect of their relationships:[2] "What does it mean that he was irritable at breakfast this morning?" "I can't believe I said something so stupid to her. She must think I'm an idiot!" "What will I do if he leaves me?" This rumination spirals and grows until it is a tornado, wiping out a woman's feelings, her rational thoughts, and her ability to see good solutions to her problems.

An excessively social identity also leads a woman to seek reassurance from others that the relationship is okay, that the other person is not angry or frustrated with her, or that the other person will always be there in the relationship. In the workplace, women who are excessively seeking reassurance may constantly ask for feedback on their performance: "Do you really think I did okay? You're not just being nice, are you?" According to work by psychologist Thomas Joiner of Florida State University, such reassurance-seeking can grow annoying and tends to make others irritable.[3] "What do you mean, 'Do you really love me?' How many times do I have to tell you before you'll believe me?!" or "For God's sake, I said you did okay! Go back to work already!" Unfortunately, the woman who is insecure about her relationships will only read this annoyance as evidence that the other person really *doesn't* love her, or she really *didn't* perform well, which can lead her to seek even more reassurance, and a cycle of tension and conflict escalates.[4]

Not surprisingly, women who have an excessively social identity are more prone to experience anxiety and depression than women with a more tempered social identity. Women who are excessively relational have poorer self-esteem, feel less in control of their lives, and are less optimistic. Thinking of yourself only in terms of your relationship to others can even harm your physical health. Psychologist Vicki Helgeson found that women with newly diagnosed breast cancer showed poorer physical functioning over three months if they had an excessively social identity.[5] These women did not take care of themselves properly, failing to follow doctors' orders about exercise, sleep, and diet, and suffered from poorer body image that became worse after their diagnosis.

For this reason, assessing how you see yourself in relation to others can be quite distressing. Before you begin the following exercises, consider your state of mind. Are you feeling overwhelmed and stressed or peaceful and calm? If you're feeling stressed, turn the page and move on to another exercise for the time being. If you're feeling calm, give yourself a few minutes to settle into a quiet place, where you feel comfortable and at home, and where you will not be interrupted—especially by the other people in your life you might be thinking about as you consider your personal identity.

Once you've settled in, think about your closest relationships, with your spouse or partner, with your children, with your parents and siblings, with your dearest friends, with your coworkers. Now, heaven forbid, imagine the most important of these relationships is gone. You are no longer a wife or partner, a mother, a daughter, a best friend to someone who is core to your sense of self. The coworker you spend all your time with at work moves out of town. You would obviously be extremely sad, but *would you be able to move on and rebuild your life without this person? Or would you be so devastated that you couldn't go on, or wouldn't want to go on?* Many people, when they lose a close relationship, say that it is like a part of themselves has died, but *would you feel totally empty without this relationship?* If so, you may be defining yourself so much in terms of this relationship that you are at great risk and need to work toward a healthier perspective on it.

Exercises to Build a Healthy Social Identity

Defining yourself in terms of your roles to others not only makes you vulnerable should those relationships end, it also can do real harm to those relationships and to the people you love. When your own self-worth is tied to who your husband is and how much he loves you, or the success and devotion of your children, you can become overcontrolling or excessively dependent. This sense of self risks smothering the people in your life, or creating resentment, and can damage your relationship.

Vanessa practically lived her life through her two children, who from a very young age showed themselves to be star students and athletes. Vanessa got completely wrapped up in their success and couldn't handle anything less than a top performance. She'd stand on the sidelines of her son's soccer games, yelling at him to run this way, kick the ball that way. Her children's teachers and coaches began to view her as a terrible meddler, who tried to control her children as though they were puppets. By the time Vanessa's children were teenagers, they had become deeply resentful of her overbearing manner. Her daughter quit all of her extracurricular school activities, let her grades go to hell, and started hanging out with kids who defined themselves by their rebelliousness, from wearing Goth clothes to sneaking out at night. Her son continued to be a top athlete at his school, but he started abusing steroids in a desperate effort to live up to his mother's expectations for him. Eventually he was caught during a surprise drug test at school and banned from participating on any sports teams. Vanessa felt betrayed by her children and totally confused by their claims that she was the one who had wrecked their lives.

Expanding Your Social Identity Exercise

Is there a relationship in your own life that is absolutely core to your sense of self? If so, take a moment to consider whether there might be risks or costs to having this level of investment in the relationship. *Are you putting yourself in jeopardy of devastation should this relationship end? Are you possibly stifling the relationship, or the person you love, by your dependency, your need for reassurance, or your controlling ways?* If the answer to any of these questions is yes, then use this as motivation to make changes to how you define your sense of self.

To make those changes you need to identify what you're getting out of your primary relationship, and find some other social context for getting those benefits. If your children's success at school or in sports provides you with a sense of achievement you yourself never experienced as a kid, or makes you feel good about yourself not just as a mother but as a *person,* you need to find another way of getting that feeling of success without putting a psychological burden on your children. If by being married to a man who is prominent in your community or in his profession you gain status and power that has become critical to your self-worth, you need to find another venue for getting that boost that is dependent on *your* talents, interests, and core values—not his. This doesn't mean you have to abandon your primary social relationship. Instead, you should branch out from it and embrace new roles and activities that do not depend on your loved ones. In fact, by ensuring that your identity is defined by yourself rather than your loved ones, you will likely improve your relationship with them.

Just as you did when you were working on building a stable and adaptable sense of self, you will need to identify the new roles you want to pursue and interests, talents, and values you want to exercise or express as part of your new multidimensional social identity. To do so, fill out the Expanding Your Social Identity Worksheet below.

Faced with her daughter's rebellion and her son's steroid use, Vanessa finally realized that she was overinvested in her children, to the point of ruining her relationship with them and pushing them to make bad choices for themselves. She reflected on how she had gotten herself into this pickle. It was pretty simple, really. Vanessa had been a star athlete in high school, and enjoyed immense popularity and admiration with other kids. She wanted to be able to give her kids that same level of popularity and status. But she was also trying to rekindle her own excitement and confidence from being admired when she was an adolescent. So when her children began to lose their star appeal, she didn't just worry about how it was affecting them; she felt as though she was a failure.

Expanding Your Social Identity Worksheet

What is your primary social identity?

List the people in your life who are integral to your identity.	List at least one area in which each relationship expresses talents, interests, or values that you take pride in.	Generate at least one activity, role, position, or other relationship in which you could express your own talents, interests, and values. Who might help you in this area? Try to identify people who are not listed in column 1.

Vanessa made a conscious choice to curtail the degree to which her own image of success was based on her children's popularity and accomplishments. She decided to sit down with them and find out what they wanted to do with their lives, separate from her expectations and hopes for them. At first, they didn't believe she was sincere when she told them she wouldn't push them to excel at sports or anything else that no longer interested them. Eventually, though, they began to talk with her about their favorite music and the classes in school they most enjoyed. Vanessa was worried that some of her children's interests might make them seem weird or uncool to their peers, but she bit her tongue in order to support her kids and build her own, independent identity.

Vanessa's ability to pull back from living through her children was only possible because she did a lot of soul-searching to evaluate what she herself wanted to be. She realized at age forty-six that "being popular" was not the goal she wanted to define her self-worth. She truly did love sports, however. She had continued to be athletic but in a casual way, playing a little tennis and running each day, but not playing competitively. Vanessa liked to win, though she knew she was out of shape and unlikely to win tennis or running competitions, even in her age group. Besides, she'd had her children's winning careers at sports to satisfy that goal. Now that she had rejected living through her children, Vanessa decided she would train to run a marathon, something she had never done in her life. The difficulty of the training made her appreciate even more the resentment her children must have felt by being constantly pushed by their mother to work harder at their sports. She told her kids this, and it increased the level of trust and communication between them immensely.

How, ideally, would you like to answer the questions "Who are you? What do you do?" Don't allow yourself to answer "I'm the wife (or partner) of so-and-so" or "I'm this child's mother." Instead, find answers that convey your deepest goals for yourself, and if you aren't pursuing those goals in some way outside of your relationships, begin today to generate ideas for how to do this. Then make a contract with yourself to carry through on one of those ideas.

Vanessa's Expanding Your Social Identity Worksheet		
What is your primary social identity? *Mother*		
List the people in your life who are integral to maintaining your identity.	List at least one area in which each relationship expresses talents, interests, or values that you take pride in.	Generate at least one activity, role, position, or other relationship in which you could express your own talents, interests, and values. Who might help you in this area? Try to identify people who are not listed in column 1.
My son Colin *My daughter Mari*	~~*Being a popular, star athlete*~~ *Being an athlete* *Being a dedicated student*	*Train for the marathon!*

Learn to Develop Several Roles in Life

Identity Strength #3: Women's identities are multifaceted, based on several roles rather than one fixed role.

You may feel you have plenty activities and responsibilities in your life, perhaps too many. *But do these activities and responsibilities fulfill all your important needs and express your values? Or are you just busy, in a narrowly focused way?*

Use the Roles Worksheet on page 178 to make a list of all the roles you play in your life. Include your roles at work, your relationships with others, your community work, your hobbies, and anything else you feel is an expression of who you are and what you value. Note the meaning or purpose of each role in expressing your values, interests, or talents. Then note whether you feel you are growing in that role, and how. Ask yourself if you are learning new skills, developing new relationships or deepening existing relationships, or finding new ways of exercising your talents or expressing your interests over time.

After you've completed the Roles Worksheet, ask yourself if the

---

Roles Worksheet

List each of the roles you play in your life. Include work roles, relationship roles, and community leadership or service roles. Then note the meaning or purpose of that role in giving you the opportunity to expresses your values, interests, or talents.

Role	Its meaning, purpose, or expression for me	Am I growing in this role?

---

roles you currently play are allowing you to use all of your core talents or pursue all of your core interests. Do you have intellectual, artistic, or humanitarian interests that are not being expressed in any of your roles? Are there new kinds of relationships you would like to have?

Janine used this exercise to recognize that many roles in her life were stagnating. On the first line, she noted her part-time work as the registrar of voters in the small town in which she lives. Registering voters gave her the chance to express her belief in promoting the democratic process. Next she listed another area of community service, volunteering at her daughter's elementary school, where she helps children whose reading skills are weak. Her tutoring work allowed her to keep in touch with developments at her daughter's school and better get to know the teachers and administrators. Janine is obviously a mother, a role she values and enjoys greatly. But when she got to describing her role as a spouse, she realized it was less gratifying to her. She and her husband often argued, sometimes about important things, like money, sometimes about petty things, like how each of them stacked dishes in the dishwasher. Yet, even in the roles in which she felt content, Janine realized she didn't feel as though she was growing as a person, intellectually or otherwise. All her roles were *comfortable enough*, but static. Nothing had changed in the past year. She could easily imagine herself doing the exact same part-time work and volunteer work in a year's time. Indeed, she could imagine being exactly the same person at the end of a decade—and that distressed her. She wanted to continue to grow as a person, and decided to find new roles in which she could do so.

As you complete the Roles Worksheet, be honest in evaluating whether your roles express your broad range of interests and values, or whether they are simply activities you have fallen into that carry little meaning for you besides fulfilling some duty.

Exercises to Build Multiple Roles

The Roles Worksheet has helped you identify the roles you currently have in your life and how they express your talents, interests, and values. *Are there talents, interests, or values that are important to you but that are not being used or developed in your current roles?* Perhaps your job is a role in which you feel you are using your education and talents and growing intellectually, and your home life is an area in which you get to nurture others to their potential, but you also have strong political or religious values you do not have much opportunity to express. *What new roles could you take on to begin to express those values?* Join a political action organization that shares your values? Teach a class in your church, synagogue, or mosque?

There are many possible roles in life, but some of the most common are:

- ❏ Parent
- ❏ Partner/Spouse
- ❏ Adult Child (for example, of an elderly or ill parent)
- ❏ Friend (to a sibling or unrelated other)
- ❏ Work Role (employee, employer)
- ❏ Community Service Role (in a religious, political, charity, or other community organization)

Check off the roles that you do *not* currently have in your life. *Do any of these immediately appeal to you? Why? What benefits could you gain by taking on this role? How would this role allow you to express or develop your talents, interests, and values?*

Exploring New Roles Exercise

Think about the appealing role you identified but do not currently have in your life. *What has kept you from taking it on?* Maybe you simply haven't gotten around to it. You know there is a political action group in your community that works on a cause of concern to you, but you haven't gotten around to going to a meeting or joining. If the opportunity to take on a role is available and you just haven't organized yourself to take advantage of it, sit down and make a concrete plan for how you will do so. *What information do you need to gather (e.g., where or when the meetings are)? With whom do you need to talk in order to get involved?* Make a contract with yourself to carry through with this plan and schedule the steps you need to take in your calendar.

Often we feel there is no time to take on another role in our lives. Our current roles fill our time to overflowing. That indeed might be the case, and sometimes we have to put off taking on a new role until another period of our life. Mothers of young children sometimes long to put their education and specific skills back to use in the workplace, while at the same time they value their time at home with their kids. Despite the frustrations, they decide to accept that getting back into a job role will have to wait for a couple of years. In many cases, however, we can reconfigure how we spend our time to make room for a new role.

If you haven't pursued a role that appeals to you because you haven't felt you had the time, think about how you might be able to cut down on the things you are currently doing to open up the time you need. Are there tasks you could delegate to other members of your family, such as getting your partner to cook dinner on the night when the organization you'd like to join meets? Are there tasks you could cut out altogether, or at least do less often, such as cleaning seldom-used

Time-Finding Worksheet				
Role	Time-Finding Task	Cut it down to . . .	Delegate it to . . .	Date Accomplished

parts of your house? At work, are there activities you do that someone else could do, so that your time is freed up? On the Time-Finding Worksheet above, list each of your current roles and list at least one task that you could cut back on or delegate to give yourself more time to pursue a new role that appeals to you.

Another frequent obstacle to pursuing a new role is that you don't have the resources or opportunity to do so. Perhaps you'd like to go back to school to gain new skills or to broaden your general education, but you don't feel you have the money. It's true that education is expensive these days, but it's also true that innovative new programs can provide educational opportunities in nontraditional, flexible venues. Internet-based classes are offered at rates that are more afford-able than those of traditional on-campus classes. Plus, the courses are often there for the taking twenty-four hours a day. And although stu-dent financial aid is tight for these programs, it's not completely unavailable. To investigate whether you might qualify, you'll need to make an appointment with the financial aid office of the college or other educational institution you are interested in attending. As you consider the resources you might need—beyond time—you might want to take advantage of the Breaking Down Obstacles Worksheet in chapter 7 (page 141).

Some roles you have not yet pursued may seem completely out of reach. For example, if you would love to be a mother but are currently not in a relationship in which that might happen or are beyond the age of childbearing, you may feel being a mother is impossible. Women are finding ways around even those obstacles, with artificial insemination or adoption. These paths to motherhood are expensive, however, and thus not open to all women. When a specific role seems completely unavailable to you, step back and ask yourself what it is about that role that appeals to you. What is it about being a mother that makes you want to take on this role? The chance to nurture a young life, to give unconditional love, to share with a child all the beauties and wonders of the world? Now think about whether there are any other ways to fulfill these desires in yourself, in addition to having your own child. Are there volunteer organizations that serve children where you could give of your love and your time? Are there jobs that involve nurturing young children, in which you could fulfill these mothering desires? The point is that a given role appeals to us because it allows us to exercise talents, pursue interests, or express values that are important to us. When that specific role seems unattainable, we can reflect more broadly on what talents, interests, or values would be tapped by that role and then use our creativity to imagine other ways to tap those talents, interests, or values.

Your Quick Reference Guide

Psychologists used to believe that our identities were fully formed by the end of adolescence, and did not undergo much change as we continued through the decades of adulthood. We now know, however, that people's identities change considerably as they pass from young adulthood to midlife and into older age. Major life events—good ones, such as the birth of children, as well as difficult ones, such as the loss of loved ones—often change how we see ourselves. The identity strength exercises in this chapter can help you transition from one phase of your life to another, helping you make conscious choices about how you define and express who you are.

Here is a summary of the assessment activities and exercises to build your identity strengths.

Building Identity Strengths

Specific Strength	Assessment Activities	Building Exercises
Identity Strength #1: Having a stable but adaptable sense of self	Think about your work, hobbies, and other activities. Imagine the most important of these disappearing. How devastated would you be? How would you define yourself? Would you be able to find other ways to exercise your talents and interests?	**Imagine Your Adaptable Self Exercise** (page 168) Identify what talents, interests, or core values are expressed and exercised in a role you fear losing. Then generate alternative ways you could express these.
Identity Strength #2: Seeing yourself in relation to others	Imagine the possibility of losing a relationship that is very important to your sense of self. Would you feel totally empty? Would you be able to go on?	**Expanding Your Social Identity Exercise** (page 174) Identify what is most important in this relationship. What interests, talents, and values are you exercising or expressing through it? Now generate ideas for how you can pursue your interests, talents, and values outside this relationship.
		Ask yourself: *Who am I? What do I do?* Find answers that convey your deepest goals for yourself, and if you aren't pursuing those goals in some way outside of your relationships, begin today to generate ideas for how to do so.
Identity Strength #3: Having several roles in life	List all your roles in life, then ask yourself if there is at least one role in which you are able to grow intellectually and/or use your intellectual talents. Is there at least one relationship that is and you	**Exploring New Roles Exercise** (page 180) Consider why you have not pursued a role that you would like or that would be good for you to have. If you just haven't gotten around to pursuing that role,

(Continued)

Specific Strength	Assessment Activities	Building Exercises
	feel is growing? Do you wish you had other relationships? Are there roles in which values that are important to you are explored and expressed, such as spiritual values, or political values, or community values?	make a concrete plan for doing so. Then make a contract with yourself to carry through with this plan and schedule the steps you need to take in your calendar. If you haven't had time to pursue a role, evaluate how you could cut back on other activities or delegate tasks to free up time.

Breaking Down Obstacles Exercise (chapter 7, page 141) If there are concrete obstacles to pursuing a role, use the Breaking Down Obstacles Worksheet to break obstacles into their smaller parts, then generate ways to overcome them. Or if the role is truly unattainable, think about ways you could satisfy your values, talents, and interests with an alternative role. |

9.

Sharpening Emotional Attunement: Building Your Emotional Strengths

When you were learning about women's emotional strengths in chapter 4, you may have said to yourself, "Oh, I'm very emotionally attuned. I'm already an expert when it comes to being in touch with my feelings!" Even so, I encourage you to jump into this chapter and explore its assessments and exercises, as a chance both to celebrate your strengths and to identify any fine tuning you might need in how you use your emotions—especially in the tricky terrain of the workplace.

On the other hand, you may have awkwardly gulped down the stories of women displaying emotional strength and said to yourself, "Sure, they're reading people's minds and soothing nerves, but there's no way I could have that effect. I'm an emotional wreck!" Don't feel discouraged. Just give the exercises in this chapter a try. You might find that you have greater strengths than you give yourself credit for. And by pinpointing which of these strengths needs the most work, you will be able to design a program to improve your overall emotional fitness.

Learn to Perceive Others' Feelings

Emotional Strength #1: Women are expert at perceiving and tuning in to other people's feelings.

For the next couple of days, at the end of the day, make a list of all the people you encountered more than just casually that day. They might be coworkers you are doing a project with, family members, or even clerks who help you with a purchase in a store. Beside each name, list all the emotions you believe that person was feeling during his or her interaction with you. *Do you have a sense of what each person was feeling? How difficult was this for you? Would you typically have noticed that person's feelings? Or does this feel like a foreign task to you?* If tuning in to others' emotions is something you find easy and even interesting, then this strength is in good shape. If this felt like an odd or strange task, then this is a strength to work on.

Exercises to Build Your Ability to Perceive Others' Feelings

Emotional Strength #1 may come automatically for some women, but if it seems difficult to you, then you need to make a conscious effort to tune in to others' feelings and learn to read them. Important clues as to what others are feeling come from their faces. As I mentioned in chapter 4, psychologist Paul Ekman has found that across cultures common facial expressions, based on how muscles contract and relax, indicate the emotion—or emotions—a person is feeling. For research purposes, Ekman has developed a detailed coding system for analyzing photographs of faces to determine what people were feeling when the photograph was taken. Sometimes emotions are shown in just an instant—mere fractions of a second—before a person attempts to hide it with the pretense of another emotion. Sometimes a person is feeling more than one thing at one time, and the face wavers between multiple emotions. And sometimes a person is incredibly expressive even though he or she is experiencing a relatively weak emotion, or vice versa. The coding system, and the database of photographs that Ekman and his colleagues have developed to train psychologists, law enforcement professionals, and others, delve into all of these possibilities.

In everyday interactions with others, however, most people don't have the time, inclination, or experience to conduct this kind of meticulous analysis. But you can use some of the universal facial cues that Ekman identified to get a better clue as to what's going on with people. Most of us know that a smile indicates happiness, but do you know how to tell the difference between a fake smile and a genuine one? It's in the eyes. When people smile in a way that creates crows' feet around their eyes, they are revealing genuine happiness. When no crows' feet are visible, this suggests they are just putting on a smile, as when someone is being polite but insincere, say, when you ask an acquaintance who's going through a divorce how they are, and they say, "Fine."

Want to know if someone is angry? Look for a flushed face, eyebrows lowered and drawn together, flared nostrils, a clenched jaw, and bared teeth. Someone who is fearful may also have a flushed face, but their brows will be drawn together, their eyes will be popped wide open, and their lips will be stretched horizontally. And sadness is characterized by a downturned face: a downturned mouth, downturned eyes. Often the whole head is downturned.

People's bodies look different with different emotions as well. Both when they are happy and when they are angry, people tend to stand tall, with their chest forward; their posture literally says, "I can take on the world!" When people are afraid, their bodies scoop inward, as if they are protecting themselves. When people are sad, their body posture often follows their downturned facial gestures; shoulders slump, and the body looks as if it could fall to the floor.

Tuning In to Others' Feelings Exercise

To practice reading the signs of others' emotions, go to a public place such as a mall, sit on a bench, and watch people. Notice the differences in people's faces, the ways they carry their bodies, how energetic and expansive they are—or how slowed down. Try to guess what other people are feeling. If you have a friend who is quite good at reading others' emotions, take him or her with you, and check to see if your impressions of other people's emotional lives match your friend's. See what cues your friend uses, and discuss how your impressions and your friend's impressions are similar or different.

Understanding Others' Feelings Exercise

Of course, people don't always want to telegraph their emotions. Especially when we are with people we may have a complicated relationship with, they may try hard to hide what they are feeling. Your spouse may suppress how he feels, and deny that he is feeling anything when you ask. Your teenager may flash from one emotion to another—fear and shame at your disapproval over her grades alongside anger that you are grounding her over them—and furiously tell you that you have *no idea* how she is feeling! Your boss may be like a block of expressionless stone that seems to say he's always in one emotional state: anger.

With these people, you can try to tune in to the situation surrounding them to discern what they might be feeling. Just as there appear to be universal connections between certain facial expressions and specific emotions, there appear to be similarities across cultures in the types of situations that elicit particular emotions, which I've summarized in the table below. Sadness and defeat are usually the result of losing something important to you and feeling helpless, or hopeless that you will ever get it back. The death of a loved one is the prototypical example of an event that causes sadness across most

Emotional Triggers

Emotion	Situation	Physical Expression
Sadness, dejection	Loss of something or someone important, feeling helpless and hopeless	Downturned mouth, eyes, face, head, slumping posture
Fear, anxiety	Threats to your well-being or the well-being of others	Flushed face, eyebrows drawn together, eyes popped wide open, lips stretched horizontally, body drawn inward
Anger	Being intentionally or unjustifiably harmed or transgressed by another person	Flushed face, eyebrows lowered and drawn together, flared nostrils, clenched jaw, bared teeth
Joy, happiness	Gaining something important to you or someone you love	Smile that creates crinkling around eyes, standing tall with chest forward

cultures. But when you lose your job, or you don't get into a school of your choice, or something else you care about is lost, you may feel sad, too. So if you are trying to understand why someone seems sad, look for something they have lost. For example, if your teenager seems blue and morose much of the time, perhaps he is sad because he feels hopeless he will ever be popular with other kids or because he is questioning whether he will accomplish important goals in his life.

With this shorthand in mind, over the next week stop and assess twice a day what you think were the emotions of each person you interacted with using the Understanding Others' Feelings Worksheet below. Then try to identify the situations that might have led to the other person's emotions. Ultimately, your goal should be not only to be able to read others' emotions but also to understand the sources of them. Understanding not only what they were feeling but also why will help you choose your responses to them more appropriately and effectively.

Understanding Others' Feelings Worksheet

List each person you encountered more than briefly, and then write down what you think that person was feeling and why.

Person	What he or she was feeling	Why he or she was feeling that way

---

Learn to Understand Your Own Emotions

Emotional Strength #2: Women understand their own emotions and the sources of these emotions.

When you finish making the list of what other people have been feeling in their interactions with you over the past couple of days, start over and list what *you* were feeling in each of those interactions, using the Understanding Your Own Emotions Worksheet below. *Is it clear to you what you were feeling, or are you unsure in many cases? Do you understand what the sources of your feelings were? Again, do you find this an easy task or difficult?* If you find it easy to recognize your emotions and their sources, this is an important strength—and it makes you healthier. If you find yourself frequently befuddled by what you are feeling and why, this is a strength that you'll want to shore up.

Understanding Your Own Emotions Worksheet		
List each person you encountered more than briefly, and then write down what emotions you were feeling in that encounter and why.		
Person	What I was feeling	Why I was feeling that way

Exercises to Build Your Understanding of Your Own Emotions

Often we feel as though we are overwhelmed with a general sense of distress but don't know just why. This makes it hard to tolerate and manage our emotions, and sometimes causes us to act rashly. Some of the same exercises you used to build Emotional Strength #1 can be useful in learning to better understand your own emotions. However, it's unlikely that every time you feel upset you are going to rush to the mirror to see what your facial muscles are doing.

Instead, the clues to our own emotions lie in our *appraisals* of what's going on in our lives. Appraisals are interpretations of events in our lives, of what other people say to us, of our memories of the past, and of our imaginations about what might happen in the future. I said earlier that there are universal links between particular situations and specific emotions. This is as true for us as it is for other people. But when it comes to understanding our own emotions, we can look not only at the concrete situation we are facing but also at how we are appraising it. Different people make different appraisals of the same situation; as individuals, we may make different appraisals of similar situations—or even the same situation—as time passes. When you were a child, walking down the street of a big city may have seemed threatening to you and so caused you to be fearful, but as an adult, you consider it exciting and exhilarating. When your husband loses his job, you may view this as a loss to you as well and feel sad, but when your boss loses his job, your appraisal might be "Yeah, the jerk is gone!" and you might feel joy.

Recognizing Your Appraisals Exercise

If you have difficulty knowing how you feel in a situation, tune in to those thoughts playing in the back of your mind like a radio in the next room. *Are you thinking about what you have lost in a situation? Or are you thinking that a situation is threatening to you or someone you love? Or do you feel you have been intentionally wronged by another person?* The clues to your feelings lie in your appraisal of the situation—and you may have several emotions competing for your attention. For example, if your daughter is about to leave for college, you may be worried about her safety (a threat appraisal), sad that she won't be at home any longer (a loss appraisal), ashamed that she didn't get into a better college (a shame appraisal), but also happy that you and your husband will have more freedom when she's gone (a gain appraisal). So you may have a jumble of negative and positive emotions that become clearer when you tune in to the appraisals playing in your head.

Go back to the Understanding Your Own Emotions Worksheet and review each of the situations you wrote down and the emotions you were feeling. What kinds of appraisals do you think you were having during each situation? How did those appraisals lead to specific feelings? Then do the worksheet again to keep track of your emotions and appraisals for the next several days. Twice a day spend a little time reflecting on your emotional experiences and the appraisals you made at the time. You will find that this becomes a more automatic process with practice, and that you will gain a greater understanding of what you are feeling, and why.

Learn to Express Your Emotions

Emotional Strength #3: Women know how and when to express their emotions.

To assess your ability in Emotional Strength #3, pick a period of days when you will be interacting with a wide range of people in your life, including family members, coworkers, and friends. For example, you might want to start this exercise on a Thursday or Friday, when you will be at work, and then continue it into the weekend, when you'll be spending more time with family or friends. Using the Expressing Your Emotions Worksheet on page 193, list whether or not you express your emotions in your encounters with the people in your life. *Did you frequently express your emotions to others or was it a rare occurrence? What emotions are easy to express, and which ones are hard to express? Under what conditions did you express, or not express your emotions? Did it happen more often with certain people than with others? When you expressed your emotions, what were the consequences? Were you honest in your expression of your emotions? Do you possibly express your emotions too much with others?*

Expressing Your Emotions Worksheet		
List each situation in which you either expressed your emotions to someone else or stifled those emotions.		
Situation, and who was involved	What I was feeling	Expressed—or not? Why not?

Exercises to Build Your Ability to Express Your Emotions

Difficulties in Emotional Strength #3 often stem from not understanding your emotions. Plain and simple, it is hard to show accurately what you are feeling if you don't even know what you're feeling or why. Thus, the first step in learning how to express your emotions more fully and appropriately is to fill out the Expressing Your Emotions Worksheet above. By working on this exercise, you may find enough insight into your emotions that the ability to express them flows naturally.

Sometimes we understand what we are feeling but feel stifled or afraid to express these feelings to certain people. You may be concerned that by expressing your emotions you'll annoy the other person or make him or her think less of you. You may not feel you have the right to express your emotions, particularly if the other person is your boss or someone with greater status or authority. By holding your emotions inside, however, you may cause the other person to misunderstand you or prevent him or her from knowing that a situation is edging to the point of distress. For example, let's say your boss has a habit of calling staff meetings at five o'clock on a Friday afternoon, just as you and most of the other staff are getting ready to leave. He's a workaholic and he'll be in the office until 10 p.m., so it doesn't occur to him that everyone else wants to leave at a reasonable hour. You get angry when he does this, and the rest of the staff does as well. In fact, some people have left the company because they don't want to put up with this manager's behavior. By not telling your boss that you are frustrated by his actions, you build up resentment that is likely to seep out in many unproductive ways, and you deprive your boss of the chance to change his behavior and possibly prevent the defection of other employees.

Assertive Expression Exercise

If there are people with whom it is difficult for you to express your emotions, write their names down on a list. Now rank these people from the least frightening to the most frightening in terms of your ability to express your emotions to them. Start with the least frightening person on your list, and for the next couple of days look for an opportunity to express how you are feeling to this person. It can be a positive feeling or a negative feeling, but don't shy away from expressing negative feelings.

When you do try to express your feelings, use *assertive* language. This is language that tells the other person how you feel and why the situation or the other person's behavior is making you feel this way, but does not take an accusatory or confrontational tone. If possible, tell the other person how you would like things to change. So if you wanted to tell your boss that calling staff meetings at 5 p.m. on Friday annoys you, you might say:

> I feel really frustrated when you call a staff meeting at five o'clock on Friday because it's the end of the week and I'd like to get home to be with my family. I'd appreciate it if we could schedule regular staff meetings at a time earlier in the day.

The important elements of this statement are (1) you take responsibility for what you are feeling and express it ("I feel really frustrated . . ."); (2) you specify the behavior or situation that is causing you to feel this way ("when you call a staff meeting at five o'clock on Friday"); (3) you explain why this behavior causes you to be annoyed ("because it's the end of the week and I'd like to get home to be with my family"); and (4) you suggest a remedy ("I'd appreciate it if we could schedule regular staff meetings at a time earlier in the day"). Not every assertive statement has to include all of these elements; the most important parts of asserting yourself are expressing your feelings and specifying the behavior or situation that is causing you to feel this way. Assertive language targets your emotion on a behavior, which makes it more likely that you'll get a change in behavior (and your boss won't get preoccupied by the fact that you think he's a jerk).

In contrast, addressing someone with nonassertive, accusatory, or aggressive language only raises his or her defenses. Let's imagine you express your concerns to your boss by saying:

> You're really inconsiderate to call those meetings at 5 p.m. on Friday night! What are you thinking!

This kind of language will likely trigger anger in your boss, not appreciation for the feelings of his employees. You call your boss names ("You're really inconsiderate!") and suggest he's annoying you on purpose. And you don't provide any kind of solution. Instead of changing the staff meeting time as you wish, he might reply, "Well, if you people were as dedicated to your work as I am, you wouldn't mind giving a little of your precious weekend to the company!"

Practice using assertive language first with the least frightening people on your list. You can even go to one of the people you feel comfortable with and ask for help in the exercise. Tell him or her you are trying to learn to use assertive language to express your emotions and focus on behaviors and situations, ask him or her to give you feedback on your statements. *Are you coming off too aggressive or too meek?* Then begin to gradually work your way up your list toward more frightening people. You might want to practice what you are going to say to these people, role-playing with someone you trust. You don't have to memorize your lines exactly—that might confuse you if you get anxious in the real situation—but you can get a sense of the most important couple of things you need to say to a given person. It can be helpful to write down what you want to say so you can review these points right before you address the person.

Note an important caveat. There indeed are some people to whom it is dangerous to express your emotions. If you have an abusive husband, expressing your emotions can lead to real harm to you or your children. If this is true for you, then you need to get help to get out of the situation, and not even think about trying to fix it by expressing your emotions.

Short of this, there are other situations where there may be real costs to expressing emotion. Women in leadership positions often feel they must suppress how they feel in order to maintain control, and women wanting to rise in male-dominated fields stifle their emotions so as not to be viewed as weak. These women are often caught in a catch-22 situation, in which not expressing their emotions leads people to think they are stone-cold bitches. During the 2008 Democratic primary campaign, Hillary Clinton was viewed by many as cold and unfeeling, but when she teared up in response to an emotionally charged question, many people said this confirmed she was too emotional and weak to be a leader.

You may want to make a list of the pros and cons of expressing your emotions to the people at the top of your list of frightening targets for expression. What could you get out of this? If it is only the catharsis of letting go and telling this person what you really feel, consider whether this is worth taking any risks you have identified in revealing yourself to this person. Talk through your reasoning with a trusted friend, so that he or she can push you to evaluate whether the risks are real or imagined and you are able to come to some satisfying decisions about when to express your emotions, and when not to.

Learn to Tolerate Distress

Emotional Strength #4: Women can tolerate distress and are thus better equipped to alleviate it.

Think back to the most upsetting situation you faced in the last month. Maybe it was when your child got hurt playing. Or when your boss yelled at you or an important sale failed to materialize. Or perhaps something more serious happened, such as your home was foreclosed on, or a loved one died, or a family member got in trouble with the law. *Did you feel as though you just couldn't stand how upsetting this was? Do you still feel that way about the situation? Did your distress feel out of control and overwhelming? Or did you feel as though you could handle that distress, as much as you didn't want to?*

We all have times when we feel overwhelmed by negative emotions. But to deal effectively with the situations that cause these emotions, we need to be able to tolerate how we feel. If you usually keep your balance and continue to function at home and at work in times of distress, then you excel in Emotional Strength #4. If your response is "I just can't stand it" and you can't do what you need to do in these crisis situations, then this is a skill that needs strengthening.

When something upsetting happens to Leisa, she feels as though she is drowning in her own emotions. For example, Leisa got into an argument with a clerk in a department store over a blouse she wanted to return. She hadn't worn it, deciding when she got it home that it was just too expensive for her to have bought. But the clerk said the blouse couldn't be returned because it had been put on clearance in the time between when Leisa bought it and returned it to the store. There was nothing on the receipt that said the purchase was nonrefundable, and Leisa had not noticed any signs indicating that no returns were allowed. Still, the clerk insisted that the store's policy was not to accept returns on clearance items. As Leisa and the store clerk went back and forth over these facts, their discussion grew into a loud argument. Other customers were waiting in line behind her, listening to everything she said.

Leisa couldn't believe how stubborn and rude the clerk was being, and she was so overcome by frustration and embarrassment that she could no longer get her words out. She began hyperventilating; her blood seemed to rush to her head. Leisa thought she was going to blow up. She finally stormed out of the store, trembling, with the blouse and receipt crumpled in her hands. Unfortunately, Leisa often has to flee from confrontational situations because she can't stand how upset she gets. Tolerating distress was clearly a skill Leisa needed to work on.

Exercises to Build Your Ability to Tolerate Distress

When we get upset, our bodies respond in predictable ways. Our heart rates and blood pressure increase, and we begin breathing more rapidly. Our stomachs may churn, and our muscles tense up. Over the course of evolution, humans and other animals have developed these bodily reactions to stress because they prepare us to literally run away or forcefully attack when threatened.[1]

Most of us are aware of our physiological responses to upsetting situations, but some of us become overwhelmed by them. All the blood rushes to our head, our heart seems ready to explode from our chests. We feel as though we are suffocating and begin to gasp for air. We are dizzy and our thoughts are confused. Such extreme responses to stress are probably born into some people. Studies have shown that genes play a role in how intense people's physiological reactions to stress are. But you can gain some control over your body's reaction to stress by changing the way you think and behave.

Body Relaxation Exercises

When we first detect that we are feeling upset, some of us panic over the very fact that we are getting upset. "Oh no, I'm starting to lose it! My heart's beating hard! I can't breathe! I shouldn't be feeling this way! What's wrong with me!" Of course, these thoughts just ramp up heart rate, blood pressure, and breathing, confirming the fear that we are losing it. This snowballing of thoughts and bodily reactions can cause a full-blown panic attack, or at the very least make our distress feel intolerable. We just want to flee the situation.

To put a halt on this snowballing effect once it has begun, you need to do exactly the thing you can't imagine doing: *relax.* You can't just tell yourself to relax (although that does help some people); you need to use relaxation exercises to slow down the physiological changes that accompany your snowballing panic. Therapists have developed dozens of relaxation exercises, but you only need a couple simple yet effective ones in your arsenal.[2]

SIX-SECOND BREATHING

When you begin to feel upset, or if you are fully engulfed by distress, stop, shut your eyes and draw in a long, deep breath. Hold it for two to three seconds. Then exhale slowly and completely, letting your shoulders and jaw drop. Feel the relaxation flow into your arms and hands. Repeat this several times. This exercise can be done anywhere, anytime—including in the thick of an upsetting situation—yet it is amazingly effective at inducing relaxation.

HEAD, NECK, AND SHOULDER RELAXERS

When you get upset, your neck and shoulder are among the first muscles in your body to tense up. Relaxing these muscles sends waves of relaxation down to your other muscles, helping to slow down the stress/distress reaction in your body.

When you feel your neck and shoulders tensing, first tighten your neck and shoulder muscles as much as possible, then hold this tension for five to ten seconds. Now completely release your muscles, feeling the tension wash out. Repeat this exercise several times, focusing on the difference between how your muscles feel when tensed and how they feel when you relax.

Another set of exercises to release tension in your shoulders, neck, and head involves gently rotating them. First, gently rotate your shoulders forward and backward. Concentrate on the sensation of your muscles relaxing as you do this. Second, gently rotate your head from side to side and from front to back, in a circular motion. Then repeat this rotation in the opposite direction. Do this very slowly so you don't strain your neck muscles. Repeat these rotation exercises several times until you feel the tension subsiding.

When you are stressed, the muscles in your forehead tend to tense up, and you clench your teeth. To relax your forehead, lift your eyebrows as if you were very surprised at something. Then relax your eyebrows as you breathe in slowly, hold the breath for a couple of seconds, and then breathe out slowly and completely. Feel the release of tension in your forehead. If your teeth are clenched, rotate your lower jaw while breathing deeply and slowly.

Thought Relaxation Exercises

The exercises above can help slow down your physiological responses, but you also have to stop your snowballing thoughts if you want to quell your distress. There are three steps for dealing with these thoughts: *Accept, Choose,* and *Focus.*

You will be using the Tolerating Distress Worksheet on page 201 to work on these steps. Think back to a recent situation in which you were quite distressed. Vividly imagine the situation in detail, and try to tap in to the thoughts you were having and how you were feeling in the moment.

Next, *Accept* that you are upset by the stressful situation and that this is a normal reaction to stress. As I said, our bodies are hard-wired by evolution to experience increased heart rate and rapid breathing when we are confronted by a stressor. But some women rail on themselves for getting upset: "I'm such a weakling! I shouldn't be this way! I can't handle anything!" These thoughts fuel our distress and motivate us to escape the situation instead of dealing with it. If these kinds of thoughts come when you are upset, note them under "Thoughts I Have When Upset." Then, under "Counter-Thoughts," write down "I accept this as a normal reaction to stress." Brainstorm other statements you can use to counter your "I can't handle this" thoughts. The point is to tell yourself you will accept this distress rather than catastrophizing it or castigating yourself for it.

Accepting that being upset is a normal reaction is just the initial step. Now you must *Choose* to deal with that distress rather than flee from it. Brainstorm things you can say to yourself when you are distressed that affirm you are choosing to stay put and deal with the situation, and you believe that you can. This might be something along the lines of "I choose to stay here and handle this and I *can* do it!" In the moment, it may be hard for you to truly believe you can deal with your distress. When that happens, try doing one of the physical relaxation exercises and then tell yourself you can handle it; as your body feels less tense and you feel more in control of its reactions, you will begin to believe that it really is possible to tolerate distressing situations.

Finally, try to switch your *Focus* from your body and its reactions to what is happening in your environment. Often we get so consumed by our feelings and thoughts of distress that we become unaware of what other people are saying or what is going on. This makes it hard to

---

Tolerating Distress Worksheet

Accept	
Write down the thoughts that make it difficult to accept and tolerate your feelings:	Write down at least one counter-thought that will help you accept your feelings:

Choose

Write down a statement about choosing to deal with your distress:

Focus

Write down a statement that will help you focus on the situation instead of your distress:

respond effectively. For example, when Leisa tried to return the blouse
to the uncooperative store clerk, she was so preoccupied with her own
distress that she didn't hear the clerk say that Leisa could go to the customer service department, which had the ability to override store
policies and thus might refund her money.

So, after you have accepted that it is okay to be upset in a situation,
and have chosen to stay put and deal with it, consciously turn your
focus to the details of what is going on. What are other people saying?
How are they acting? Try not to attend to your interpretations of what's
going on, such as "I can't believe she's being so unreasonable!" or "This
is not going to work out well!" Instead, try to focus on the concrete
details of what's happening, down to what color shirt the other person
is wearing, how she cocks her head, what kind of gestures she is using.

Why am I asking you to do this? Because research by psychologists
Ozlem Ayduk and Ethan Kross shows that when people take a "distanced" perspective on a distressing situation, watching the situation
unfold as if they were a fly on the wall and concentrating on the concrete details of what's happening, they become less upset over the
situation and can respond to it more effectively.[3] In contrast, when
people take an "immersed" perspective on the situation, focusing on
how they are feeling rather than on what's concretely happening, their
distress escalates and they are less able to respond effectively.

Leisa filled out the Tolerating Distress Worksheet as shown on
page 203.

If Leisa had taken a distanced perspective on her interaction with
the uncooperative store clerk, she would have noticed that the woman
seemed even more upset than Leisa was. The clerk was surrounded by
other customers, who were becoming increasingly angry about waiting for the argument to finish, and her cash register area was a mess.
The clerk felt overworked and besieged. By distancing herself from her
own distress, Leisa would have been able to understand why the clerk
was overreacting to her request. She would have calmed down and
heard the clerk suggest trying the customer service department. She
could have turned around and walked directly to that department,
where she would have been able to return her blouse.

Leisa's Tolerating Distress Worksheet	
Accept	
Write down the thoughts that make it difficult to accept and tolerate your feelings:	Write down at least one counter-thought that will help you accept your feelings:
I can't breathe. I can't say what I mean. I'm shaking with anger. I'm going to explode.	*I'm having a normal stress response—my body is trying to get as much oxygen into circulation as it can, and my muscles are tensing up, as part of the 'fight or flight' response.*

Choose
Write down a statement about choosing to deal with your distress:
I'm not spooked, and I'm not going to lash out. I can handle this—and I've handled much tougher things! I can do this.

Focus
Write down a statement that will help you focus on the situation instead of your distress:
I need to keep my focus on my goal and pay attention to the real obstacles. What can I do? What did the person say I can do? What else could I do to get to my goal? What is in the way of this person helping me? Could I get her to help me to my goal?

Learning to *Accept, Choose,* and *Focus* when you are distressed takes practice. In psychotherapy, clients often role-play distressing situations with their therapists, trying to conjure up distressing moments so they can practice using these skills along with helpful relaxation exercises. You can ask a trusted friend to help you do the same. Tell your friend the details of a situation in which you felt overwhelmed by your distress, and have him or her take the role of the other person—the perpetrator of your distress—while you try to relive the situation from your vantage point. But this time, try to use your relaxation exercises, and practice accepting, choosing, and focusing rather than getting overwhelmed. You can also practice these effective responses in anticipation of some event coming up that you expect to be distressing, such as a job evaluation meeting with your boss, or a conversation you need to have with your teenager over a subject of high conflict between you, like the rules for using the family car. Have your friend take the role of the other person and practice how you are going to maintain control over your distress by relaxing and then accepting, choosing, and focusing. This can be immensely helpful in preparing you for difficult situations and keeping you from getting nearly as upset as you might have been.

Learn to Manage Your Feelings

Emotional Strength #5: Women excel at managing their feelings.

An important determinant of whether we can tolerate distress is if we know how to manage feelings of distress so that they are reduced rather than amplified. When you think back on the distressing event you remembered in the previous exercise, *how did you manage your feelings? Did you consciously and actively do things to make yourself feel better and increase your ability to handle the situation? Or did you just let the feelings go until they dissipated on their own? Did you do things that probably made you feel worse, such as drinking alcohol or sobbing uncontrollably for a long period of time?*

Another way to evaluate your skills at managing feelings is to imagine some very difficult situation arising on the job or at home, a situation that makes you very upset. Then use the Managing Feelings Worksheet on page 205 to check off all the things you would typically do in response to your feelings in this upsetting situation.

Now, whether or not you checked off these specific responses, circle actions number 4, 5, 6, 7, 8, 10, 11, and 13. These responses tend to reduce your distress and help you cope more effectively.

Next, whether or not you checked off these specific responses, mark an X alongside the check-boxes for actions number 15, 18, and 19. These responses can make you feel good in the short term, but tend to make you feel worse over the long term.

Managing Feelings Worksheet

Imagine a very upsetting situation that makes you feel distressed. Think about how you would respond to your feelings about this situation. Check off each of the responses you think you are likely to engage in.

❏ 1. I bottle up my feelings so they don't show.

❏ 2. I yell at someone to let my feelings out.

❏ 3. I do something extreme, such as drive down the highway really fast, to release my feelings.

❏ 4. I take a walk or do something pleasant to calm myself down.

❏ 5. I try to breathe slowly or relax my muscles to calm myself down.

❏ 6. I try to see the situation in a different way.

❏ 7. I talk to someone I trust about the situation.

❏ 8. I take steps to change the situation.

❏ 9. I focus on who is at fault in the situation.

❏ 10. I pray or meditate.

❏ 11. I exercise to make myself feel better.

❏ 12. I focus on how badly I feel.

❏ 13. I realize that these feelings will pass eventually.

❏ 14. I get angry with myself for not handling the situation better.

❏ 15. I avoid thinking about it.

❏ 16. I get preoccupied with thinking about the situation.

❏ 17. I wonder why things like this happen to me.

❏ 18. I eat something I enjoy to make myself feel better.

❏ 19. I drink alcohol to make myself feel better.

The rest of the actions—numbers 1, 2, 3, 9, 12, 14, and 16—tend to heighten your distress and make it harder to deal with difficult situations.

For the time being, focus on becoming aware of whether your natural inclination is to minimize your distress, reduce your distress in the short term with potential ill effects later on, or churn up more distress. In the following section, I'll explain strategies for increasing your number of calming responses and decreasing your number of distress-inducing responses, so that you will feel better able to manage your emotions and deal with difficult situations.

Exercises to Build Your Ability to Manage Your Feelings

Unhelpful and unproductive responses to feelings, such as numbers 1, 2, 3, 9, 12, 14, 15, 16, 18, and 19 on the Managing Feelings Worksheet, tend to fall into three categories. First, some of these responses focus your attention on your feelings of distress in a situation, and as we've just discussed, this kind of "immersed" perspective fuels your distress, making it more difficult to respond effectively to the situation. Second, some of the responses involve bottling up your feelings for the time being—but eventually your emotions will explode. Plus, chronically suppressing your emotions causes wear and tear on your body. Third, some of the distress-increasing responses involve fleeing the situation in a dangerous manner, such as driving fast down the highway, or perhaps drinking alcohol.

Some actions, however, *increase* your ability to tolerate distressing situations and respond to them successfully. These include finding ways to relax, either at the time you are distressed or more generally, so that you don't get upset as often or as easily. We discussed some specific strategies for relaxing in the exercises to tolerate distress earlier in this chapter. The remaining actions that decrease distress fall into two categories: reappraisal strategies and problem-solving strategies.

When I was discussing how to better understand your emotions, I said that *appraisals* are interpretations of a situation—why you think something happened, what you think it means, and so on. Seeing a situation as threatening triggers feelings of anxiety and fear. Interpreting a situation as a loss triggers sadness. And believing that someone has intentionally provoked you triggers anger. *Reappraisals* are attempts to see the same situation in a different light, one that leads to less anxiety, sadness, or anger. Mountains of research show that reappraisal is an effective tool for managing your feelings.[4]

Practicing Reappraisal Exercise

You can learn to use reappraisal to manage your feelings by getting into the habit of asking yourself, when you are feeling upset, "How am I interpreting this situation?" Then ask yourself, "What is another way of looking at this situation?" For example, imagine your mother calls and says that she and your dad have decided they are not going to come to your house for Christmas, although they have been doing so for the last several years. She says they aren't coming because airline tickets have gotten so expensive these days. Your initial interpretation, however, is that she has never liked your husband and she's just using the price of airline tickets as an excuse not to be in the same household with him for a weekend. This appraisal leads you to be angry and frustrated with her.

But ask yourself, "What is another way of looking at this situation?" You could just accept her stated reason for not wanting to come for Christmas. You might even wonder if something has happened to your parents' financial status that has them worried about money. Perhaps she and your father are getting old enough that they find airline travel intimidating. They tire easily, your father gets confused and frustrated when there are delays, and your mother's ankles swell up on the plane. Or perhaps it's not your husband they are avoiding by not coming but your Aunt Gertrude, who also comes for Christmas and drives your mother crazy with complaints and excruciatingly detailed descriptions of her endless medical procedures. By collecting a series of re-appraisals, you will quell your anger a bit. That will give you the emotional space to calmly ask your mother if there is anything else going on that you should know about, such as financial problems, health problems, and the like.

Think back to a time during the last week when you felt quite upset. As you have done in previous exercises, tune in to the thoughts that were going through your head, as though you are listening to a radio playing in another room. *What were your appraisals of the upsetting situation? Did you feel threatened by something in the situation? Did you think you had lost something important to you? Did you interpret another person's behavior as intending to cause you harm?* Now take that same situation and ask yourself, "What is another way of looking at this situation?" It is not always easy, initially, to come up with a reappraisal. One way to help yourself is to ask, "How might someone else see this situation?" If you can't come up with a new way of thinking

Reappraisal Worksheet		
Situation:	Your Initial Appraisal: What did you think was going on at the time?	Your Reappraisals: What other explanations might account for the situation?

about this situation, you can ask a friend for help. Describe the situation in detail to her, and then ask her how she would interpret it. It may be very different from your interpretation. If she comes up with the same appraisal as you initially did, ask her to help you come up with alternative ways of looking at it.

Then, for the next week, use the Reappraisal Worksheet above to practice generating reappraisals for difficult situations. Anytime you feel distressed about something—whether you're angry, sad, anxious, frustrated, overwhelmed—write down in the first column what the situation was. Then tune in to what's going through your mind; that is, what your initial appraisals or interpretations of the situation are. Then try to generate at least one reappraisal for that situation by asking yourself, "What's another way of looking at this situation?" It is usually helpful to use the worksheet soon after the upsetting situation happens. Otherwise it can be tougher to tune in to your initial interpretation of the situation and understand why you became upset over it.

Studies show that practicing reappraisal with the help of worksheets such as this can significantly improve your ability to manage your feelings. In fact, clinically depressed people can overcome their depression by learning reappraisal in the course of cognitive therapy.[5]

After you've been using the Reappraisal Worksheet for several weeks and feel confident of your ability to brainstorm a reappraisal of each difficult situation you encounter, choose one of the difficult situations from your first week of using the worksheet and give yourself three minutes to come up with as many reappraisals as you can. The next week, repeat the process, trying to come up with additional reappraisals. As you become more skilled at using reappraisal, you will likely grow less likely to get stuck on your initial appraisal, and you'll quickly come up with other possible explanations for the situation.

Problem-Solving Exercise

Another powerful tool for managing your feelings is to learn to take a problem-solving approach to distressing situations. Essentially, instead of seeing a situation as a threat or a loss, or a provocation, you try to see it as a problem to be solved. Focusing on problem-solving diverts your attention from your negative feelings to the actions you can take to get some control over the situation or change it. For example, when Leisa, the woman with the blouse to return, ran up against the uncooperative store clerk, she could have taken a problem-solving approach by focusing on how she could get around the obstacles the clerk was putting in her way. She then could have asked to see the clerk's manager, or have just left the clerk and gone straight to customer service. Either of these actions would have helped her manage her emotions better than focusing on how angry she was with the clerk and how unfair the situation was.

As with reappraisal, a problem-solving approach doesn't come naturally or automatically to many of us. But we can ask ourselves a simple question to encourage a shift from brooding over a situation to problem-solving: *What's one small thing I can do that might change this situation for the better?*

Imagine that it drives you nuts that your middle-school child is always volunteering you for tasks at school. Her class needs treats for a party, and she volunteers you to bring cupcakes. She and her friends need a ride to and from the basketball game and she volunteers you to be the driver. You've reprimanded her for this several times in the past, but you always give in, so now you're angry with yourself as well as with her. What's one small thing you could do that might change this situation for the better? Screaming at her won't work, and you don't want to strand her and her friends at the basketball game. But you do want to set some limits and get her to be more considerate about making these requests. You could say to her, "I'll make the cupcakes (or drive you to the basketball game), but I'm charging you for this service. I'm going to deduct money from your allowance for every cupcake (or friend in the car), and every time you volunteer me to do something like this without asking me well in advance, I'm going to charge your allowance." I predict she will grasp the lesson pretty quickly.

Crisis situations are particularly appropriate for taking a problem-solving approach as a way of managing your feelings. If your child falls off a playground structure and is writhing in pain, you should be thinking what you can do to take care of him rather than focusing on how afraid you are. If you arrive at the airport to begin a family vacation only to find your flight has been canceled, the best way to manage your feelings is to go into problem-solving mode. That means you don't stand there screaming at the ticket agent. Instead, you rack your brain for ideas for how to get your family to your vacation destination and enlist the ticket agent's help to achieve your goal. In general, if you can keep focused on solving the crisis rather than on how upsetting it is, you will be able to draw out people's creativity and cooperation to address the situation.

To practice problem solving, go back to the situations you listed on the Reappraisal Worksheet, and for each one ask yourself, "Is there any small thing I might have done in that situation to change it for the better?" Then for the next week when you encounter a distressing situation ask yourself this question and see if you can take a problem-solving approach to it. Problem solving doesn't work in all situations—there are some problems that just can't be solved, such as the loss of a loved one. But the vast majority of situations lend themselves to some problem solving.

Your Quick Reference Guide

Women's emotional strengths are among our greatest assets. Building your emotional strengths frees you to use all your other strengths more fully. Having good emotional strengths can also improve your health, since having chronic negative emotions you don't express and that you feel are out of control tear away at your body and create disease. So as difficult as some of the exercises in this chapter can be, doing them can reap benefits across all areas of our lives.

Here is a summary of the assessment activities and exercises you can use to build your emotional strengths:

Building Emotional Strengths

Specific Strength	Assessment Activities	Building Exercises
Emotional Strength #1: Perceiving others' feelings	At the end of each day make a list of people you've interacted with and what emotions you think they were feeling. How easy or hard is it to know what others are feeling?	**Tuning In to Others' Feelings Exercise** (page 187) Go to a public place like a mall and watch people's expressions on their faces and in their bodies. Try to guess what emotions they are feeling.
		Understanding Others' Feelings Exercise (page 188) Learn the links between certain situations and specific emotions. Then practice trying to discern what types of situations other people are facing, and what they may be feeling as a result of these situations.
Emotional Strength #2: Understanding your own emotions	At the end of each day, make a list of how you were feeling in your interactions with others. How easy or hard is it to know what you are feeling?	**Recognizing Your Appraisals Exercise** (page 191) For each situation in which you feel emotional in some way, reflect on the appraisals you are making of those situations and how those appraisals are leading to your emotions.

(Continued)

Specific Strength	Assessment Activities	Building Exercises
Emotional Strength #3: Expressing your emotions	For a few days, make note of situations in which you felt emotional in interaction with someone. Keep track of how frequently you expressed those emotions, and with whom it was easy and with whom emotions were difficult to express.	**Assertive Expression Exercise** (page 194) Rank people in order from who is the least frightening to most frightening in terms of expressing your emotions. Then begin with the least frightening person and look for an opportunity to express your emotions to this person. Then move through your list to more and more threatening people. Learn assertive ways of expressing your emotions: describe specifically what you are feeling and the behavior or situation that is making you feel this way. You may also suggest a remedy that would make you feel better. Practice using assertive responses to express your emotions to the people in your life, starting with the least frightening person and moving through the list to the more frightening ones. Make a list of the pros and cons of expressing your emotions to specific people to help you decide whether it is advisable to express your emotions.
Emotional Strength #4: Tolerating distress	Think back to the most upsetting situation you faced in the last month. How well were you able to tolerate that distress? Did it feel overwhelming, or could you handle it?	**Body Relaxation Exercises** (page 198) Practice six-second breathing and head, neck, and shoulder relaxers to gain control over your physiological responses to upsetting situations. **Thought Relaxation Exercises** (page 200) Imagine an upsetting situation in the past, then imagine how you would *Accept* that you got upset,

Specific Strength	Assessment Activities	Building Exercises
		Choose to deal with your distress rather than flee it, and *Focus* on what is happening in the moment rather than on your body.
		Practice taking a "distanced" perspective on upsetting situations, focusing concretely on what is happening rather than on your own reactions.
Emotional Strength #5: Managing your feelings	Evaluate what kinds of responses you tend to have to upsetting situations.	**Practicing Reappraisal Exercise** (page 206) Practice using reappraisals of upsetting situations by asking yourself, "What is another way of looking at this situation?" or "How might someone else see this situation?"
		Problem-Solving Exercise (page 209) Practice taking a problem-solving approach to upsetting situations by asking yourself, "What's one small thing I can do that might change this situation for the better?"

10.

Connecting More Effectively: Building Your Relational Strengths

Relational strengths—understanding others' points of view, listening actively and patiently, putting others' needs first—come relatively easily to most women so you might feel as though this is an area where you don't need much work. Perspective-taking, active listening, patience, and balancing others' needs are essential tools to being a good parent and partner, and we get many opportunities to practice and hone these skills in our family lives. Even if that is the case, you could most likely benefit from practicing how to strike the right balance between empathizing with loved ones and friends and ensuring that your own needs and rights are met. In addition, you may find that you have great relational strengths in some settings, such as with your family, but need to practice using those strengths in other settings, such as on the job or in your community activities. Relational strengths are just as important in the workplace as they are with family and friends, whether you are a relatively low-level employee or a person with authority over others. Relational strengths lead to more successful negotiations, partnerships, and employee motivation, and developing these strengths can help you move your career forward and be a better leader.

Learn to Be Empathic

Relational Strength #1: Women are able to take others' perspectives.

People who are able to put aside their own perspective momentarily, who do not assume that others see things the way they do, are better able to anticipate and respond to others' needs and concerns. Thus taking another person's perspective—contemplating his or her motivations, goals, influences, priorities, and emotions—is an essential skill both for good personal relationships and for negotiating mutually beneficial agreements.

It is especially difficult to take another person's perspective when we are in conflict with him or her or feel wronged by that person. In those cases, we are prone to defensively say to ourselves, "I deserve to get what I want!" or "How dare he treat me that way!" or "I can't believe she behaved so badly!" In the previous chapter, I discussed how to better understand the emotional environment of the people in your life. Now it is time to test and develop your powers of perspective-taking—understanding others' goals and issues and finding common ground between you and them.

To assess your skill in Relational Strength #1, recall any incidents over the past month in which you were in conflict with another person (for example, over a sale or a contract) or another person made you feel annoyed, offended, or hurt. Say, for example, that your boss presented a project to the company's board of directors and received accolades for it—and failed to acknowledge that you had come up with the project's concept and contributed half of the research for the final presentation. Or, say that when you announced with pride you had bought a new, well-reviewed car, your father responded by saying you had made a stupid decision because you let the car dealer overcharge you. If no such incidents come to mind, think about a recent situation in which someone you are close to, such as a family member or close friend, was annoyed, offended, or hurt by someone else. For instance, perhaps your child was teased by a schoolmate she thought was her friend.

In such situations, it's easy to focus only on your own, or your loved one's, perspective. But spend a few moments thinking about what might have been motivating the other person in this incident. *Was he driven by some outside constraints that caused him to act as he did?* For example, perhaps your boss wasn't given an opportunity to discuss the teamwork involved in preparing the project. Indeed, we've all been in meetings in which we're supposed to present an idea to decision makers and the decision makers do all the talking. Perhaps he wasn't given much of an opportunity to say much of anything at all. *Is it possible that he misunderstood where you were coming from?* If in the past you've generally eschewed taking credit for projects in order to build camaraderie across the departmental team, your boss may not realize that you wanted to be singled out for your contribution on this project *because* it was being presented to the board, with whom you have very limited contact. *What goals might he have had that led him to act as he did?* Maybe your boss has his own performance evaluation looming, and last year he was told that he needed to demonstrate more innovative thinking.

If you found it easy to answer these questions, and remember thinking about the other person's point of view during the situation itself, then you should rate yourself as "Outstanding!" on this skill. If, however, it seems foreign or even wrong to you to be concerned with where the other person was coming from, then you may want to enhance your skills at perspective-taking. Being able to take another's perspective does not mean you have to allow that person to "win" or accept how the person has acted toward you. Instead, it allows you to respond more consciously and effectively to that behavior, for your own benefit.

Exercises to Build Your Ability to Take Others' Perspectives

Getting inside other people's heads—seeing the world as they do, appreciating the stresses and obstacles they face, understanding how their background affects who they are now—should be easier for you to do with the people you know best, especially your family members. You have known them all or most of your life and have intimate knowledge of many of the critical events in their lives. Still, it is amazing how often we feel we don't know where a loved one is coming from, why he says the things he does or how she can behave so badly. And with the people we live with on a daily basis, we often don't take the time to know what is going on in their lives now that may be driving their behavior. We're so busy with the activities of life that we don't know our husband's workplace has become more stressful in recent weeks or that our child is being harassed by a bully at school.

Getting Inside Others' Heads Exercise

So a good place to work on building your ability to take others' perspectives is at home. Take some incident in the last week or so in which you were mystified by the behavior of one of your family members. For example, Barbara couldn't believe it when her seventeen-year-old son Paul left the garage door open and the back door to their home ajar one night when he came in after she had gone to bed. Their neighborhood wasn't terribly safe, and she had preached to her son countless times about the importance of securing all the doors at night. All she wanted to do was to scream at him when he woke up the next morning. Why should Barbara be concerned about seeing her son's perspective in this case? One reason is that he had recently been telling her she doesn't understand him or what kids are like. Another reason is that if she could comprehend why Paul had acted so irresponsibly, she might be able to help him be more responsible in the future. Raising her voice rarely worked with Paul, so she needed to find other ways of getting through to him.

The first question Barbara and you can ask when you are trying to gain insight into another's behavior is "What situations might be influencing how this person acts?" Just as your own behavior is affected by your appraisals or interpretations or expectations, other people's behavior is, too. And just as your behavior is shaped by your environment and the conditions you face, other people's behavior is, too. So when you are trying to understand where another person is coming from, try to imagine what might be influencing him or her to act this way, or how he or she might be responding to the environment around him or her.

When Barbara posed this question to herself, she remembered that Paul had been out late in order to practice for a county-wide debate competition on the weekend. He was hoping to get a scholarship to college, since their family had little money for tuition, and he had been told by the team's coach that past students who had placed first in the debate had gone on to win a prestigious and generous scholarship from a local benefactor. Maybe, Barbara thought, he was preoccupied with how badly the practice had gone for him last night and had just blanked out about shutting and locking the doors. This didn't excuse the behavior, but it helped Barbara calm down and feel less like screaming.

When her son got up that morning, she took a deep breath and told him firmly but not angrily that he had left the doors open and she was frustrated and disappointed. Then she asked him, "What was going on last night that you didn't remember to shut the doors?" Notice that Barbara didn't presume that her hypothesis that her son had been worried about the upcoming debate match was correct. Having perspective-taking ability doesn't mean you assume you know exactly what's going on in another person's head. If Barbara had said, "You were too busy worrying about the debate match on Saturday, weren't you?" her son might have reacted defensively, "*No*, that wasn't it at all!" and stormed off. Taking another person's perspective means you are receptive to being enlightened about thoughts, behaviors, motivations, and influences that are very different from your own. So Barbara asked an unassuming question, and Paul answered, "I'm sorry! I was thinking about needing that stupid scholarship, and then I got a text message from Sarah [his girlfriend] saying she thinks we're too young to be dating. I just was spaced out when I came in last night." Rather than simply creating conflict by screaming at her son, Barbara opened the door to talking with Paul about the things that were going on in his life. This might not guarantee that the garage door gets closed next time, but it did increase the level of communication and trust between Barbara and her son.

For the next week, whenever someone you are close to does or says something that takes you by surprise, ask yourself, "What thoughts or situations might be influencing how this person acted?" Try hard not to impose your own perspective on his or her behavior, with thoughts like "Well, I would have . . ." What *you* would have thought or done is not relevant. Your job is to try to understand what is driving the other person's behavior. With practice, you are likely to find that your initial negative reactions to others' behaviors are softened. You will also probably notice that you are having more productive conversations with others and they are more willing to cooperate with you.

Negotiating from Multiple Perspectives Exercise

Although not every situation calls for making a deal—Barbara wouldn't consider setting up a schedule for the days on which Paul could and could not leave the garage door up—negotiation is an area in which it really pays to learn how to take others' perspectives. As I described in chapter 5, studies show that negotiations in which each party tries to take the other's perspective result in more satisfying agreements for both partners.

Think about an ongoing conflict in which you need to negotiate or reach a shared agreement. For example, you and your teenager must share a car and need to negotiate the schedule of use. Or you have to develop an agreement with another department in your company over the split of responsibilities on a big joint project. Using the Negotiating from Multiple Perspectives Worksheet overleaf, write a description of the conflict or issue that needs negotiating. Then write down the other person's position, including all of the various points that he or she might raise in support of that position. Next, rank what you think are the most important goals or concerns for the other person in this negotiation—what does he or she need to get out of the negotiation the most, and what is less important to this person. Then go through the same process for your own position—describe it, including points in

Negotiating from Multiple Perspectives Worksheet	
Describe the conflict:	
State the other person's position:	**State your position:**
Identify and rank, from most important to least important, the other person's goals and concerns:	Identify and rank, from most important to least important, your goals and concerns:
1.	
2.	
3.	
4.	
5.	
6.	
7.	
8.	
The shared agreement:	

support of your position. And rank your goals and concerns, from the most important ones that you can't give up to the least important ones.

As you fill in this worksheet, keep in mind that external factors might influence the other person's position in this negotiation. If, for instance, the head of the other department knows that her top project manager is going through a crisis at home, she will not disclose that in stating her position, but it will definitely affect what she's willing to offer and what she's willing to concede as she negotiates the allocation of project resources with you.

Now take a look at both lists. *Are there areas where you might find common ground?* Circle these components in both of your positions. Next, look for areas where you can balance the other person's concerns with your own. *Is there any issue among the other person's top three remaining goals or concerns that you are willing to concede in exchange for something you want or need?* If so, draw an arrow between these. Now, at the bottom of the worksheet, write up a description of a possible shared agreement on all of these points—the areas in which you have found common ground or issues you could concede or trade off.

Finally, really push yourself to take the other person's perspective. Imagine conceding all of the unresolved issues on the other person's list—without getting anything from your list in exchange. *What might you gain from this?* As you brainstorm answers to this question, consider not just this negotiation but future negotiations you might have with the person, and the advantages you might have in the next negotiation if you concede a bit in this one.

June went through this exercise before going to see her boss about a salary raise. She had only received the standard raises that everyone in her catering firm had gotten for the last five years, even though her work had received high praise from the firm's clients and had brought in more new clients than anyone else's. June felt she deserved a bigger raise this year, but knew that the company was pinched financially because it was investing thousands of dollars in upgrading its food-preparation facilities. Taking a moment to imagine herself in her boss's head, she then completed the Negotiating from Multiple Perspectives Worksheet as shown on page 222.

In doing this exercise, June noticed several areas of overlap in her concerns and her boss's concerns. Like her boss, she wanted the facilities upgrade and didn't want her raise to stop those renovations. So that meant the money for her raise needed to come from somewhere else, such as in savings to the company. Perhaps she could offer to substitute teleconferencing for traveling to clients' offices to discuss catering

June's Negotiating from Multiple Perspectives Worksheet	
Describe the conflict: *I want a bigger raise this year but the company is strapped for cash.*	
State the other person's [my boss's] position: *I can't give you a bigger raise because any extra budget money for the next year will go to facilities upgrades. That will benefit your work so you shouldn't be asking for more.*	State your position: *I have earned the company more money by producing work that clients appreciate and that draws clients. I deserve to be paid more than the standard raise that everyone gets.*
Identify and rank, from most important to least important, the other person's goals or concerns.	Identify and rank, from most important to least important, your goals or concerns.
1. *Budget can't go into the red.*	1. *To be recognized for quality of work.*
2. *Have to upgrade facilities.*	2. *Want more money to buy a nicer house.*
3. *Don't want to alienate or lose valued employee.*	3. *Do want the facilities upgrades so my working environment is better.*
4. *Don't want to create dissension among employees by giving one a bigger raise than others.*	4. *Don't want to damage relationship with boss or other employees.*
5. *Don't want to look bad to my superiors*	5.

assignments, or she could investigate pieces of equipment for the new facilities that were just as good as those currently in the budget, but cheaper. Like her boss, she didn't want to alienate the other employees by seeming to be treated more favorably. On the other hand, she wanted recognition for her work, and thought that such recognition might motivate other employees. Perhaps the company could start a bonus program, in which employees who brought in new clients got a financial bonus that would be built in to the cost structure of the contracts with the new clients. Even if she couldn't get a greater increase to her base pay than the other employees, getting substantial bonuses by bringing in new clients would help her meet her goal of buying a new house.

June wrote out these ideas in the section of the worksheet labeled "The Shared Agreement." Then she rehearsed how she was going to approach her boss in a way that respected his perspective but asserted her own position as well, and led to something like the shared agreement she thought was possible. When she went in to see him, she said, "Jim, I understand how important it is to upgrade our facilities, and how expensive that is. I want the upgrades as well. But I feel strongly that I deserve some financial recognition for the success the company has had with clients, old and new. I'd like to tell you some of my ideas for accomplishing both your goals and mine."

When you are first learning to negotiate from multiple perspectives, you might find it difficult to see the other person's position, let alone to figure out the various component parts of that position and how that person values each compared to the others. If you're having trouble, ask a trusted friend to role-play a realistic conflict with you so that you can hear another person's perspective directly.

Learn to Listen to Others

Relational Strength #2: Women actively listen to others.

One way to find out if you need work in Relational Strength #2 is to ask the people in your life with whom you have regular, intimate conversation what they think. In a private moment with your spouse or partner, or with your child, ask whether he or she feels you listen well. You'll need to work hard at being as non-defensive as possible—don't object if your loved one hedges or tells you outright that there are times you don't listen well. Instead, be quiet and listen. Try to find out (without putting your loved one through the third degree) in what situations you tend to listen well and in what situations you don't listen well. For example, perhaps your child feels you listen well when you are at home and things are quiet, but when you are driving him to school, or your child calls you at work, you are preoccupied and don't listen. This may be understandable, but children often communicate important things at inconvenient times, and if you want to know what's going on with them, you have to listen, no matter what else you'd rather be doing.

At work, we tend to be highly motivated to listen to our bosses. It's your coworkers and especially the people who are subordinate to you that you are most likely not to listen well to. It can be hard to find out if you are a good listener at work, because the people who work under you may be too intimidated to tell you about your problems in listening, and your peers may not want to stir up a conflict. To test your listening skills at work, spend a couple of days trying to actively listen at times when others, particularly your peers or subordinates, are talking with you. *How difficult is it to listen well? Does it feel like something you do often? Or is it a startling, new experience, suggesting listening is a skill you may need to improve?*

Exercises to Build Listening Skills

Nothing teaches you the benefits of active listening more than doing it, and seeing the benefits firsthand. So try these exercises to motivate yourself to listen more.

Silence Exercise

If you have discovered you are a talker and not a great listener, spend one or two days pretending you have laryngitis and can't talk. Suppress all talking even when you really want to. While you are faking laryngitis, notice what you might have missed if you had been talking. Do your children open up and say things you are surprised to hear? Does your spouse fill the quiet air at dinner with enlightening information about what's happening at work? Do your coworkers and employees venture new ideas or opinions that take you by surprise? Keep a diary of the things you hear that you probably wouldn't have heard if you hadn't kept quiet yourself. *What did you or others gain when you listened more actively? Were others more confident or more trusting? Did listening give you an insight into where they are coming from?*

Now, take note of the benefits of listening more and talking less, using a set of index cards to write them down. For example, when Barbara and her son had argued on an earlier occasion about leaving the garage door open, Barbara presumed she knew what Paul had been thinking. She lectured him at length, and every time Paul tried to say something, Barbara cut him off. He stormed off, saying, "You never listen to me." That had gotten Barbara's attention. So when Paul asked for a ride to the next practice, Barbara agreed without hesitation—and without a word. On the ride, she pretended she had laryngitis, but with her smiles at him, her laughter at what was on the radio, and her friendly gestures—including reaching out to Paul in a gentle, loving way—she made it clear to her son that she wasn't giving him the silent treatment out of anger. Paul took Barbara's cue and began to talk about his topic for the debate match, and about how much he wanted to do well since it seemed that the scholarship he was gunning for always went to the student who won the tournament. Barbara took note of what she had heard on the drive: "Paul isn't sure he knows everything he needs to know about his debate topic to be sure he wins at the debate match," and "Paul feels a lot of responsibility for getting a scholarship to pay for college."

Afterward Barbara took her cards and wrote down the benefits from actively listening:

> *Listening Plus: Paul doesn't bottle up his insecurities. He trusts me enough to share his fears.*
>
> ---
>
> *Listening Plus: Paul is growing into a very responsible grown-up. I understand that sometimes he's irresponsible, but sometimes he's responsible, too.*

Pulling these cards out before her confrontation that morning, Barbara was able to remind herself not to jump to conclusions and to give Paul a chance to explain himself. And that led to him telling her about his distressing text message from his girlfriend, Sarah.

To make sure you don't mentally mix your "listening plus" cards up with your "negative thoughts" cards from chapter 7, use a different card color, such as blue or yellow, for these cards. Use as many or as few cards as you need, but try to capture all of the benefits, each on its own card. You'll want to hold on to these cards and keep them handy—review them as motivation to spend more time listening actively at home and at work, especially when you know you have an important conversation coming up in which your instinct might be to talk rather than listen.

Rubber Band Exercise

Reflect on what it is that compels you to talk so much in such situations. *Are you expressing your opinions or showing your knowledge in an attempt to look good? Are you trying to control the situation?* Sometimes this is a good idea. If you really do have the best solution to some problem at work, you should pipe up and push your point of view for the good of the company and your own career. If you truly believe that your spouse or partner, or your child, is making a bad decision, you should tell him or her so. But if you are constantly forcing your opinion or just talking over others, there can be negative consequences to your relationship with others, to their desire to listen to anything you say, and to their development of independence and confidence.

So for the next week, wear a small rubber band on your wrist, and each time you find yourself jumping into a conversation, not listening to what others are saying, or cutting others off, snap that rubber band to remind yourself to just be quiet and listen.

Learn to Be Patient

Relational Strength #3: Women are tolerant and patient.

The tests to determine whether you are patient are similar to those for determining whether you listen well, because these two strengths are linked—you can't listen if you are impatient. So you can ask the people in your life outright if they find you to be patient or impatient with them. Again, be prepared to be unpleasantly surprised. We often believe we are much more patient than other people perceive we are.

Another test is to observe yourself for a week, watching for times when you feel frustrated or agitated, as though you are ready to jump out of your seat—in short, impatient. *How often do these situations arise? With whom do they tend to arise?* If in one week no such situations occur, you are a very patient person! If you find them occurring frequently, at home or at work, patience may be a strength you need to cultivate.

Karen was shocked to find out her family did not see her as a patient person. She asked her husband and two children if they thought she was patient. None wanted to answer. That was her first clue that the answer to her question was not "Yes, you are very patient, Karen." She told her family, "I promise I won't get angry. I want to know when I'm not patient so I can be better." Eventually, her daughter said, "Mom, you're pretty patient on the weekends, but during the week you always seem in a hurry and are rushing us. I know we're slow, but you don't even let me finish my sentences sometimes. You finish them for me so we can get going." Empowered by his daughter's honesty, Karen's husband, Joe, added, "You can be so impatient during the week that I don't feel I can just talk to you about what happened during the day."

Karen thought of a million objections to what her daughter and husband had said. It was her job to get her children to school and to work—they always seemed to be running late or forgetting things, so of course she had to hurry them along. And with her husband, didn't he understand that in the evenings she had a lot to juggle, including cooking, washing dishes, doing laundry, and helping the kids with homework? How could Joe expect her to sit casually and chat about the workday?

But Karen decided to stifle her objections and calmly thanked her family for being honest with her. Then she observed herself for the next week and realized that she *always* felt rushed and agitated with her children and her husband. It was as if they pressed the "Slow" button and moved like barnacle-encrusted turtles. Karen also realized that urging along her husband and kids didn't make them move faster but only created hostility between her and them. Moreover, she was missing out on some important moments during the week due to her impatience: Joe trying to tell her that he was worried about his parents' health, her son's struggle understanding new concepts in his science class, the body image concerns that kept her daughter in front of the mirror for an hour each night. Karen was very clear by the end of the week that patience was one skill that definitely needs improvement.

Exercises to Build Patience

Why are you always in such a hurry? This is the question you should ask yourself if you find you are an impatient person. You may answer, like Karen, "Because there is so much to do!" But then the question is whether getting all those things done is worth the damage to your relationships—at home, at work, with your friends—caused by your impatience. If the answer to that is "no," then you need to think about how you can cut back on the things that make you feel so hurried and pressured so that you can slow down, listen, and be present with the people in your life.

Priority-Setting Exercise

If you feel you are impatient at home because there are simply too many chores to get done, activities to get to, and so on, make a list of all these things. Then sit down with your family and rank these in terms of how important they are. Getting homework done will be high on the list, as will be getting food into the house. But watching TV or keeping the garage clean will (with hope) be low on the list. Your daughter's music lessons are high on the list because music is very important to her, but you might want to put ironing her blouses lower on the list. Think about whether there are any activities near the bottom of the list you can eliminate altogether, or at least cut back on. Also think about whether you worry too much about doing everything just right: you push your child to do all the extra-credit homework and turn in projects that look professionally done; your house always has to look like something out of *Better Homes and Gardens*; your meals are so elaborate they could land you a show on the Food Network. Is all of this really necessary? By insisting on near-perfection in areas of our lives, we put pressure on ourselves that makes it hard to be patient with others who might not see the need for all that perfection.

If you are impatient at work, think first about who is the most frequent target of your impatience. If one of your employees seems to do everything at a snail's pace, consider whether she needs additional training or equipment (such as a faster computer) to be able to work more efficiently. Or perhaps she's too loaded down with tasks and you need to work with her to streamline her duties and prioritize so that she gets the important ones done in the time frame you expect. If she's just slow (or even lazy), then you may need to have a talk with her about your expectations and whether she's able to meet them.

If you simply want everything to be done faster than it tends to get done, then you need to check your own priorities and expectations. Do you really have to get projects in before the deadline? What benefits do you see from doing this? You might be trying to build your company's reputation as a rapid delivery service. But are there possible costs, for example, in the quality of the work that gets done or the loyalty of your employees, who are always being pressured to work faster? Think about whether some projects deserve your impatience because there are many more benefits than costs to delivering the project quickly or soon. On the other hand, there may be other projects that don't deserve your impatience because there are many more costs than benefits to rushing the work.

Relaxation Exercises

Across all areas of your life, you can improve your patience by learning to relax more. Go back and review the relaxation exercises in chapter 9. Then when you find yourself becoming impatient, use them to calm yourself and make a decision to be more patient. The Six-Second Breathing Exercise is especially good for this because you can do it without other people noticing. When you are sitting at dinner and your husband is talking about his day but you are becoming impatient to do the dishes, breathe in slowly, hold the breath for a couple of seconds, then breathe out again while slowly feeling your body relax. As you are breathing out, focus your attention on what he is saying and how you can become more engaged in conversation with him.

Learn to Put Others First—When Appropriate

Relational Strength #4: Women are able to put others' needs before their own.

This is another strength that women often err in expressing too much, as well as too little. Some women put aside their talents, interests, and needs to support and promote a partner or to take care of a child or elderly relative, and end up feeling unfulfilled, frustrated, and resentful. On the other hand, some women pursue their own interests and careers so doggedly that they put on blinders as to how their pursuits are affecting others and what they are giving up in their relationships with others for those pursuits.

So how do you know if you are striking the right balance between putting yourself versus others first? There is no universal standard. Different women have different values and standards for the balance between focusing on their own interests and focusing on the interests of others.

To determine what your standards are (in an ideal world) and whether you are meeting them, try this exercise. Ask yourself, *Is there anything I would like to be doing in my life right now that I'm not doing because I am putting others' needs first?* You might answer that you aren't working full-time because you are caring for your small children or your parents, or doing volunteer work in the community. Perhaps you aren't traveling around the world because your partner's job doesn't allow him to travel with you. Or maybe you'd like to quit work and write a novel, but the company you own employs a lot of people who would be out of work if you quit. Whatever the specific circumstances, ask yourself, *How much do I value my interests that I am giving up? How much do I value what I am doing instead of pursuing my interests?* If these valuations are equal, or you value what you are doing even more than what you are giving up, your values appear to be in balance and you probably are appropriately putting others' needs first. If it pains you greatly to think about what you are giving up relative to what you are getting in return, then you may be putting others' needs before your own to an unhealthy degree.

Exercises to Build Your Ability to Put Others First When Appropriate

If you have identified interests, talents, and values you are neglecting because you are putting others first, and feel that these are too important to neglect any longer, it's time to work on Relational Strength #4.

Imagine Balancing Exercise

On the Balancing Worksheet on the next page, write down the interest, talent, or value you are not pursuing because you are putting others first. Then generate some ideas for how you could begin your pursuit. Perhaps you gave up your job as a teacher to take care of your dad, who has Alzheimer's disease. Under "What I'd like to be doing" you would write down "Teaching," and under "How to get started" you might write "Take a class at the community college to renew my teaching certificate" or "Check into open positions in the public schools."

Next, list any concrete obstacles to pursuing your interests, such as not having enough money to hire a caretaker for your father when you are away. Set aside any worries you might have about what others will say about your decision to put your own needs and desires first. Then,

---

Balancing Worksheet

What I'd like to be doing:

How to get started:

Possible obstacles:

Ways around these obstacles:

1.
2.
3.

Possible objections from others:

Ways in which pursuing your own needs will benefit others:

1.
2.
3.

---

brainstorm manageable, small steps you can take to address these obstacles, using (if necessary) the Breaking Down Obstacles Worksheet on page 141 to come up with at least three ideas. For example, you could call the local senior center to see if they have any respite services where volunteers come into your home for a few hours each week to allow you to get away to do important tasks, such as taking a class at the community college.

When you start to put these ideas into action, the people whose needs you've been prioritizing are likely to object to your taking any time away from them for yourself—no matter how much or how little. For example, your father may say he is not comfortable having a stranger in the house and wants you to stay home with him all the time. These kinds of objections, more so than concrete obstacles, are often what keep us from striking the proper balance between our own needs and the needs of those we love. So, now think about the objections others might raise, and add them to the Balancing Worksheet.

It's important at this point to consider whether making changes that put some of your needs forward might also benefit the other person. If you are growing resentful of your father because you feel stifled by staying at home and caring for him, this will likely seep into your relationship with him. Indeed, caregivers sometimes even become hostile and abusive to the elders they love as a response to the stress and frustration of full-time caregiving. This is why senior care organizations provide respite services, which allow caregivers to take the time away from caregiving that they need. Pursuing your interest in teaching may be so gratifying to you that you gather renewed energy and joy to give to your father. Finally, consider at least three ways in which pursuing your needs could benefit the people whose needs you're pulling back on your priority list, and add them to the worksheet.

If you are one of those rare women who has tipped the balance between self and others toward a singular pursuit of your own interests at the expense of others and decide you want that balance to be more even, the question you have to ask yourself is: "Which of my pursuits am I willing to give up to put another's needs first?" Pursuits that are of relatively low interest or value to you should be the first to go. If you are president of both the Chamber of Commerce and the Garden Club, the Chamber of Commerce position is probably more important to the continued success of your business than is the Garden Club. Women in business are especially prone to loading themselves up with community leadership positions, some of which contribute to their business success, some of which reflect important personal values, and some of which were not much more than accidents, things they have fallen into and don't care much about. Identifying which activities you could drop without much impact can free up time you can give to others' needs.

You may feel you need to make more radical changes to strike a balance between putting yourself first versus putting others first. If your child develops a serious physical disorder that requires significant lifestyle changes, frequent doctor visits, changes at his school, and so on, you may feel you can't manage his health adequately while working full-time. Quitting your job may be the right thing for you to do, but take some time to consider the costs as well as the benefits of making such a big change. There are not only financial costs but also costs to your well-being, intellectual growth, and career advancement. If you think you can manage that, then great. But there may be smaller changes you can make to give yourself the time and space to care for others as you see fit while not abandoning your own needs wholesale.

Your Quick Reference Guide

If you feel a bit tired and sore after doing these exercises, or don't feel as though change is coming quickly enough, remember that building strength takes time and repeated practice. You are trying to break old habits you may have had all your life, or gain skills you've never had before. Keep taking those small steps, day by day, and using imagery to get a fix on the positive outcomes you are moving toward, and you will get there.

Here is a summary of the assessment activities and exercises to build your relational strengths:

Building Relational Strengths

Specific Strength	Assessment Activities	Building Exercises
Relational Strength #1: Taking others' perspectives	Reflect on a recent situation in which you felt wronged by someone. How hard or easy is it to understand what might have	**Getting Inside Others' Heads Exercise** (page 217) For the next week, whenever someone you are close to does

Specific Strength	Assessment Activities	Building Exercises
	led this person to act in this way toward you?	or says something that takes you by surprise, practice asking yourself, "What thoughts, feelings, or situations might have influenced how this person acted?"
		Negotiating from Multiple Perspectives Exercise (page 219) Imagine reaching a shared agreement by approaching a conflict with another's perspective in mind.
Relational Strength #2: Listening to others	Ask others in your life whether you are a good listener. Spend a couple of days trying to listen to others and ask yourself how hard or easy this is.	**Silence Exercise** (page 224) Spend one or two days pretending you have laryngitis and can't talk. Keep a diary of the things you hear that you probably wouldn't have heard if you hadn't kept quiet. Note how your active listening has benefited you and others on "Listening Plus" index cards, which you can refer to for motivation before important conversations and meetings.
		Rubber Band Exercise (page 226) For the next week, wear a rubber band on your wrist, and each time you find yourself jumping into a conversation, not listening to what others are saying, or cutting others off, snap that rubber band to remind yourself to just be quiet and listen. Keep a log of what you are hearing that you would have missed if you had been talking. Reflect on what compels you to talk all the time.

(Continued)

Specific Strength	Assessment Activities	Building Exercises
Relational Strength #3: Being patient	Ask others if you are a patient person. Observe yourself for a week, watching for times when you feel frustrated, agitated, and impatient. Notice where and with whom you are most likely to be impatient.	**Priority-Setting Exercise** (page 228) If you are impatient because you feel there is too much to do, make a list of your obligations, activities, etc., then rank them. Generate ways of eliminating the low-priority ones so you feel less rushed. Reflect on your expectations for how quickly things need to get done and how many things you should be doing. Cut back as much as possible. **Relaxation Exercises** (chapter 9, pages 198 and 200) Practice relaxing when you become impatient.
Relational Strength #4: Putting others first when appropriate	Ask yourself, "Is there anything I would like to be doing in my life right now that I'm not doing because I am putting others' needs first?" Then ask yourself, "How much do I value the interests I am giving up?" and "How much do I value what I am doing instead of pursuing my interests?" Ask yourself, "Have I been singularly pursuing my own interests to the detriment of others' needs?"	**Imagine Balancing Exercise** (page 231) Identify activities or interests that you feel you are sacrificing in order to serve other people's needs. Generate ideas for how you could begin pursuing these activities and interests. Break down obstacles to generate the small steps you should take to balance your own needs with those of others. Identify the benefits to others of putting your own needs first so you can answer any objections. Consider what you'd be willing to give up or what low-priority activities you could eliminate to make room for others' needs.

THREE

Unleashing Your Power

11.

Leading Like a Woman

We used to think that good leaders were masculine leaders—forceful, directive, decisive—John Wayne in the boardroom. Increasingly, leadership gurus are arguing that the modern world requires a very different type of leader, one who can generate innovation in the face of rapid technological change, work with diverse groups of people, and empower, support, and engage others. Bernard Bass of the Center for Leadership Studies at Binghamton University in New York has labeled this a "transformational leadership style."[1]

Transformational leaders communicate the values, purpose, and importance of their organization. They are optimistic and excited about their organization's objectives and inspire others to be just as enthusiastic. They focus on the development and mentoring of others. They gain the respect and loyalty of others.[2] Nearly forty studies show that transformational leaders are more effective leaders—they make more money, produce more successful products, and accomplish more of their organization's goals.[3]

Do the qualities of a successful transformational leader sound familiar? They should, because women's quintessential strengths dovetail perfectly with these qualities. Indeed, psychologist Alice Eagly of Northwestern University compiled nearly four-dozen studies comparing the leadership styles of men and women and found that, across the board, women were significantly more likely to lead in a transformational style.[4] "We're looking at a different paradigm of leadership, and it plays naturally to the strengths of women," says

Regina Sacha, vice president of human resources for FedExCustom Critical. "The tide has turned. The leadership skills that come naturally to women are now absolutely necessary for companies to continue to thrive."[5]

Bringing It All to the Table

Women's mental strength of determined optimism cultivates a positive mood in everyone around them. In turn, these positive moods, combined with women's ability to see many paths to their goals, enable them to be more creative and persistent in finding solutions to problems. Their ideas for new products or ways of selling those products tend to be more innovative, since they aren't concerned with "doing it the way it's always been done." And women's optimism makes other people want to be around them, to help them, and to emulate their "can-do" attitude.

Rosa Parks became a leader by refusing to do it the way it's always been done and by remaining optimistic that she would effect change in the face of tremendous powers against her. In the 1950s, the city of Montgomery, Alabama, held an ordinance on its books that required African Americans to give up their seats on the city buses to white patrons if ordered to by the bus driver. Parks, and most other African-American riders, had complied with this rule many times, because this was a way of life in the segregated South. Indeed, on one rainy day, a bus driver insisted Parks get off the bus after she had paid her fare and reenter from the back door; when she stepped off the bus, the driver closed the door and drove off, leaving her to walk five miles home in the rain.

On December 1, 1955, Parks was riding in the designated area for African-American patrons when a number of white patrons entered the bus. The bus driver, the same man who had left her standing in the rain after she had paid her fare, came back to insist that she and three other African Americans give up their seats to the white patrons. The other three moved, but Parks refused. She was arrested and tried for disorderly conduct. The incident triggered the Montgomery bus boycott, one of the turning points in the civil rights movement. Parks later recounted:

> I did not want to be mistreated, I did not want to be deprived of a seat that I had paid for. It was just time . . . there was opportunity for me to take a stand to express the way I felt about being treated in that manner. I had not planned to get arrested. I had plenty to do without having to end up in jail. But when I had to face that decision, I didn't hesitate to do so because I felt that we had endured that too long. The more we gave in, the more we complied with that kind of treatment, the more oppressive it became.[6]

Rosa Parks not only rejected the idea that she and other African Americans had to follow the rules and do things the way they had always been done, she also held a deep and stubborn belief that by her actions she could change the world. Her refusal to give up her bus seat was just one incident in her long history of fighting for the rights of African Americans. Prior to her arrest, she had worked to free African-American men falsely accused of rape and was a secretary to the president of the Montgomery NAACP. Later in her career, she founded the Rosa and Raymond Parks Institute for Self-Development to encourage youth to reach their highest potential by learning dignity, pride, courage, and perseverance.[7]

Parks was known as a woman with "quiet strength." She believed in her ability to change the world, but she did not believe in self-aggrandizement. Women's tendency to focus on getting the job done rather than promoting themselves keeps everyone focused on the task at hand. Women reach out to others and build teams of complementary strengths. As a result, projects are accomplished on time, outcomes reflect everyone's best efforts instead of who won the battle to be top dog, and morale is built instead of destroyed in the process.

Women's identity strengths allow them to adapt to the changing circumstances of the marketplace and to their particular company or organization. They can be flexible without losing sight of the group's primary goals or of their own values and interests. This is a critical ability in today's fast-changing and diverse world, where consumer trends come and go with amazing speed, and successful companies have to balance the need to compete on a global level with the need to respond to local business conditions.

Women's multiple roles create balance in their lives, preventing them from investing their identity too much in the company, and giving them many sources of strength and support. This balance helps them keep an even keel emotionally and gives them a healthy perspective on the pressures and politics of the workplace. Because women's identities are intertwined with their relationships with others, promoting others makes them feel they are promoting themselves. This makes them outstanding mentors who build their subordinates' talents and aren't afraid to give others credit that is due.

Mary Kay Ash, who founded the billion-dollar company Mary Kay Cosmetics, is celebrated for inspiring her employees to greatness. A believer in the Golden Rule, Ash built an organization powered by women whose skills and talents were often overlooked by traditional corporate leaders, and taught these women how to use their skills and talents for their own benefit and a profit. But Ash also respected her employees' personal and family lives as well as their contributions to the company, and created opportunities for employees to balance the demands of home and work. Take Anne Newbury, a schoolteacher who wanted to be a stay-at-home mom, who decided to try working for Mary Kay Cosmetics in 1969. She rose to the position of Mary Kay Inc.'s independent executive national sales director and has earned commissions totalling over $7 million. "Mary Kay taught us more about leadership, about mentoring and coaching, than anything else," Newbury said. "I would have done anything that she ever asked me to do. Not only because I admired her and loved her, but because when I look back over what my life could have been if I hadn't been drawn to her influence, I shudder. Not just financially, but emotionally and spiritually. She helped me to believe that I could be anything in the world that I could ever dream of becoming."[8]

Women's emotional strengths are a foundation of their effectiveness as leaders. A recent review of forty-eight studies involving more than seven thousand participants showed that people who are more emotionally intelligent—that, is who are better skilled at understanding others' feelings and their own feelings, and managing these feelings well—are more successful as leaders.[9] Women's ability to perceive others' feelings gives them a barometer of how things are going with the people who are critical to the success of their organization. As a result, they can head off trouble in the early stages, and recognize when an employee has found his or her niche in the company. Because women grasp their own emotions, they are able to trace their moods and mindset to a variety of triggers. When they are disturbed by something at work, such as an employee showing up late one morning, they can separate their feelings about the incident from their feelings about other areas of their life, such as their child divulging on the way to school that he had forgotten to do his homework the previous night. As a result, women are able to acknowledge their moods and react more appropriately to frustrations, for example, reprimanding the late employee but not completely blowing up at her.

Women's ability to express their emotions means they can praise others when appropriate, building their trust and loyalty, and express disappointment when appropriate, communicating a need to change. Women's ability to tolerate and manage their own emotions means they can hang in there and deal with difficult situations, or can handle an employee being upset or having personal problems, and then they can take a deep breath and return to focusing on the job.

As Connie Jackson, the chief executive of St. Bartholomew's and the Royal London Charitable Foundation, argues, "Strong leadership starts with being able to pull together a group of people—who may not have anything in common—and getting them to buy into a vision of themselves as a collective group who can achieve uncommon results."[10] Women's relational strengths build cadres of devoted workers who are growing and thriving, putting their best efforts into the group. Women's ability to take others' perspectives means they appreciate employees' concerns and talents, and can work to minimize the concerns and build their talents. Women's perspective-taking abilities also give them an advantage in business and political negotiations, as I detailed in chapter 5. Women's listening skills lead them to gather more information that is crucial to understanding current problems and anticipating potential problems. Says Susan Rice, the chief executive of Lloyds TSB Scotland, "To learn you have to keep asking. It's all about asking questions. The people I work with will say that the process of my asking them questions helps them clarify their own thinking and they actually come out a little sharper. That takes a lot of trust. My job, as I see it, is to set a clear strategy, ask the right questions, and encourage our managers to be the experts in their business."[11]

Women's patience prevents them from making rash decisions or accusations. They are willing to work with employees who are having trouble learning new skills or duties and who have family demands or troubles that are impacting their jobs. Women are not just focused on their personal gain but the gain of everyone in the group. This inspires loyalty and a willingness to go the extra mile for the organization.

Doris Morrow, a fifty-two-year-old Missouri state senator, packages all women's strengths together into an exceptionally transformational leadership style. Doris started a small business when she was in her twenties, making clothes for large women. Although Doris was herself only five-foot-five and eight stone, her mother had been large and had never been able to find stylish clothes that fit her. Doris loved to sew and had designed and made most of her mother's clothes for decades. At first, Doris's business consisted only of herself, a sewing machine, and an ad in the newspaper in her midsize Missouri town. Within five years, however, Doris had ten employees and more business than her company could handle. Doris deeply appreciated the women who worked for her—some were young and working in their first job, some were older homemakers trying to earn a few dollars, some were immigrants who had once worked in sweatshop conditions in large clothing manufacturing companies. Doris provided them with a clean, safe, and cheerful working environment, with top-of-the-line equipment. She encouraged them to come to her with ideas for new styles, and some of her company's most successful lines were based on her employees' patterns. Doris had a good eye for the strengths and weaknesses of her employees, and tried to channel them into tasks that played on their strengths. If that wasn't possible, she arranged for training to improve their skills in areas of weakness. As a result, her employees were fiercely loyal to her, producing top-quality clothes that became nationally respected.

In her experience as a business owner, Doris ran into innumerable obstacles, particularly with zoning ordinances, tax laws, and bureaucratic practices that were implemented in ways that impeded the growth of small companies such as her own. When Doris, in her late forties, was comfortable financially and her company was buzzing along under a new general manager she had trained from the ranks of seamstresses, she decided to do something to reduce the burdens on small businesses. A retirement in the state senate had created an open seat and Doris made the bold decision to run for office, even though she had never been involved in politics before. In her campaign, Doris steadfastly refused to "go negative," instead running on a platform of "positive change." To many people's surprise she won the election.

Four years into her term as a state senator, Doris had logged some stunning legislative successes, due largely to her focus on "positive change" rather than on criticizing failing programs. While many of her colleagues spent their time ranting and raving about how stupid or corrupt other people were, Doris worked with local officials to understand the original purpose behind seemingly nonsensical zoning laws or licensing requirements. She made it clear to the local officials that she respected them and valued their opinions, and as a result they were happy to work with her to reform these laws in ways that benefited both government and business. She developed a young staff in her senate office that was as loyal to her as the garment workers in her company, and this staff generated innovative ideas to increase Missouri's support for small businesses. When other politicians attacked Doris for policies she had proposed, she calmly and confidently challenged them to suggest alternatives to her proposals. Usually they had none that were nearly as developed as Doris's. Doris was becoming the epitome of an effective leader in the "Show Me" state of Missouri, because of her relentless focus on uplifting people and promoting progress.

The Fruits of Women's Strengths as Leaders

Women use their strengths to lead others and effect change in a million ways every day. Like Doris Morrow, women are now being elected to political office in increasingly significant numbers, in part because people across the country believe that women possess more integrity than men. Allthough the U.K. still has a long way to go, there has been an increase in female representation in Parliament: in 2009 almost one in five Members of Parliament were female, whereas until the late 1980s the percentage of female MPs in the U.K. had never reached more than one in twenty.[12] The percentage of women holding elective offices in the United States has risen from 3 percent in 1979 to 16.8 percent in 2009.[13] After the 2008 elections, seventy-three of the 435 seats in the U.S. House of Representatives and seventeen of the one hundred seats in the Senate are held by women—the highest level thus far in American history, in a year when the number of women running for election did not set a record. Twenty-four percent of statewide elective offices (governor, lieutenant governor, attorney general, secretary of state, etc.) are held by women, with seven women holding the top spot in a state's executive branch. Voters, weary of lying and corruption, selfishness, and backstabbing negativity, believe that women will inject the public forum with more honesty, more constructive dialogue, and an increased concern for the common good.

Voters' beliefs are supported by some hard evidence. Studies show that women are significantly less likely than men in similar positions to commit white-collar crime, such as embezzlement, forgery, fraud, and tax evasion.[14] They also show that women's greater integrity is directly tied to their willingness to put others' needs first.

Women are also using their strengths in business, particularly by starting their own companies. In the U.K., there are approximately 620,000 majority women-owned businesses generating around 130 billion pounds turnover.[15] In 2008, there were 10.1 million women-owned firms in the United States, employing 13 million people and generating nearly $1.9 trillion in annual revenues.[16] Women-owned firms make up 40 percent of all firms in the country. These firms are doing well, matching or exceeding the growth rate of male-owned firms. The *Financial Times* magazine reported that recent studies conducted by Catalyst and Mckinsey in the U.S. and Europe have found a correlation between the number of women in a company's leadership and the company's profitability, and Nick Wilson of Leeds University Business School has found that having women on the board can reduce a company's risk by twenty percent.[17]

In the United States, organizations founded and run largely by women have had major influence on education in the United States. The PTA was founded in 1897 by Alice McLellan Birney and Phoebe Apperson Hearst as the National Congress of Mothers. The fact that women at that time did not even have the right to vote did not stop them from believing that by working together they could improve the education and well-being of children across the country. By 1919 there were thirty-seven state-level branches of the group, and in 2009 there were over 25,000 local associations with over 5 million members.[18] Over the years, the PTA has fought for and won the passage of laws against child labor, reforms of the juvenile justice system, the creation of kindergarten classes and hot lunch programs, the installation of fire sprinkler systems in classrooms, and hundreds of other reforms. On the local level, PTAs, largely composed of mothers, work to ensure that their children's schools are safe and provide the best education possible.

Women often reject the idea that they are leaders. In the Los Angeles barrios a group of women came together to oppose prison construction. Juana Gutierrez, a member of the group, organized other women's activities and lobbied politicians. Still, she said, "I don't consider myself political. I'm just someone looking out for the community, for the youth."[19] Yet the impact of women's work to change their communities, their businesses, and the world is vast. People live better lives because women see what is needed, work together to bring about change, and inspire others to do the same.

How are you leading others toward positive change? Think about your formal leadership roles: Are you an employer or do you manage other people's work? Do you help to organize groups at your child's school or your own school, your religious institution, or in your community? Do you hold a political office? Think also about your informal leadership roles and the ways that you guide and influence others in your family, your friends and neighbors. Leadership doesn't just mean organizing other people. Leadership includes anything you do to make changes in line with your values, goals, and interests. Acting as a good role model to your children is being a leader. Taking food to a neighbor who is a shut-in is being a leader. Writing a letter to the editor of your newspaper is being a leader. Use the Leadership Roles Worksheet below to catalog and appreciate all the ways you lead in your daily life. Don't feel confined to writing a neat list or fitting everything on the page—push yourself to be as specific or as expansive as you can to describe the leadership roles in your life.

After you've listed all your leadership roles, think about new ways you could lead that would express your values, interests, and goals. What could you begin doing that you are not doing now to have a positive impact on some problem you see or to create some new opportunity for yourself or others? Use your powers of positive imagery to see yourself in these new roles, making change and improving lives.

Leadership Roles Worksheet

1. List all your formal leadership roles, such as employer, manager, officeholder, community organizer, and the like:

---

2. List all your informal leadership roles—the ways you influence others in your family, among your friends and neighbors, in your community, and on the job:

---

3. List any new leadership roles—either formal or informal—that would help you fulfill your interests, values, and goals for yourself and others:

In the process of evaluating how you are already a leader, you may have found yourself saying, "But I'm not very good at giving negative feedback" or "I'm not very good at handling others when they're upset or dealing with setbacks" or having other negative thoughts. Or, in contemplating new leadership roles you might want to take on, you may have hesitated, worried that you don't have the skills or strengths to be effective in a particular role. You can use the exercises in Part II of this book to enhance your effectiveness as a leader by building your unique psychological strengths. For the remainder of this chapter, I'll tell you the stories of several women whose leadership effectiveness was being undermined by weaknesses in their mental, identity, emotional, or relational strengths. Then I'll offer my recommendations for how they could tailor a strength-building program to harness their ability to be effective, transformational leaders.

A Leader's Problems

Gwen had always been a grease monkey. Growing up with four older brothers who loved cars, Gwen was an expert on the insides of an automobile engine long before she was old enough to drive a car. It didn't matter if it was a foreign car or made in the USA, Gwen could take it apart and put it back together without as much as a single screw misplaced. Although some of the other girls could not fathom her love of cars and the boys jeered at her, Gwen insisted on taking courses in car mechanics in high school and went to work in her uncle's large service station after graduation. Her skills were so good, and she was such a reliable and loyal employee, that her uncle eventually promoted her to manager of the service floor, with responsibility for organizing the work of five other mechanics in the shop.

Despite Gwen's substantial talent at mechanics, however, she often doubted her abilities, perhaps because she had been told so many times that girls could not be car mechanics. When she encountered a new model of car, she worried that she would not be able to identify and fix the problem. Gwen was especially prone to feeling incompetent when she was dealing with the complex computers in many of the newer models. If her initial attempts at solving the problem didn't work, she would feel as though she'd hit a wall, overwhelmed and ashamed. Sometimes she'd even go home early because she couldn't think of what to do next and didn't want anyone to see that she was flailing.

Gwen was always able to figure out how to fix a car in the end, which accounted for her uncle's faith in her. But now that Gwen was a manager, her tendency to become hopeless when she ran into difficulties and her unwillingness to ask for help from others was harder to hide. The other mechanics would come to her when they couldn't fix some problem to see if she had any ideas. If she didn't instantly see the solution, she beat herself up for being a failure. She'd tell the mechanic that she'd think about it, then bury her head in some papers, and he'd walk off dissatisfied that she wasn't much help.

Gwen clearly needed to build her mental strengths of looking for paths around obstacles, enlisting help when needed, and determined optimism. Here's how she might use mental strength-building exercises.

First, she should spend a few days tuning in to the thoughts that go through her head when she feels stymied by a problem. She'd probably hear herself saying things like "I don't know what to do! I'm incompetent! They'll find out I'm a fraud! I'll get fired!" Gwen could write these down on "negative thoughts" index cards, then work to come up with counter-thoughts to each of them, such as: "The other mechanic doesn't know what to do either, that's why he came to me." "Just because I don't instantly know the answer doesn't mean I'm incompetent." "I am not a fraud." "If I don't know how to do something, I can find out." Gwen should keep her cards with thoughts and counter-thoughts in her drawer at work and pull them out periodically *before* one of the mechanics comes in to talk with her about a problem, to build her confidence.

To deal with the feelings that she's up against a wall when she encounters something she can't fix instantly, Gwen needs to practice breaking down each problem into smaller pieces and concentrate on generating possible solutions to these smaller issues one at a time.

She might devise a general plan for approaching an unknown problem, for example:

1. Write down the symptoms of the problem (such as the noises the car is making, how it is not functioning properly).
2. Generate some ideas for what these symptoms might be signaling.
3. Think through which of these ideas best fits the particular configuration of symptoms this car has.
4. Think about what tests to do to determine which of these ideas is correct.

These are essentially the procedures that Gwen uses implicitly to solve problems, but when she gets overwhelmed she doesn't think of them, so formalizing them in writing will likely help her.

Finally, Gwen really needs to overcome her reluctance to ask for help. She might think about who would be the least threatening person to ask for help when she needs it, whether it is her uncle or one of the mechanics who is especially friendly. Then she should make a specific plan to ask this person for help on a problem, even if she thinks she could eventually solve it by herself. She could rehearse what she would say in her mind ahead of time, then she should reward herself for asking the question, no matter what happens. Since Gwen feels incompetent when working with car computers, she could enroll in a class on automobile computers to increase her knowledge and comfort level with them. Gwen could also increase her motivation to ask for help by telling herself that she could probably improve the service station's record by building an atmosphere and system whereby all the mechanics worked together to solve problems, rather than working alone.

How could you build your mental strengths and improve your leadership ability at work, in your community, or in your volunteer work? If you are not optimistic about your leadership abilities, start by identifying the ways you are discouraging yourself with the thoughts that run in the back of your mind. Then counter those thoughts by banishing them or generating alternatives to them. If you have trouble seeing your way around obstacles, try to reduce them to their smallest components, then generate actions you can take to overcome these. If you get obsessed with getting your way instead of getting the job done, make a pact to focus on team-building and cooperation rather than your status in the group. And if you have trouble asking for help, push yourself to do it anyway—with a not-so-threatening person first, then with those people who are scarier to approach.

Seeing Yourself as a Leader

Women's difficulties in implementing their identity strengths in leadership roles often stem from a lack of experience or comfort with being thrust into authority positions over others. "I don't really see myself as a leader" is something you'll often hear from a woman who gets promoted at work or is asked to take on the leadership of an organization. Every woman has the right to *choose* not to be a leader, but no woman should feel she doesn't have the right to *be* a leader. Women can overcome weaknesses in their identities as leaders by reminding themselves of their core values and interests, and viewing their leadership role as a way to fulfill these values and interests.

Women also run into problems in leadership when they are too oriented toward their relationships, to the point of letting others exploit them or of trying to make everyone happy. This can play out in their relationships with people they are supposed to be leading, and in their attempts to balance their family roles with their leadership roles, as it did in Sandra's case.

When she was in her early thirties, Sandra began pursuing her master's degree in education. She wasn't sure what she wanted to do with the degree once she had it, but she thought it was a good thing to have if she ever decided she didn't want to be a classroom teacher any longer. Sandra focused on education administration, and she found her studies so interesting that she kept taking classes after she had completed the requirements for a master's, eventually earning a Ph.D. When the position of vice principal of her school opened,

Sandra decided to apply, and landed the job. She was still getting used to the job when the principal was diagnosed with cancer and had to take a leave of absence. Sandra was asked to become the interim principal, and although she was reticent, the school board urged her to take the job in order to maintain some continuity in the administration while the principal was away.

Sandra soon developed an identity problem. She still thought of herself as one of the teachers, and was buddies with several of them, but her position as principal required that she sometimes make decisions they didn't like. When this happened, some of the teachers would needle her, saying, "You've changed" or "I would think you'd understand our point of view." Sandra especially had trouble giving any kind of negative feedback to teachers she'd known for years.

Sandra's home life was also a source of stress. Her husband, Phil, worked long hours, which left Sandra to pick up her two children, get them to sports practice and music lessons, and cook dinner for the family. She'd been able to juggle this when she was a classroom teacher, but as principal she couldn't just leave in the afternoon to drive the kids around town. She'd tried hiring someone to do the driving, but had trouble finding a reliable person, and resented that her husband seemed oblivious that her responsibilities were now too great to be expected to juggle the child care and meal arrangements on her own. Sandra also had to give up her regular exercise class because of all the extra work and she resented this as well.

Sandra had a good opportunity in being appointed interim principal, but she was going to crash and burn professionally and personally if she didn't shore up her identity strengths. She was feeling conflict between her identity as one of the classroom teachers and her identity as principal. One way to resolve this conflict was for her to ask herself, "What core values or interests am I fulfilling by being the principal?" At heart, Sandra wanted to help children learn, to develop their academic skills early so that they could build on these skills in high school and college. She deeply believed that a strong early education gave children essential keys to achieving their ultimate goals in life. This had made her a beloved and effective classroom teacher.

Now, as principal, Sandra had the opportunity to improve the quality of early education on the much broader scale of the whole school. She needed to see her interactions with the teachers—the decisions she made and the feedback she gave them—in light of these core values. This would help her get the motivation to do what she needed to do, and make her more persuasive in arguing for her point of view.

Sandra also needed to recognize that she was being excessively concerned about her relationships with others. This made her reluctant to be in conflict with the teachers at school. Focusing on her overarching goals of improving children's education should help break Sandra's concern about staying on good terms with the teachers. When she has to deal with disagreements with the teachers under her, she could frame her point of view in terms of their shared goals of educating the children rather than focusing on her discomfort with the confrontation. Sandra should also begin to build a network of peers—other principals, perhaps others who are women or who had worked their way to principal after serving as a teacher in the same school. These peers could help her sharpen her vision of herself as a principal and give her practical tips on how to deal with challenges on the job, including dealing with teachers who don't like her decisions. Finally, Sandra might want to have an honest, frank conversation with some of the teachers at her school about the changes in their relationship, acknowledging that these changes aren't always comfortable but shoring up their basic friendship and citing their shared interests in helping children.

Sandra's desire to avoid conflict was also a driving force in her struggle to balance multiple roles alone instead of confronting her husband about needing to pull his weight in the management of the family. Focusing on her primary goals should help her have the courage to talk with Phil. Sandra should first sit down and write out what she thinks Phil's arguments will be: he has always worked ten- to twelve-hour days, and his employer wouldn't understand him suddenly cutting back; the interim principal position wasn't permanent and he didn't want to restructure his work hours when the stress Sandra was under was temporary; he had no interest in carting the kids around, and Sandra had worked it out by hiring a driver.

Then Sandra should decide how she might respond to each of these arguments, and how she is going to express her point of view to Phil. She might begin by saying that although the interim principal position is temporary, she wants to go into administration permanently, so they do need to work out a long-term solution. She might note that Phil isn't required to work so many hours, he just does, and his status in his company is strong enough that he can restructure his workday somewhat without risking his job. Sandra might also express that she feels it is an issue of fairness for them to work out a more equitable division of labor now that her career is getting more demanding. Then Sandra should enlist Phil in generating ideas for how they might re-juggle family activities so that both of them carry their weight but still have time to perform their jobs well.

Finally, Sandra should take stock of the many things she does for her family, and what she does entirely for herself, with an eye toward a proper balance. Her exercise classes are important to her because she wants to keep fit and healthy. They are also one of the few things she does entirely for herself, and this alone makes them valuable. Sandra should generate ideas for how she could build those exercise classes back into her regular schedule—for example, by organizing a class in the gym after school for the staff. This would cut out the time she'd need to travel to the health club's class and build camaraderie between herself, the teachers, and the staff.

If you, like Sandra, are having trouble seeing yourself as a leader and as a result are not working effectively with others, you can also use the strength-building exercises in chapter 8 to build your identity strengths. Ask yourself what talents, interests, and core values you want to express in your role as leader. Then look back to other roles you have filled in your life to see how you were pursuing these talents, interests, and core values. Seeing the continuity between your previous roles and your current leadership roles will help your new roles seem less foreign to you and remind you why they are important. They will also help you manage the people you now lead by communicating the values and goals you hold dear and your vision for how your group can fulfill those values and goals.

If a new role as leader is creating an imbalance in your life by taking up all your time and energy, evaluate which of your other roles you aren't willing to give up and make a concrete plan for creating more balance in your life. If there is imbalance between how much you are putting your own needs first or others' needs first, reaffirm the values and goals that led you to this leadership position, and then make a plan for how you are going to balance those values and goals with others' needs.

Emotions as Leadership Tools

When women feel they need to work on their emotional strengths to improve their leadership, it's usually because they feel they are too emotional and want to get better control over their emotions. Such was the case with Claire, a twenty-five-year-old campaign organizer for the Democratic candidate for U.S. Senate in her home state. She was passionate about her job; she cared deeply about the values the candidate stood for and she really wanted her to win. She was the only paid staff person in the office she ran, however, because her candidate wasn't flush with money. Having to rely primarily on volunteer help drove Claire crazy. People would show up late, or not at all. Many of the volunteers had trouble taking direction, doing whatever they wanted rather than their assigned tasks or sitting around debating the issues with one another instead of going out to citizens to persuade them to vote for the candidate. Frequently, Claire would lose her cool and yell at a volunteer, who then never came back. When she tried to suppress her anger, Claire felt she was going to explode, and snide remarks slipped out anyway. As Election Day grew near, Claire found herself less able to handle the ups and downs of the campaign. When her candidate was doing well in the polls or gave a rousing speech to a large crowd, her spirits soared. But when the poll numbers were down or there was unfavorable news coverage, she was despondent.

Claire's passion for her candidate was commendable, but her lack of emotional strengths was undermining her effectiveness as a political organizer. To gain control over her anger at the volunteers, Claire should develop and practice assertive ways of expressing to the volunteers their responsibility for fulfilling important tasks to ensure the candidate's victory. She should start her assertiveness campaign with the least fragile and reactionary volunteer (and perhaps the one she would care least about losing), before moving to people with whom she might find it more difficult to be assertive.

For example, say there is a volunteer named Rick who spends more time schmoozing with his peers than calling potential voters. Claire might decide to say to him, "Rick, I've noticed that you are not getting through your assigned calls most evenings. I understand this is a tedious job but we both want to win this election. Can I have a commitment from you to get your calls done before you move to any other tasks around the office?" She should say this a few times by herself or with a friend, practicing how to deliver the question in an even but firm tone of voice. Then, on a night when she feels calm, she should approach Rick and deliver her message. If Rick responds that he thinks he is being assigned too many calls or that he would prefer some other task, Claire might say, "Calling is really the most important task we have at this stage of the campaign. What can we agree upon as a reasonable number of calls for you to do in an evening?" If she can get Rick to name what he thinks is reasonable, he'll feel more obligated to meet that goal. And it will be better for Claire's blood pressure and emotional control to let Rick do fewer calls but have some confidence that he will get them done than to keep expecting him to do as much as the others but discover that calls haven't been made by the end of the evening.

Claire can use many different exercises to improve her ability to deal with her own roller-coaster emotions about the campaign. She should first accept that her deep feelings about this campaign cause her to get extremely upset at times, then choose to learn how to cope with her emotions better, and finally focus on developing new strategies for coping. Then she could memorize some relaxation exercises and employ them when she is feeling upset. She could tune in to the thoughts that make her so upset by keeping a diary of these thoughts for a week. She might discover that she catastrophizes losing the campaign: "Everything I care about will be lost!" "The world will go to hell in the next six years if we lose!" "I will feel like a failure if this campaign loses!" Then she could develop reappraisals—counter-thoughts to her catastrophizing thoughts—and write them down: "I can find other ways of promoting my values even if this campaign loses." "Things will not be good if my candidate loses, but the world will not end." And "My candidate losing doesn't mean I am a loser."

Claire should think concretely about what she would do if her candidate loses to continue promoting the values she holds dear. If, for example, her candidate is very pro-environment—and this is something Claire cares deeply about—she could look into positions with environmental action organizations or alternative energy companies that might hire her after the election. Or, if Claire's main passion is improving access to health care for all, she could investigate lobbying firms that advocate for health care reform. The point is to have a set of ideas about how she can continue working toward her goals and values once this campaign is done, regardless of how it turns out. This will diffuse her feelings about the campaign, making it easier to manage her emotions when things aren't going well.

Building your own emotional strengths to become a good leader primarily involves first tuning in. You can tune in to the emotions that others are expressing by being quiet and attentive more often, and learn the links between subtle cues such as facial expressions and body postures and the emotions they convey. You can tune in to your own emotions by keeping track of the thoughts that run behind them. This will give you a better understanding of why you overreact or underreact in certain situations. Secondly, you need to make choices about how you are going to respond to the emotions of others and your own emotions. We often think that emotions are automatic and uncontrollable, but we do have a choice as to how to respond to them. Learning assertive ways of expressing your emotions and responding to the emotions of others builds honesty and trust in organizations. Developing new strategies for managing when you are upset makes you feel more in control in any situation in life, including leadership situations.

The Relational Leader

Women's relational strengths are some of their greatest assets in leadership positions. Most women do an outstanding job taking others' perspectives, whether it be on the job, in political or community organizations, or in spontaneous groups joined together around a common cause. They listen patiently to others, appreciate their points of view, and work toward mutually satisfying solutions to problems.

Not every woman is so blessed, however. Consider, for example, Frances, a forty-three-year-old executive in a major accounting firm. Fran's superiors and coworkers consider her extremely intelligent and competent. She's brought in a greater number of new accounts than any other associate at her level of the company, and her clients raved about her meticulous work and her excellent recommendations for reorganizing their financial records.

Despite her many successes, however, Fran had not been promoted to partner in the firm. Other people at her rank, all men, had been promoted with fewer years and fewer accomplishments behind them, but Fran had been passed over for promotion again and again. The senior partners, it seemed, had a problem with Fran's aggressive style of interacting with her coworkers. Fran believed that in order to succeed within her company she had to be more self-aggrandizing than her male counterparts. This behavior earned her the nicknames of *bitch, bully broad,* and *dragon lady*—never mind that she might have gotten away with this style, or even prospered because of it, had she been a man. The senior partners felt that Fran only cared about her own success and not about the greater success of the company. They also felt, rightly, that she couldn't inspire her coworkers because they tended to mistrust—and avoid—her.

Fran had a staunch ally among the senior partners in Don, a sixty-four-year-old New Yorker who appreciated Fran's straightforward, no-nonsense style. Don knew what his colleagues were saying about Fran behind her back. He also knew that his fellow partners were worried that Fran would become even more abrasive if she were promoted. So one day Don invited Fran to lunch to talk about her harsh style. At first, Fran bristled at the notion that she should soften her approach. "What do you want me to do, wear a pink dress and high heels and go around with an insipid smile on my face all day?" Fran barked. Don assured her that that was not what he had in mind, saying, "Listen Fran, I just think you could relax a bit and consider how it feels to be on the receiving end of your style. I want to see you promoted, but it isn't going to happen until the other senior partners can feel comfortable being in the same room with you."

Fran thought about what Don said over the next couple of days. She didn't like the idea that she should have to change the way she interacted with her colleagues, but she recognized she would have to if she were ever going to be promoted. Fran also knew that some of her family members and friends found her difficult at times, and she acknowledged that she often felt lonely and isolated from others.

How could Fran change her style of relating to others while remaining true to herself? Fran had weaknesses in all her relational skills: she didn't even try to take the perspective of others but was singularly focused on herself in most encounters; she didn't listen to others and was extremely impatient; and she put her own self-promotion above others' to the point that people did not trust her. First, Fran should determine when and where her weaknesses emerge most often. She could do this by keeping track of key interactions over the next week in a diary, observing what kinds of situations caused her to become irritable and how other people reacted to her outbursts. She would probably realize that it wasn't just occasionally that she lashed out at others—it happened every day, sometimes multiple times per day. Often her outbursts focused on people who were moving too slowly for her tastes—her secretary not getting a letter ready quickly enough, the cashier at the supermarket taking a long time to check out her groceries, her sister taking forever to tell her some story about their parents.

Fran should then devise some ways to stop her impatient, self-centered outbursts. To become better able to understand and appreciate the impact of her outbursts on others, she could keep track of these outbursts for a few days, each time asking herself, "What may have prompted this person to act as he or she did?" Her initial answer to this question may be "incompetence," but she should continue to ask herself, "What other thoughts, motivations, influences, or situations might have led to his or her actions?" For example, when her secretary fails to get a report finished, Fran might consider that it's because she's loaded the secretary up with ten other jobs this week. If Fran can get into the habit of taking others' perspectives, this will take her a long way toward being more patient and understanding when their needs or interests should come before her own.

To further improve her abilities to be patient and to put others' needs before her own when appropriate, Fran needs to take stock of her priorities and goals. Sure, she wants to get promoted at work, but does she want to do it by hurting others and ruining all relationships? Is being so mean really accomplishing her goal of being promoted? Concretely, Fran should ask herself, "What impact are my angry outbursts having on others?" and "How could I react differently to have a better outcome?" Fran knows that being impatient with her secretary and yelling at her results in tears—and no progress toward getting work done. She might conjure an image of herself talking calmly with her secretary about which of the ten projects can be postponed so that the report can get done. Similarly, Fran should build an image of herself acting in more calm and empathetic ways toward others and still being very effective on the job. This can motivate her to pause, take a breath, and consider others' needs and opinions before lunging forward with her own point of view.

Fran suffers from what psychologist Alice Eagly calls a "gender role mismatch": a disjunction between personal style and the style that society prescribes for women. Fran's superiors were evaluating her negatively because her naturally aggressive personality was viewed as inappropriate for a woman. To be sure this is unfair, and it represents a form of gender discrimination. Unfortunately, this is often how the world works. By recognizing this fact, Fran can improve her relational strengths and gain that long-elusive promotion. In the process she can learn how to be more patient and caring, substantially improving her relationships with family and friends as well.

Similarly, you can build your relational strengths for better leadership, whether you tend to be too self-focused like Fran, or too focused on pleasing and accommodating others. You can increase your perspective-taking skills by getting into the habit of asking yourself what kinds of thoughts or situations might be driving the behavior of the people you lead. You can improve your listening skills by just being quiet more often and noticing what you've been missing, rather than feeling you always have to be talking and directing traffic at work. More patience can come from realizing that speed isn't always the most important thing at work; even though building cooperation and good will among members of a team can be slow going, it can have benefits far beyond just meeting a deadline. If, like Fran, you are singularly focused on your own gain to the detriment of others, you need to realize that this can backfire, as it nearly did with Fran's promotion. On the other hand, if you are letting others abuse you for the sake of their gain, you need to clarify your own interests and goals, and make concrete plans to stand up for these, using the assertiveness exercises in chapter 10.

The bottom line is that you *are* a leader, probably in ways you don't even realize, and you *deserve* to be a leader. Moreover, the world *needs* you as a leader. It needs your talents to improve the functioning of businesses, communities, families, and individuals. It needs to hear your values and opinions as we all sort out how to work together. Imagine yourself a leader. Then *become* an effective leader by exercising all your mental, identity, emotional, and relational strengths.

12.

Parenting Like a Woman

Parenting is both extremely difficult and extraordinarily wonderful. Just as you are about to tear your hair out over the latest incomprehensible act committed by your child, you catch the sight of those beautiful eyes, that lovely smile; you hear the lilting giggle. And your heart melts. Sometimes you wonder why you ever wanted kids—until the sound of a sleepy "I love you, Mommy" hits you as you tuck him into bed at night, or you feel the thrill of standing by as your teenager reaches one of the most important goals in her life.

All of women's psychological strengths are put to use in their work as mothers. Every day, women apply their mental strengths in creatively solving problems facing their families. Women channel a can-do attitude to their children, serving as role models and building their children's own sense of competence and self-efficacy.[1] Women's determined optimism also helps them to maintain a steady, persistent hope when fighting for the resources their children need to survive and thrive. For instance, Catherine just knew that her son Jake, who was born with Down syndrome, could develop more fully and quickly if he received better quality training than he was getting through the public school system. However, she couldn't afford the tuition to the private school for children with special needs in their city. Although lots of people told her just to be happy that Jake was doing as well as he was, Catherine repeatedly petitioned the school board to either increase the level of services to Down syndrome children in the public schools or provide vouchers so they could afford to go to the private school. At this point, Catherine worried that she was losing momentum, so she enlisted help from other parents who were struggling to find ways to access the same special training for their children. Catherine rallied these parents to write letters to board members and to turn out at school board meetings to protest for a change in the policy. When a straightforward voucher system was not gathering enough votes to pass the board, Catherine and the other parents considered the options for getting what they wanted, but on the board's terms. The parents eventually persuaded a majority of the board to adopt a voucher system that funded part-time attendance at the private school, which allowed their children to receive the special services they most needed. Catherine never wavered in her fight for her child's education, even when success seemed out of reach.

Focusing on getting the job done instead of getting their own way can help women navigate the authority battles children so often launch with their parents. When a child says, "Why can't I wait until Sunday night to do my homework? That's when all the other kids do it!" a woman drawing upon her mental strengths will avoid saying, "Because I said so!" and focus on ways to reach the goal the child can accept: "You are exhausted by Sunday night and you know you don't do your best on your homework then. You get it done faster and better if you work on it Saturday morning. Then you can relax for the rest of the weekend."

Women's ability to see many paths toward goals can help children maintain a flexible, problem-solving attitude when they run into obstacles. Psychologist Carol Dweck has found that when adults respond to children who are having difficulty with a task by guiding the children's attention to finding alternative solutions, children remain more positive about the task, generate new ideas for solving it, and keep trying until they conquer the problem. In contrast, when adults respond to children's difficulty with criticism, children are more likely to give up on the task and feel bad about themselves.[2] "Maybe you could think of another way to do it" is far more motivating than "What's taking you so long?"

Women's understanding that there are many pathways to success also helps them to appreciate that their children are different from each other and from their parents, and may travel very different paths to happiness in their lives. For men, this sometimes can be harder to realize and acknowledge. While both women and men sometimes invest too much of their identity in their children, men tend to do so by expecting their children, particularly their sons, to follow in their footsteps—in business, in politics, in lifestyle, even in worldview.

Insisting that your child pursue the same career path or lifestyle that you chose can create a tremendous, perhaps lifelong, conflict. Two brothers who were three years apart in age, Bill and Alan, were as different as night and day in their temperaments and interests. Bill hated school but loved to work with his hands. Ever since he was big enough to carry a hammer, he had excitedly followed his father, George, a contractor who owned a business building and repairing houses. Bill soaked up everything George taught him, and by the time he was a teenager, he was George's most valuable worker, highly skilled, with a passion for every aspect of construction. Alan, on the other hand, loved school and books. George would try to get him to come along with Bill to the job sites to help out, but Alan only wanted to stay home and read or do his homework. George didn't hide his disappointment with Alan, and the two had gotten to the point that they barely spoke to each other. The mother of the family, Colleen, was Alan's refuge and supporter. "You can do anything you want to do," she would tell Alan. Colleen repeatedly confronted George, insisting that he respect and support Alan's interests as much as he did Bill's. George never did really understand why Alan was so different from Bill, but he finally backed off when Alan won a full academic scholarship to college. If not for Colleen's appreciation, Alan would have felt isolated, and might have become rebellious or despondent—derailing his chances for the scholarship and the opportunity to pursue his own dreams.

The Appreciative Parent

The parent-child relationship is complicated and ever-changing. Children's basic needs, their ability to communicate those needs, and their desire for independence or coddled security seem to vary on a daily basis. One minute your kids are infants, completely dependent on you, able to express themselves through the coarse language of crying and smiling. The next minute they are toddlers, wanting to "do it myself," and talking a blue streak that only a parent understands. You sail through the relatively calm years of middle childhood only to crash into the roller-coaster ride of puberty (and coarse language of a very different sort). "Mom, you're embarrassing me" and "Get off my back!" might be followed a few hours later with "Mommy, can you rub my back?"

Women's identity strengths help them navigate the many phases and changes children go through as they move from infancy to childhood to adolescence to adulthood. Having multiple roles helps women balance their identification in their children with investments in other areas, such as work or volunteer activities, so that their own self-esteem doesn't get too dependent on their children's successes. Having multiple roles also gives women a release valve from the pressures of parenting. Many women find it a relief to go to an office for a few hours, where they can exercise and be appreciated for their intellectual talents—and talk about more lofty topics than whether it's okay to eat a whole bag of tortilla chips before dinnertime. By cultivating a stable but flexible core identity of their own, women become aware of how a person's traits, talents, interests, and values—more so, say, than a family name—can provide continuity over a lifetime and the room to grow and transform from one stage of life to the next. Because women form identity based in large part on social roles, they understand that their personal choices will affect their children, directly and indirectly. For example, women who were heavy drinkers or smokers in high school or young adulthood tend to adopt more healthy habits when they become mothers, both because they have responsibilities to care for their children and because they want to stand as positive role models.[3]

Further, research shows that emotional strengths of women have enormous influence on the development of their children's skills in this area. The parent-child relationship is a dance of emotions, in which parents and children share turns leading and following, responding to each other's moves more or less smoothly. When children are infants, parents coo at the slightest sign of their child's attention, and this is eventually reciprocated by the child's first smile and attempts to verbalize back. As children grow older, the dance gets more complex, but still involves parents and children sharing ups and downs of emotions and interests, expressing feelings to each other, getting each other excited, and calming each other down. Children whose parents are more responsive and skilled in this dance grow up more emotionally healthy and able to make good decisions about their behavior.

Being able to tolerate distress and manage emotions helps mothers deal effectively with the inevitable crises that arise with children. Whether it is a scraped knee, a lousy report card, or a failed love affair, mothers can empathize but remain calm while they help their child move past a crisis. In their day-to-day relationships with their kids, women's sensitivity and wisdom in expressing and managing emotions are also on ample display. According to psychologist Nancy Eisenberg of the University of Arizona, when parents respond reassuringly to their children's emotions, their children become better skilled at handling a wide range of stressors in life. In one study, Eisenberg followed 180 school-age children and their mothers over a two-year period.[4] At the first assessment, mothers and children viewed a series of pictures depicting positive and negative scenes, and then researchers rated the mother's emotional expressivity in discussing the pictures with her children. Those children whose mothers expressed greater warmth (smiling and laughing, asking their children how they felt about the scene, responding positively to their children's expressions of emotion) tended to be better at regulating and expressing their own emotions; these children were also more persistent in overcoming obstacles. Moreover, the children whose mothers were especially warm continued to show great skills at regulating their emotions and coping with stressful situations two years later. So by being emotionally expressive, tuning in to their children's emotions and channeling these emotions in appropriate ways, mothers help their children grow to be emotionally intelligent themselves.

Mothers utilize their ability to express emotions to praise their children for achievements and good behavior, while at the same time setting clear boundaries and rules. One evening when Alana was watching her son Tim play football with his high school team, she noticed that whenever the team made a touchdown, they would turn to the fans of the opposing team and rudely gloat by thumping their chests. When they got home from the game, Alana commended Tim for his play—he had been instrumental in one of the team's touchdowns that night—but also told him she thought the team's behavior toward the opposing fans was unacceptable and not in line with their family's values. Tim admitted that he was uncomfortable with the practice but felt pressured by the other boys to join in. They talked about ways Tim might encourage his teammates to act in a more sportsmanlike manner, or at the very least, find a way to not participate in the rude behavior even when the other boys urged him on and he felt a lot of pressure to fit in.

Women's relational strengths—their ability to listen, be patient, and take others' perspectives—give them the fortitude and patience to steer through the twists and turns of their children's development. Women understand what forces might be driving their children's behavior, and they take as little of that behavior personally as possible. Harnessing relational strengths may be especially valuable to the mothers of adolescents. Recent research suggests that the areas of the brain that help people manage their emotions continue to develop through adolescence and young adulthood.[5] So young teenagers are flooded with hormones, which make them volatile and increase their sexual interests substantially, well before the prefrontal areas of their brain, which control decision making and help regulate impulses, develop fully. This disconnect between teenagers' hormones and their impulse-checking capacity may account for much of the trouble they get into.

By taking the time to appreciate a teenager's mindset, women provide more than a safe haven from the tribulations of junior high and high school. Adolescents whose parents are not able to negotiate their competing needs for personal autonomy and an intimate, dependable relationship with their parents are more likely to develop mental health problems.[6] Patience and perspective-taking allows mothers to weather the irritability and confusion all children feel as their bodies change rapidly and as they struggle to understand who they are.

In the previous chapter, I showed you how women can improve their strengths in each category—mental, identity, emotional, and relational—to become better leaders. In this chapter, I want to focus on specific challenges that parents often face, and how women can use and improve their strengths to meet those challenges more effectively.

Handling the Inevitable Crises of Parenting

Much of the time, we can muddle through parenthood despite having obvious weaknesses in our psychological strengths. You may not be great at assertively expressing your own point of view, but if you have children who are easygoing and implicitly understand your values and rules, your difficulties with assertiveness may be of little consequence. You may be emotionally volatile and clueless as to others' feelings, but if your family is sufficiently calm and tolerant, you can get away with it.

Weaknesses of any kind tend to become apparent under stress. Tiny cracks have been known to bring down airplanes when they are put under intense or repeated pressure. Similarly, when crises happen in families, deficits in your psychological strengths can threaten to bring you or your family down. Yet you can repair the cracks in your psychological strengths, even in the midst of a crisis, by utilizing the strength-building exercises in Part II of this book. Let me illustrate with the story of Maura and her son, Eddie.

Maura, twenty-eight, lived in San Diego, where she raised her six-year-old son, Eddie, as a full-time mom. Eddie had been a high-energy kid even before he was born. Maura reported feeling him move in her womb long before the obstetrician said it was likely she could, and by the ninth month of her pregnancy, Maura couldn't sleep at night because Eddie was kicking so much. All of that was forgiven when Eddie emerged into the world, a brown-eyed beauty with a full head of black hair just like Maura's. As a young child, Eddie was generally a good-natured kid, and he never seemed to intentionally frighten or annoy Maura; as soon as he realized he had done something wrong, he would readily come to her to say he was sorry. But Eddie's ball of energy couldn't be contained, and he was always racing down the driveway on his tricycle or climbing over the backyard fence and disappearing into the neighbor's yard. Maura sometimes grew emotionally frantic dealing with his adventures. In her bouts of anxiety and frustration, she would scream at Eddie to behave, causing him to cower and cry. She would then collapse into a heap herself, call him over to her, and hug him as she started crying, too. Maura had many cracks in her emotional strengths, especially in tolerating and managing her own distress, and in expressing her emotions appropriately to Eddie.

By the time Eddie was in elementary school, Maura was getting phone calls from his teachers, with complaints that he frequently disrupted the class by running around when he should be sitting quietly. Maura felt completely incapable of handling this crisis. She had no idea what to do, and couldn't think past her own feelings. Inevitably, one of the teachers suggested that Eddie had Attention Deficit Hyperactivity Disorder (ADHD) and should be on medication to control his behavior. Maura had secretly hoped that some pill would control Eddie, since she didn't believe she could do it herself. So Maura took Eddie to the pediatrician for an evaluation. Instead of diagnosing ADHD, the pediatrician told Maura, "Listen, there is nothing medically wrong with Eddie. He just needs more discipline. I don't mean harsher punishment. I just mean you need to learn to enforce reasonable rules with him so that he can begin to control his own behavior. He's perfectly capable of this."

Maura was stunned, disappointed, and completely overwhelmed. How in the world was she going to get Eddie to control his behavior? She hadn't been able to do this for six years, and there was no reason to think she could do so now. For a couple of days, she tried to push the pediatrician's remarks out of her mind, but after another complaining phone call from Eddie's teacher, Maura realized she had to do something to improve her strengths as a parent. She didn't believe she could do it on her own—Maura knew enough to enlist help—so she called the pediatrician back and asked for a referral to a child psychologist, which the pediatrician gladly provided.

The next week, Maura and Eddie went for an evaluation with Dr. Robin Whitehall, a thirty-five-year-old psychologist who specializes in treating children with disruptive behavior. Whitehall began by having Maura observe when Eddie's behavior was most out of control and when he was better able to control himself, using an hour-by-hour diary. She also had Maura write down how she responded to Eddie during these situations. This diary was a tool to help Maura get a handle on the answer to the question "When and where do I get into trouble?" After a couple of weeks, Maura began to notice a pattern in her own behavior. When Eddie started running around, she would begin to plead with him, saying things like, "Eddie, honey, please don't run through the kitchen. Mommy is trying to cook dinner." When he wouldn't comply with her request, Maura would become impatient and start yelling vague threats, such as, "I said stop it, Eddie! Or else!" If Eddie kept at it, Maura would eventually bellow, "I said get out of here! Right now!" That's when Eddie would run off crying, followed shortly by Maura, now also crying and apologizing profusely.

Maura brought her diaries into the next session with Dr. Whitehall and confessed that though she recognized this pattern in her behavior with Eddie, she didn't know what to do about it. So Whitehall encouraged Maura to sit back and think about what she would like her interactions with Eddie to be like. Maura spent a while creating a positive image of her and Eddie playing together at the playground, talking about his day at school, and working together on some project. Then Whitehall had Maura recount a recent encounter when she had gotten upset with Eddie. Maura was resistant at first, not wanting to bring on those feelings of helplessness and despair. She trusted their psychologist, however, and after a while was able to re-create the last difficult encounter with Eddie, imagining herself being patient, talking with him calmly, and Eddie doing as he was told.

Then Dr. Whitehall helped Maura brainstorm three small steps she could take to improve her patience with Eddie. First and foremost, they decided that Maura needed to keep herself calm when Eddie became obstreperous. Whitehall taught Maura some quick relaxation exercises that she could do in any circumstance to slow down her emotional reactions and keep from getting overwhelmed. These involved slow, deep breathing and clenching then relaxing her fists, focusing on the release of tension when she opened up her hand. As she did these exercises, Maura would repeat the word *calm* to herself slowly and quietly.

Second, Dr. Whitehall suggested that Maura imagine assertive ways she could respond to Eddie other than pleading or yelling threats. Initially, Maura couldn't think of what she might do differently, but with a little encouragement she imagined herself simply and calmly telling Eddie what she wanted him to do—and what the consequences would be if he didn't comply. It took some practice (Maura rehearsed what she would say, with Whitehall role-playing the part of Eddie), but Maura finally found the right words: "Eddie, I want you to go into the living room to play while I am cooking dinner. If you don't, I will take you up to your room for a time-out."

Finally, Dr. Whitehall suggested that Maura's third strategy for change had to be following through on disciplinary action if Eddie didn't comply with her requests. Maura's typical response of tearfully apologizing for blowing up at Eddie had only been reinforcing his bad behavior. So the psychologist and Maura rehearsed what would happen when Eddie refused to stop running through the kitchen. Again, after some practice, Maura figured out what to say: "Eddie, you didn't do what Mommy asked, so go up to your room right now for a fifteen-minute time-out." As Dr. Whitehall praised Maura for her accomplishment, she beamed with pride. But when Whitehall asked, "And what if he doesn't go to his room at that point?" Maura sunk down in her seat, defeated. The psychologist pushed Maura to return to her positive image of her interaction with Eddie. Maura quickly realized she needed to state a consequence for Eddie's disobedience— and follow through on it. In her imagination of the encounter with Eddie, she said, "Eddie, if you don't go to your room for fifteen minutes, you'll lose your hour of TV time tonight before bed." Maura knew this would be a potent threat, because Eddie loved that hour of television each night.

Maura had obviously already enlisted the aid of Dr. Whitehall, but she decided she would also talk with Eddie's teacher, to let her know that she was taking steps to change Eddie's behavior and to ensure that the teacher was doing what she could to help Eddie gain control as well. The teacher was skeptical—she still believed Eddie needed to be on medication. But she knew about Dr. Whitehall's approach and told Maura that her new strategies for responding to Eddie matched the teacher's own approach to handling him in the classroom. This was good, because it meant the two of them would be giving Eddie consistent messages about what was acceptable behavior and what the consequences of unacceptable behavior would be.

Maura had ample opportunities the next week to practice her new responses to Eddie's out-of-control behavior. In the first couple of incidents, her resolve faltered and she reverted to yelling or pleading. But she regained her resolve by the third episode, when Eddie was racing around the grocery store knocking things over. She stood for a moment by her grocery cart and did her relaxation exercises to calm herself. She then firmly told Eddie he was to stop running around and stay by the cart, or they would leave the grocery store immediately and he would be in time-out for thirty minutes at home. When he continued to race around, knocking over a display of cans, she left the cart right there in the aisle, took Eddie by the hand to the car, and when they got home, sent him up to his room. He was so stunned by his mother's new behavior that he went to his room immediately.

Dr. Whitehall encouraged Maura to notice how she felt about herself and what went through her mind as she began to change her way of responding to Eddie. Maura realized that at first she felt guilty and worried that her firmness would damage the relationship somehow. But then Maura told herself that her relationship with Eddie had not been positive for some time, as her anger over his defiance had been growing. Moreover, Eddie's lack of control was interfering with his progress in school and with his friendships with playmates. This strengthened Maura's commitment to sticking with the strategies for change she had developed. Within a few months, the entire pattern of interaction between Maura and Eddie had changed. He was more appropriate in his behavior at home, and this spilled over into more appropriate behavior at school.

Maura enlisted professional help to overcome her weaknesses in parenting Eddie. Dr. Whitehall helped her improve her emotional strengths substantially by evaluating what types of situations gave her the most trouble, using positive imagery to realize how she wanted to interact with Eddie, and employing several small exercises and steps toward fulfilling her positive image. As a result, Maura's relationship with Eddie improved and she grew more confident in her parenting skills, losing her sense of hopelessness that she would ever be able to help Eddie control his behavior.

You may not have the means to enlist professional help if you face a crisis such as Maura's. But you can use the assessments and exercises in Part II to design your own program of strength-building. Remember to first ask yourself "When and where do I get into trouble?" to evaluate the specific situations that cause you to feel distressed or in which you have the most difficulty being effective with your child. Then think about "What is my positive image for change?" to create goals for yourself and your relationship to your child. Finally, focus on "What small steps can I take to bring about positive change?" Then savor the improvements in your relationship to your children, and in their health and well-being, that come from your small steps.

Changing Yourself to Help Your Children Change

As clichéd as it seems, parents are role models for their children. For example, research shows that parents' drinking behavior substantially influences their children's use of alcohol.[7] When kids see their parents drink to excess, they are more likely to emulate this behavior and become binge drinkers themselves. Similarly, kids who hear their parents talk about dishonest behavior, such as cheating on taxes or stealing office supplies at work, are more likely to see dishonesty as acceptable. On the other hand, when children see their parents making positive changes in themselves by improving their mental, identity, emotional, and relational strengths, children can be inspired to make positive changes as well.

When she was twenty-five years old and a graduate student in English literature at UCLA, Traci fell madly in love with Jim, who was pursuing his MBA. They dated for a year, lived together for a year, and then got married just after Jim finished his degree. Traci had completed her graduate courses and was starting work on her dissertation when the couple moved from California to New York City so that Jim could accept a promising job in the financial industry. Traci was sure she could write her dissertation even from their small apartment—the Internet made it possible to do most of her research from wherever she was, and she had secured library privileges at New York University through contacts from her thesis advisor. Traci found it lonely to be cooped up in their apartment all day, however, so took a part-time job in a department store just to get out and see people. "I can write my dissertation on my days off and at night," she assured herself and Jim.

Finishing her dissertation became much harder, however, when Traci had her first child, Steven. He was a relatively easy baby, but nursing Steven every two hours each night left Traci sleep-deprived. During the day she would take Steven to parks and playdates to escape the apartment and get him some fresh air. Two years later, their second child, Emily, was born, and then a third child, Clark, came two years after that. Traci truly had her hands full with three children under the age of seven. But she loved being a mother. She reveled in every milestone her children reached—their first words, learning to walk, entering preschool. Traci wanted the very best for her children, and Jim's lucrative position on Wall Street meant the couple could afford it. She spent countless hours researching private schools, visiting facilities, interviewing administrators and teachers, and talking with other mothers about the pros and cons of different schools.

As her children grew older, Traci found herself more and more often in battles with them over their grades, what they could wear, who their friends were, and their extracurricular activities. Traci earnestly believed in her children's potentials and she wasn't going to let them waste their talents. Each child played multiple musical instruments and participated in a sport at their school or as part of a private club. When any of their grades dipped, Traci instituted a rigorous study schedule, hired tutors, and visited the child's class to observe the teacher's instructional style. Traci's behavior wasn't too different from the mothers of many of the children in the elite private school that her children attended. There was a true competitive spirit among the mothers as to whose children received the most honors, performed in the symphony orchestra, played the most minutes as striker on the soccer team, and so on. Traci had gotten caught up in this culture. Instead of listening to her children's preferences and taking their perspectives, she imposed her own image of what they should be in every aspect of their lives. She let her children's successes and failures stand in for her successes and failures. As a result, she was micromanaging them, insisting that they run their lives according to her rules rather than focusing on helping them fulfill their own interests and dreams.

The battles over who was running the children's lives became fiercer as Traci's kids reached adolescence. Her oldest, Steven, now thirteen, announced he wanted to go away to boarding school, specifically to escape his mother's clutches. The idea of any of her children not being at home left Traci with a black hole in her psyche—what was she going to do, *who would she be*, if her children weren't there?

As her form of rebellion, Traci's daughter had embraced an acutely neurotic attitude toward pretty much everything in her life. "I am stupid!" Emily would say if she got less than an A in a class. "I am ugly!" she whined, and insisted on buying more clothes. Try as she might, Emily was no longer improving at either music or sports, which she interpreted as "I have no talent!" There were also signs that Emily might be developing an eating disorder. She'd eat a big meal at dinner, then disappear into the bathroom. Emily's weight was clearly dropping: even though she was growing, clothes that had fit her last year were hanging like loose sacks on her this year.

One day when Traci was arguing with Steven over a C on an algebra test, Steven screamed, "Mother, get a life! You are nothing but a controlling bitch and I hate you!" Steven stormed out of the room, leaving Traci in bewildered silence. Steven had never used language like that in all their battles, nor had he ever suggested that she needed to get a life. Traci decided to blame his behavior on puberty.

When she told Jim about the incident later that night, he kept an uncomfortable silence rather than agreeing with her that Steven had been irrational. "You agree, don't you, that Steven was out of line?" Traci asked. "I agree that Steven was rude and disrespectful to you," Jim said, "but I think you try to control the kids too much." Then Jim tried to hide behind the newspaper he was reading.

"What are you talking about?" Traci asked. "I only want what's best for the kids! Don't you want them to be as successful as other kids?"

"I want them to be happy," Jim said, "and I don't think we can determine that for them. They have to be who they were born to be, not what we say they should be, or what other people want for their kids."

Traci was furious with Jim for not supporting her and retreated to the guest bedroom. She was up all night thinking about what Jim said and worrying about her relationship with Steven and Emily's mental health. Was she really one of those overcontrolling, overinvested mothers who didn't let her children be themselves? Were her kids not living their lives as they wanted to? Traci paused to wonder what they would do if she didn't program every activity for them and realized she didn't really know what their preferences would be. She tried to imagine what it would be like if she backed off and let the kids do the activities they wanted to do or if she didn't sit with them every night while they did their homework, making sure it was done perfectly. She realized she didn't know what she'd do with herself—would she read a book, watch some television, maybe do some writing? What would "get a life" mean for her? She had long since given up the hope of finishing her Ph.D. dissertation. All of her activities were oriented toward the kids or Jim and his job. It frightened her to think she didn't know who she was beyond the kids' mother and Jim's wife.

Things had to change—Traci had to change. The first thing she needed to do was to understand better who her children were—what their real interests were, and what their joys and worries were. When the kids got up the next morning, they saw that their mother looked terrible—her eyes were red and swollen and she was pale and drawn. She decided not to tell them she had been up all night, but that she had come down with some bug. Rather than bounding around the apartment directing how the children dressed and making sure they had their homework in the backpacks, Traci quietly asked them to get themselves ready as she had another cup of coffee. "Mom must really be sick," Steve said to the other two.

While the children were at school, Traci wrote each of them a letter apologizing for not being a good listener, and telling them she wanted to know what they ideally wanted to be doing in terms of activities and school. She asked them to list what they really liked about school and their activities, and what they disliked. She made it clear that she was open to their dropping some activities if they weren't interested in them or were too stressed out by too many things to do. Then she took a nap.

When the kids got home from school that day, they read the letters and their mouths dropped open. "You're kidding, right?" Steven said to his mother.

"No, I really mean it. There was a kernel of truth in what you said to me yesterday, Steven, although you said it very rudely. I want to know what you guys want, and I want to learn to back off." Steven was suspicious and Emily was confused. Nine-year-old Clark grabbed the opportunity, however. "Well, Mom, I hate violin and I never want to play it again." Traci felt herself twinge—*everyone's* child played violin in their social group, and Clark wasn't too bad at it. Could she really let him stop taking lessons? Traci shut her eyes and saw Clark at his last recital. Then she realized he had a grimace on his face while he was performing and was totally bored when the other children took their turn in the spotlight. Traci shut her eyes again and recalled when Clark was playing baseball, the look of complete delight on his face, the fun he had joking around with the other boys. She opened her eyes and said, "Okay."

"You're kidding," Steven said again. "You'd really let Clark stop violin lessons?"

"Yes, if that's what he really wants," replied Traci. "Now tell me what's important to you."

"I'm not sure, I'll get back to you." Steven didn't want to commit to anything just yet, until he understood what his mother was up to.

Emily had been silent throughout the conversation, and Traci decided not to rush her. Later that evening, she went to Emily's room to talk. "Honey, I really am sorry I've pushed you so hard. It seems like maybe you've been pretty upset lately." Emily cried quietly, saying nothing. Typically, Traci would have peppered her with questions, but this time she just sat on the side of the bed, stroking Emily's hair.

"Mommy, I'm a mess and I'm so scared. I'm doing that eating thing that they talked about in health class. I'm really hungry at dinner so I eat, but then I get worried I'll get fat and I go in the bathroom and throw up. It's like I can't stop. I start feeling out of control and the throwing up makes me feel a little better. But it's so gross!"

Traci had to hold back her own tears and take several deep breaths so she could talk. "Honey, control is not the most important thing. I'm learning that really quickly. And your body is changing. You're becoming a young woman but that doesn't mean you'll get fat. The most important thing is to be healthy." Traci paused for a few moments. "How are things going at school, honey?"

"The other girls are really mean. They are all so skinny and know how to dress really good. It doesn't matter what I do, I can't fit in with them. They call me names and take stuff out of my locker. The other day one of them hit me in the girls' bathroom."

Traci jumped in before she could catch herself. "Why didn't you tell me this when it happened, Emily?"

"Because I knew you'd come to school and make a big deal about it, Mom, and then the other girls would make fun of me even more," Emily said. This stopped Traci in her tracks. Her overcontrolling ways had led her children to hide things from her, leaving them to fend for themselves rather than let her help them.

"Is there anything you like about your school?" Traci decided to ask.

Emily shot back, "No. Nothing. The kids are mean, the teachers are boring, and the classes are too hard. I always feel dumb compared to other kids." Here Emily was, at the top-rated private school in the city, and she was miserable. And Traci had had no idea. Emily had hid everything she was feeling from her. "I know you want us to go there, Mom, but I'm just not cut out for it. I'm not good enough."

After she picked her heart off the ground, Traci said, "Emily, if that's not the right school for you then we have to find one that is better for you. Everyone has their place, and maybe that's not the place for you." Emily brightened at the idea she might be able to switch schools. She sat up and talked with her mother about what she thought she might really like—a school that was for artsy kids like her, who liked to wear funny, funky clothes and write poetry and talk about philosophy. By bedtime, Emily and Traci were giggling about silly things other girls did to be popular, making plans to investigate different schools, and hugging a lot.

The next day, Traci decided to work on her own life. "Steven says I need to get a life," she said to herself. "He's right, but where do I start?" She thought back to the years before the kids were born and what she enjoyed doing then. Her love of literature had led her to pursue the Ph.D., and although she enjoyed the chance to read and think critically about books, she really had no desire to be a writer. She had expected to get a job as a professor at a university, but she now realized that teaching college students didn't interest her. When the kids were little, she had enjoyed finding books to read to them and teaching them to read on their own. She had even started a book club for them and their young friends, but that folded as the kids got so busy with other activities. Traci made a plan to talk to one of the other mothers at her children's school—she had a job in publishing—about what kinds of jobs or volunteer activities might involve children's literature.

Traci had also been athletic before her children were born. In high school and college, she had run track and been on the varsity volleyball teams. In the last several years, she had exercised at the gym primarily to stave off aging. All the fun in being physical was gone. That moment, Traci called her health club to inquire about women's sports teams, and discovered they had a volleyball team that was part of a women's league in the city. She made an appointment to talk with the coach about trying out for the team.

It took a couple of weeks of Traci working hard to keep quiet and listen to her children, asking them for their opinions rather than pushing her own, and arranging for Emily to transfer to a school that seemed more appropriate for her before Steven came around. Late one night, after Traci came home from her first practice with her new volleyball team, Steven came to talk with her in the kitchen. "Mom, I'm proud of you," he started. Traci put down her glass of juice and looked at him in disbelief. "You really do want to change. I didn't think it was real, and I'm still not sure it will last, but it's good so far." That was the end of the conversation for that night. Steven left his mother speechless and went to bed. Over the next weeks, he was noticeably less cranky with her and even let it leak he was infatuated with a girl named Kelly.

Traci's lack of identity and relational strengths had come close to ruining her relationship with her children, and possibly even ruining their lives. Her sense of self had been embroiled in what school her children went to and how they measured up to their peers academically and socially. In the meantime, she had lost track of who she was except for being her kids' mother. She had completely ignored her children's perspective on what they should be doing in life in favor of programming them to fit the image of a perfect child that her culture had prescribed. To make them perfect, and therefore make her perfect, she had impatiently micromanaged their every move. As a result, the children were living inauthentic lives—they weren't who they wanted to be but instead ping-ponging between striving to be who their mother wanted them to be and fighting against that very same thing. Emily's mental and physical health were suffering, and Traci was losing her connection with Steven altogether.

Traci made radical changes in herself and her relationship with her children by taking several small steps. First, she started listening. She gave the kids room to tell her what they liked and disliked, what their worries were, and what changes they wanted in their lives. She tried to get inside their heads, imagining their worlds from their perspective. And she allowed them to make substantial changes in their lives, even ones that went drastically against the "right program" for kids in their social group.

Second, Traci decided to get a life. She reconnected with the interests and values she had before she became a mother, and evaluated which of these she might like to pursue now. She made concrete plans to create roles and activities in her life outside of being a mother. Within a year after deciding to get her own life back, Traci was working as a development editor for a publishing company specializing in children's books.

If you worry that the way you are living your life is not a good model for your children or is hampering their development into independent, happy people, take stock of which of your psychological strengths needs work. Ask yourself if you, like Traci, need to improve your identity strengths so that you are living a balanced, rich life that includes them but is not solely based on them. Is your own style of expressing and managing your emotions a positive model for your children? Or are your emotional strengths lacking, so that you sometimes suppress your emotions and refuse to be honest, and other times lose control over them altogether? From your behavior toward your children, are they learning patience and perspective-taking skills or impatience and self-centeredness? In making family decisions, do you focus on teamwork and satisfying everyone's interests as much as possible? Or are you autocratic, sure that you know what's best for everyone?

Once you've taken stock and identified strengths that need work, imagine what your life, and family, might be like if you were stronger. Then use the exercises in the strength-building program to take many small steps toward that new and more positive family.

Employing Strengths to Help Our Daughters

One of the richest, and most volatile, relationships a mother can have is with her teenage daughter. Adolescent girls can see their mothers as the embodiment of everything they *don't* want to become and as the major obstacle to doing things *their way*. On the other hand, adolescent girls need, and long for, a close relationship with their mothers, to give them stability through the massive changes their minds and bodies are going through, and to help them make good choices. All of a woman's strengths are tested in her relationship to her adolescent daughter.

Daughters tend to mirror their mothers' strengths. Although there may be a genetic component to this phenomenon, my colleagues and I have observed mothers and children interacting in our laboratories and found that mothers communicate strong messages to their children about how to handle difficult situations, and daughters pick up on these messages even more than sons do. Sometimes mothers model how to confront difficult circumstances with confidence and resolve, and how to generate ideas for solving problems. Other times they model a helpless, overly emotional response to difficulty. Because the coping styles that mothers teach their daughters, both directly and indirectly, are recapitulated in their daughters' own behavior, one of the most important steps to growing our daughters' strengths is to recognize our own strengths and weaknesses—that is, the messages we send to our daughters—and to hone those areas that need improvement.

Over the last forty years, as women have behaved more assertively, claiming their rights to work, to be educated, and to have children when they choose, girls have catapulted in assertiveness, outpacing the growth that their adult role models have shown. Girls take their messages not only from their mothers but also from aunts, older sisters, grandmothers, female teachers, Girl Scout leaders, community leaders, and media stars.

Mothers, of course, have the most contact with their daughters and therefore the greatest opportunity to provide support and inspire positive change. Mothers have the power to help their daughters chart a healthy path through the rough and dangerous years of childhood and adolescence. Consider Patti, for example, a petite blonde, blue-eyed sixteen-year-old from Boise, Idaho. Patti had lost touch with what she thought and felt, becoming totally focused on doing what it took to become popular. She found high school a confusing, overwhelming place. It wasn't the academic work—she did well in most of her classes—but rather the other kids. Patti felt as though everyone else understood how to dress, how to act, who to talk to, and which extracurricular activities to get involved in while she floundered, more or less clueless. She spent countless hours reading magazines for teenage girls, trying to understand the "rules." Every month she tried some new program that promised to make her prettier, skinnier, more popular. And each month she felt like a failure because she either couldn't carry out these programs or found them ineffective.

On a recent weekend, Patti and her best friend, Megan, went to a party hosted by one of the school's most popular kids, whose parents were out of town. They normally wouldn't have been invited, but it was an "open-house" party, which allowed them to just walk in, no questions asked. Lots of other kids were drinking heavily and some were smoking. Some guy eased up next to Patti and asked if she wanted a drink. Patti hadn't drunk much in the past but she didn't want to put this guy off, so she said, "Sure." Patti felt nervous about whether she was doing the right thing, but Megan encouraged her to go with the boy over to the bar.

Patti ended up having four drinks that night, which made her extremely drunk. When she got home later, she tried to slink in the back door but stumbled around, making a lot of noise. Her mother, Julie, came down to investigate and found Patti sitting on the kitchen floor, leaning against the cabinets, a tear slowly rolling down her cheek. At first Julie was alarmed: "Honey, what happened, what's wrong?!"

Then Julie smelled alcohol on Patti's breath. Her immediate reaction was anger, even rage. Julie's dad had been an alcoholic and to smell alcohol on Patti felt like the fulfillment of her worst nightmare. Fortunately, Julie's emotional strengths were good and she rallied them to respond to her daughter in a way that would connect with her instead of driving her away. Julie drew in a deep breath, shut her eyes, and said to herself, "She's not my father. She's my daughter. I want to keep my cool."

Patti started to tell Julie about her evening: "There was this guy. At a party." Patti started crying more vigorously and put her head in her hands. Julie had the horrifying thought that Patti had been sexually assaulted and started to demand the boy's name. But again, she caught herself, took another deep breath, and said, "Okay, and what happened?"

"He came over to talk to me and he offered me a drink. I didn't really want to, but he was cute, and I didn't want him to think I was dumb. So I had a drink. And then we kept talking and I kept drinking. Mom, I just want to throw up! Please make my head stop spinning!"

Julie asked calmly, "Did anything else happen with this guy?"

"No, after a while he went over to talk to some other girl. Megan brought me home. Oh Mom, it doesn't matter what I do, boys just aren't interested in me!"

Julie realized at once that Patti wasn't an alcoholic; rather, she was upset that she wasn't more popular with the boys at school. She put Patti to bed, knowing that this was not the time to have a meaningful talk.

The next day, when Patti was sober and feeling extremely grateful to her mother for not becoming angry, Julie sat Patti down for a talk. Julie knew that Patti needed to work on centering her identity in her core interests and values, rather than in being popular with other kids. She thought one small step would be to help Patti generate ideas for positive ways of meeting new kids and expressing herself. She asked her daughter, "Honey, maybe we could think of some things you could do to get to know more boys. Do you have any ideas?"

Patti got a bit defensive and said sarcastically, "I could be like the popular girls. I could wear sexy clothes, I could flirt. But you wouldn't let me, and I probably would screw it up anyway, just like at that party!"

Julie understood that this kind of hostility was the result of Patti's insecurity. She also knew that her relationship with Patti was still strong enough that, if Julie could avoid overreacting to Patti's outburst, she could probably get her to work toward positive change. Julie paused for a moment, calmed herself, and drew on her mental flexibility to suggest, "No, that doesn't really sound like you. I wonder if there are other things you could do, things you would like to do, that would give you more chances to meet boys who like the same things." Thus Julie artfully challenged Patti to strategize creative steps for change.

Patti was a bit surprised that her mother didn't become angry at her rude remark, and she quickly realized that her mother had made a good suggestion. "Well, I like writing. I've thought about joining the school newspaper or the yearbook. And I like singing. But I don't know how to join. They probably wouldn't take me anyway."

Staying patient, Julie encouraged Patti to enlist others' help by saying, "What are some things you can do today to find out about the newspaper, or the yearbook, or the singing clubs at school?"

"I guess I could ask the teachers who are advisors for the clubs," Patti responded. "I could also ask some kids who are in the clubs." Julie agreed these were great ideas and got out the school handbook to identify the relevant faculty advisors. Patti was somewhat resistant, but Julie persisted and soon they had learned the names of several people Patti could talk to about different activities. They made a plan for how Patti would approach these people at school on Monday.

A few months later, Patti was involved in the school chorus and writing for the newspaper. She was meeting lots of new teenagers, boys and girls, who had interests similar to her own. Patti noticed that she no longer had any desire to understand "the rules" that so many of her peers were obsessed with and instead felt proud that she was doing things she cared about, rather than just doing what would make her popular.

To help her daughter, Julie made use of all her strengths. She used her *mental flexibility* to generate ideas about how Patti could get involved with positive peers and activities. She stuck firmly to her values about drinking, but also recognized her great desire to help Patti learn from this situation. She called upon her *emotional strengths* to control her anger and recognize the confusing emotions Patti was feeling. She exercised her *relational strengths* to stay connected with Patti even when Patti was behaving obnoxiously.

Our daughters have the freedom to pursue educational and professional opportunities that their grandmothers never dreamed possible. At the same time, our daughters are under tremendous pressure to be sexually active, to try drugs and alcohol, and to starve their bodies into impossible shapes and sizes. As mothers, grandmothers, aunts, teachers, and friends, we can help today's young women navigate a world of seemingly endless freedom and pressure by exercising our own strengths and nurturing theirs. As they then grow into strong and effective leaders, parents, and lovers, they will serve as inspirational models and teachers for their own daughters—and help shape a new generation of strong, confident leaders ready to change the world.

Parenting can bring the greatest pleasures of life, but it's not easy. For millennia, women have been using their patience, their creativity, and their empathy to raise children in warm, caring, safe environments— and to overcome any obstacles to their children's healthy development. You can use all your strengths as a woman to strategize new techniques for fostering rich, meaningful relationships with your children and creating environments in which your kids can truly thrive and grow.

13.

Loving Like a Woman

Women are great lovers. Whether it is in marriage or other romantic partnerships, close friendships, or bonds with a sibling or other family member, women use their mental, identity, emotional, and relational strengths to build resilient, intimate, mutually rewarding relationships.

Close relationships are essential to mental and physical well-being. As we saw in my study of recently bereaved people, those who had strong and supportive relationships with family and friends suffered from less depression and anxiety and were better able to rebuild their lives in the two years following their loss.[1] When people come together around a crisis such as loss, relationships can grow and flourish, as each person appreciates the other on a deeper level. This is reflected in a comment by Fran, a woman in my bereavement study whose cousin died from complications due to AIDS:

> We had incredible support from family and friends, unbelievable from our church and our pastor. And even school friends. He was very touched by the expressions of concern from friends of ours who would come in and visit him. It was a very close time for my family; that is, my husband, children, and my parents. My mother and I worked in tandem, and our relationship was altered as a result of this. We kind of emerged from this experience as peers. We're much closer. That has been absolutely wonderful.[2]

Having good relationships can also make you physically healthier. People with good relationships have more healthy cardiovascular and immune systems, take better care of themselves, rebound better after surgery, cope with cancer better, and live longer lives. In contrast, people who lack good relationships—those who are socially isolated, or in relationships that are not supportive and positive—get sick more often, recover more slowly from illness, and die earlier. Further, people with bad relationships are less likely to take care of themselves, for example, by following doctors' orders or giving up smoking.[3]

Because women's many strengths bestow them with particular skill at nurturing close relationships, being in a relationship with a woman seems to have even greater positive effects than being in a relationship with a man. Women report giving more support in marital relationships than men, but receiving less—and their husbands agree with this assessment.[4] Yale psychologist Margaret Clark found that people in general see the women in their lives as more communal in relationships, caring for others' welfare, and responding to others' needs and desires without preconditions.[5] Women are viewed as more responsive and committed to others' needs, and better able to understand others. As a result, people act in more communal ways toward the women than the men in their lives, going the extra mile to care for them when needed. This is true across a variety of relationships: with mates, siblings, parents, and extended family.

On the other hand, perhaps because women's own identities are so woven into their relationships with others, they are at greater risk of the negative health effects that come if conflicts arise in a relationship. When married heterosexual couples were asked, in a lab study, to talk about a topic about which they disagreed, both men's and women's heart rates rose with the level of conflict, and their immune responses fell. In general, though, such effects of marital conflict were greater on wives than on husbands.[6] In another study that followed 189 women and men with congestive heart failure over four years, researchers found that those with more positive marriages had higher survival rates than those with poorer marriages. Again, the effect of marital quality on survival was greater for women than for men.[7]

In this chapter, I will explore why and how women's mental, identity, emotional, and relational strengths make them so skilled at loving
others, to the benefit of the men and the women in their lives. Then
I will tell you how you can enhance your strengths to build stronger
and more fulfilling relationships with your friends, lovers, and family
members.

Being Generous with Love

One of women's key mental strengths is optimism, and optimists tend
to have terrific relationships. Women's mental strength of optimism
leads to longer-lasting friendships, greater satisfaction in romantic
relationships, and less likelihood that these relationships will dissolve.[8]
Women's optimism may also lead others to give more support to
them. Optimists are better liked by other people—they are just more
pleasant to be around than pessimists.[9] As a result, others may be more
interested in being their friends and more willing to help them out in
times of need.

Optimists tend to be generous in their evaluations of others, and
this helps to build positive relationships.[10] For example, when a spouse
is late coming home from work, an optimistic woman will give him
the benefit of the doubt, imagining what may be happening out of his
control: "He must have gotten stuck in traffic, but I'm sure he'll be
home as soon as he can." This sets the stage for a more friendly home-
coming than if a woman grumbles to herself, "He doesn't even try to
get home on time."

A recent study of dating couples confirmed that optimists tend to see
the best in their partners. Compared to pessimists, optimists perceived
their partners as more supportive and their relationships as more satisfying. The partners of optimists, for their part, also saw their
optimistic others as highly supportive, and they too were highly satisfied with their relationship. It seems that optimism creates a good
relationship feedback loop. In this same study, when the researchers
asked the couples to discuss an issue of conflict between them, they

ᅟ

LOVING LIKE A WOMAN 291

found that the optimists and their partners were more positively engaged in resolving the conflict during the conversation and as a result reported feeling more satisfied with the outcome of the conflict.[11]

Women's determined optimism, with its focus on seeing many pathways to a goal, keeps them engaged with their relationship even when times are tough. For example, in the financial crisis of 2008, Kirsten and Greg found themselves staring down a foreclosure on the little bungalow they had bought in Sacramento, California. A couple years earlier, as they were shopping for a house in the hot real estate market, they had let themselves get talked into a subprime mortgage with an adjustable interest rate. At the time, it seemed like a good idea. They were in their late twenties, recently married, and could only afford to make a down payment of 10 percent. The adjustable rate gave them a chance to own a home. Plus, though they were just starting out in their careers, they had both been quickly promoted and fully expected that they would see another leap in their salaries before any interest rate change kicked in. But just as their mortgage payments ballooned, Greg lost his job as the manager of a local vegetable farm. Kirsten and Greg had little savings to see themselves through this crisis. Greg became despondent, but Kirsten refused to give up, believing there must be some way out of the mess. She called their bank and when she didn't get much help there, she called a local agency that helped people refinance their houses. Greg was sure they couldn't get any help because he was unemployed, but Kirsten persisted, working out a plan with the agency's financial counselor to get their mortgage payments down.

Then Kirsten set to work helping Greg find a new job. He had put minimal work into the effort, again voicing pessimism that there were any jobs to be had in the economic downturn. Kirsten scoured the Internet everyday for employment opportunities and dragged Greg to an unemployment workshop that was run by their local synagogue. Within a month he had landed work with the state park service, clearing brush on hillsides near housing developments to reduce fire risk. The job didn't pay as well as his job as a farm manager, yet between Greg's paycheck and Kirsten's, they were able to afford their renegotiated mortgage.

For the few months the couple was caught in their personal financial crisis, Greg had ceaselessly moaned to Kirsten: the economy was in the pits, so there would be no jobs and he should just collect his meager unemployment check; the banks were in no position to refinance people's mortgages, so giving up the house was their only option. He seemed to find solace in these dire predictions, perhaps because they justified his lack of motivation to do anything about his situation. Kirsten refused to get into an argument about how right or wrong Greg was in his opinions. She kept her sights singularly focused on getting the job done: renegotiating their mortgage and finding employment for Greg.

Kirsten also called upon her strength in enlisting help when it is needed. Greg didn't believe there was help to be found, or perhaps was too proud to ask for it. Kirsten, on the other hand, took any and all the help she could get. Like many women, she saw it as her right and duty to get help from others—in her case, from the agency that helped renegotiate the loan and from their synagogue community.

Women frequently turn to others to help them specifically with problems in their close relationships. Women turn to their female friends to get insight about their mate's behavior and to blow off steam about their frustrations. These conversations among women tend to be highly intimate, providing women with a sense of being validated and understood.[12] People, in turn, seem to be more willing to provide emotional and practical support to women than to men, in part because they see women as more likely to reciprocate.[13]

Being concerned and responsible for others can certainly become a burden for women, yet most women are able to balance the social aspects of their identities with their own personal needs and interests. Psychologist Caryl Rusbult of the Free University in the Netherlands has shown that this personal-relational balance is an essential feature of successful relationships. A perfect balance can't always be maintained—sometimes you have to pay more attention to your own needs than to your partner's, as when you have an important deadline at work that requires you to stay late and work weekends. Other times your partner's needs are more pressing than yours; for instance, when an illness strikes. Rusbult discovered that healthy couples are able to tip the balance in favor of the personal or the relational for a while, then restore equilibrium by putting more time and attention into the domain that has been slighted.[14] For example, if you've spent the last two weeks working unreasonable hours to meet a deadline, once the deadline is passed you may suggest a long weekend with your partner so the two of you can reconnect.

To ensure that they do not grow too self-sacrificing in their love, women cultivate a vibrant, flexible personal identity that remains at their core, even as the relationships that help define that identity change. As a couple moves from one city to another, as parents age and need assistance, or as relationships are lost through death or dissolution, women can draw on this core sense of self to maintain peace and confidence.

A strong personal identity also allows women to make good choices for themselves in times of crisis. You may recall the story of Wendy, the forty-three-year-old homemaker we met in chapter 2. When she finally had enough of her husband's abusiveness, she filed for divorce. She then proceeded to build a new life for herself and her children with much fewer resources than her husband had previously provided. Wendy's courage and fortitude came from a steadfast belief in herself as a survivor and a clever problem solver. Although Wendy suddenly was forced to find paid employment to support herself and her children—a totally new role for her after many years out of the workforce—she was able to draw upon her identity to imagine herself succeeding even when she was most afraid of failing. Her self-respect grew tremendously as she conquered her changing circumstances.

Building Richer Connections

Emotions serve as signals to oneself and to others that something important has happened or is about to happen. Thus women's ability to perceive others' emotions and take others' points of view allows them to respond with empathy, which builds trust and gratitude in their relationships. Say, for example, your best friend has been unusually grumpy for the past several days. If you accurately perceive that her behavior is due to a combination of sadness and anger over a negative performance review at work, you can respond by validating her anger and reassuring her that she can improve her evaluations for the future. In response, she is likely to become less grumpy and be grateful to you for understanding and supporting her. If, on the other hand, you haven't got a clue as to why she is grumpy, your instinct may simply be to pull away and avoid her until her mood improves. This is not likely to help her, nor is it likely to strengthen your relationship.

Similarly, women's strengths at understanding, expressing, and managing their own emotions are huge assets in their relationships with others. Accurately disclosing your emotions to others creates relationships characterized by trust and mutual understanding.[15] Even two strangers brought together in laboratory studies feel closer to each other when one person discloses something emotional about him- or herself.[16] In established relationships, disclosing your feelings leads to greater intimacy and closeness. Women tend to disclose more emotional information in the context of their relationships than men do; indeed, when men do disclose emotional information about themselves, it's more often to women than to men.[17]

Because women understand and express their emotions, others are better equipped to come to their aid appropriately. Women clearly signal when they are sad, and others know to comfort them. They signal when they are afraid, and others know to protect and calm them. When women are interacting with people who are not good at perceiving others' emotions, this ability to know and clearly signal what they are feeling gives others the opportunity to respond in ways that will be helpful and will foster their relationship.

Johan was hopeless when it came to understanding other people's emotions. If his wife, Lois, became upset, Johan was instantly overwhelmed, worrying that he was the source of her distress, but also frustrated that Lois couldn't just hold in her emotions as he did. This caused a number of conflicts between them in the early years of their marriage, as Johan reacted defensively and Lois became annoyed that he focused on himself rather than on her needs when she was upset. But over time Lois developed the practice of straightforwardly telling Johan exactly what she was feeling and why—filling in all the blanks for him rather than giving him any room to misperceive what she was feeling. Although Johan still didn't really want to know or have to deal with Lois's feelings, he appreciated the clarity and the explicit directions Lois gave him as to what he could do to make her feel better.

Expressing positive emotions in the context of a relationship is clearly good for the relationship.[18] People like to hear that they are appreciated and loved, and that you enjoy being with them. Women are more comfortable being effusive in relationships. This builds a positive glow around the relationship. It also invites others to be positive themselves.

Sometimes you have to express negative emotions in relationships as well. Not doing so can be dishonest, and can lead to miscommunication between people. People who are better at expressing their negative emotions appropriately have larger social networks and more intimate relationships with others.[19] Of course, it's important that the expression of negative emotions be done in non-accusing and non-threatening ways, and when the time is right. People who chronically talk about how sad or angry or afraid they are, regardless of others' attempts to help them, eventually become ostracized and rejected.[20] But the ability to let your partner or friend know when you are frustrated or unhappy, and why, gives him or her the opportunity to support you, make amends, or clear up misunderstandings before they grow into large problems.

Being able to tolerate distress and manage emotions allows women to stay in the game when conflict arises, working toward a resolution rather than running away or stonewalling. Long-lasting relationships are characterized not by the avoidance of conflict and expressions of negative emotion, but by the willingness to constructively engage in conflict.[21] That is, couples who stay together are not afraid to argue. They don't run away from conflict or hold back their frustration or anger with each other when it is strongly felt. They can accept their own distress and their partner's distress, enough to be able to stay in a confrontational conversation until they can reach some mutually satisfying resolution. They also know enough to sprinkle some positive remarks into the conflict, validating the partner and expressing optimism that the conflict can be resolved.[22] Researcher John Gottman found that men have a tougher time than women tolerating and managing the high levels of emotional and physical arousal caused by these conflicts, and instead are more likely than women to withdraw and shut down.

The emotional richness that comes from women's willingness to be emotional and to let others be emotional adds color and spice to their relationships. People feel known, understood, and validated by women. That is in part because women are good at perceiving their emotions, but it's also because women's relational strengths in taking others' perspectives and listening to them open further avenues for communication and intimacy.

Taking other people's perspective helps women to imagine and understand their actions and influences, and allows women to be more generous in attributing motives to others' behaviors. Instead of blaming or accusing, they realize the possibility of misunderstandings or external concerns that may have contributed to another person's behavior. In a series of studies, psychologists Ximena Arriaga and Caryl Rusbult had couples involved in romantic relationships imagine a scenario in which their partner engages in some egregious behavior, such as the following:

> You feel neglected by your partner, who has been very busy lately. You nevertheless make dinner plans for an approaching evening, to which the partner reluctantly agrees. Your partner arrives for dinner half an hour late, not ready to dine, explaining that he or she must cancel dinner because of a . . . project that is due the next day.[23]

Half of the participants were asked to visualize the incident from their own point of view, considering how they would feel and how things would look to them. The other half in the study were asked to visualize the incident from the partner's point of view, considering how the partner would feel and how things would look to the partner. Those who took the partner's point of view reported feeling more positive emotions and were more willing to make amends with the partner. They were also more generous when contemplating why their partners acted this way, noting, "My partner isn't deliberately behaving badly—it's just one of those things" rather than the self-centered perspective: "My partner does not try hard enough to take into account my needs and feelings." Given these emotional and relational benefits, it's not surprising that studies show that women are more motivated than men to take others' perspectives.[24]

Women's perspective-taking also contributes to their ability to put others' needs first when appropriate.[25] For example, in the context of a heated argument, people often say hurtful things, which motivates partners to reciprocate with their own hurtful comments, and conflict escalates. Resolving these difficult interactions requires one partner to step out of tit-for-tat hostility and act in a more constructive, conciliatory manner. Women's perspective-taking allows them to put aside their own self-interest in a conflict to take into account the long-term interest of maintaining the relationship and their partner's needs and concerns. This more accommodating behavior isn't simply an avoidance of confrontation, it reduces tension between the couple and makes it more likely that the conflict will be resolved.

Having a partner who actively attempts to take your perspective also appears to make people communicate more clearly and be motivated to resolve conflicts. When you trust that your partner won't jump to conclusions about your behavior but will try to understand where you're coming from, you are more motivated to behave well and fulfill your partner's trust. Relationships in which one or both partners have high levels of perspective-taking ability are more healthy and satisfying for both partners.[26]

Finally, the relational strengths of listening and patience nurture relationships. Listening gives you insights into your partner's or friend's perspective and communicates that you care enough to pay attention. In studies in which romantic couples are observed talking with each other, women tend to be more attentive than men to what their partner is saying.[27] Active listening enables deeper intimacy, which has been found to be a great predictor that a couple will stay together and be happy over time.[28] Patience helps women stick with friends and partners when they are going through life changes of their own, such as Greg's response to losing his job at the farm, or a midlife crisis that triggers the purchase of a pricey sports car. Patience, combined with perspective-taking, helps women to forgive others for wrongs against them, and the ability to forgive is strongly associated with closeness and longevity in relationships.[29] When women are able to forgive their partner for transgressions, the couple argues less and their marriage grows more satisfying.[30] Of course, there are some transgressions that are less forgivable than others. Forgiveness is a choice, and women must call upon all their mental, identity, emotional, and relational strengths to decide if that choice is a good one in a particular circumstance.

Even in the best relationships, there are usually things we'd like to change. We might want more openness and honesty in the relationship. We'd like to be appreciated more, or have our partner be more affectionate. We'd like some habit of our partner, or our own, to change. Sometimes there are more major problems in relationships, such as mistrust or even dislike. In the next section, I'll talk about how women can utilize their psychological strengths to bring out the best in our relationships.

Bringing Out the Best or Worst in Others

The renowned sculptor Michelangelo believed that the sculpting process chipped away the outer layer of stone to reveal the true form hidden beneath. So when confronted with a block of marble from the Italian town of Carrara, Michelangelo saw, lingering beneath the exterior, the form of the *David* and began his work to release the form from the stone. Similarly, in any relationship—whether a marriage or other romantic partnership, friendship, or family bond—we can choose to look past the rocky exterior to see the our partner's true personality and behaviors, and take the time to chip away to that psychological space. Psychologists Steve Drigotas, Caryl Rusbult, and their colleagues have labeled this process the "Michelangelo phenomenon."[31] We hope that our "sculpting" frees our partners, friends, and family to show their best form—the person they ideally can be and want to be.

Sometimes, however, our interactions with others only bring out the worst in them—pettiness, hostility, selfishness. At the heart of many troubled relationships is the belief that there is something wrong with the other person, that the form beneath the stone is inherently flawed, and it is his or her responsibility to change. We tell our friends, "He's so irritable all the time" or "He doesn't seem to care about anyone else but himself" or "It drives me crazy when he . . ." (fill in the blank with your partner's most annoying habit). Often we complain to our partner about what is wrong with him, in hopes that he will gain insight that will cause him to change. Instead, all we get is an argument, anger, and defensiveness.

Indeed, sometimes the people in our lives do need to change. But we seldom see the ways we draw out and reinforce bad behavior from others, and fail to draw out and reward good behavior in the ways we respond to them and the expectations we hold.

When they were first married eighteen years ago, Elena and Mark were madly in love. They shared interests in food, wine, hiking, and beachcombing. They lived in the San Francisco area, so pursuing all these passions just meant a short drive to the Napa or Sonoma Valley, or the hills along the beach around Santa Cruz. They would talk for hours about everything and nothing, just happy to be together sharing activities they both enjoyed. Both were also passionate about their careers—Elena and Mark were both working for technology start-ups. Elena had her dream job as the marketing director in charge of conceptualizing sales campaigns that would appeal to tech-savvy "early adopters." Mark was satisfied with his new position developing applications that would make valuable information easily accessible to doctors.

Over the years, as the two helped to launch their companies' products while also beginning a family, the fun and passion of their early
years of marriage eroded. Instead of talking into the wee hours, the
couple spent their time together coordinating schedules, negotiating
household and child-care duties, and staking out ground in their frequent arguments over how to raise their two children. Mark was more
of a disciplinarian than Elena, and she thought he was too strict with
the kids and expecting too much of them. Mark thought Elena let the
kids get away with murder, and resented constantly being told what he
was doing wrong as a father. By the time the children were adolescents,
the household was mostly a place of tension and discord. Mark would
come home from work, frustrated over some interaction he had had
or some problem he hadn't been able to solve. This made him ripe for
overreacting to a snide remark from one of the kids, or a bill that Elena
had forgotten to pay and was now overdue. Elena came home from
work expecting a battle, primed to get angry and defensive at the first
sign that Mark was being critical. The second Mark would snap at one
of the kids for dropping his dirty clothes beside the laundry basket
instead of in it, Elena would mutter loudly, "Here we go again," to
which Mark would shoot back, "You think it's okay for him to just
drop his dirty clothes wherever he feels like it." The battle would be
launched. Their children would slink away to avoid their parents, and
Elena and Mark would either trade barbed accusations or clam up in
a taut silence that would last through the rest of the evening.

Mark may have been nitpicking or looking for a fight by griping
about the clothes scattered next to the laundry basket, but Elena threw
fuel on the fire by responding in a sarcastic way to him. She couldn't
stop herself from viewing Mark as a hypercritical person; she saw
everything he did in terms of that image, and reacted to him accord-
ingly. This brought out the worst in Mark—including unfair criticism
of the kids, and unfair accusations against Elena that she is content to
raise slobs.

If Elena wants to break this pattern, and more generally improve
her relationship with Mark and the atmosphere in the family, she
should call upon her strengths as a woman. First, Elena needs to

determine when and where her interactions with Mark are most troubled. If she kept a diary for a few days, or thought back over specific instances in the last few weeks, she'd realize that the roughest episodes occurred on weekday evenings. On those days, she and Mark were usually tired from work, and still had dinner to cook, laundry to do, bills to pay, and so on. The kids sometimes needed help on their homework or rides to and from school events. So the evenings were anything but relaxing—in fact, they were full of opportunities for disagreement. On Saturdays, Elena and Mark went their separate ways to do chores, and only came back together at the kids' sports matches, after which they would typically slink home to eat whatever they could throw together for dinner. On Sundays, the family tried to do things together, like going hiking. Then on Sunday nights, as they geared up for school and work the next day, the pattern of criticism and argument often set back in.

So it was clearly the weekday nights, and Sunday night leading into the new week, where Elena could see the most opportunity for change. To determine what kind of change she wants to happen, Elena should apply her immense creativity to building a more positive image, not just of what she wants weekday nights to look like or of her relationship with Mark and the kids, but of Mark himself. When she imagined Mark in her mind's eye now, she saw a hypercritical, hostile man. But what about the fun, loving guy she had married? Was it possible that these aspects of Mark's character were still there, buried beneath the ugly, rough surface that Elena typically saw these days? Mark's best qualities sometimes did shine through, when the family was out together on a Sunday, doing something relaxing and pleasant. Then Mark would be joking with the kids, letting them teach him new skating tricks, making it clear that he loved them very much.

We're more likely to bring out our partner's best self, his ideal form, if we have a vision of his best self that corresponds to his vision for himself.[32] This is where women's perspective-taking ability and listening skills can be extremely useful. The first small step Elena should take is to think back to the last few weekday nights when things had gotten tense between her and Mark, and ask herself, "What might have happened at work, or what might he have been thinking or feeling, that caused him to act the way he did?" She might have realized that each of the nights' arguments broke out, Mark had come home exceptionally tired, having given big presentations on those days. She might also remember that his idea for a new software line had been rejected by the company's top management. Then Elena could ask herself, "If Mark imagined what he'd have liked those nights to be like, and how he would have preferred to act, what would that image look like?" In other words, Elena could try to tune in to Mark's own positive image for weekday nights and himself on those nights. This image would probably involve being asked about his day and being listened to when he talked about it, having light banter with the kids, and everyone relaxing in a warm, supportive atmosphere.

Over the next couple of days, Elena could muster her listening skills to observe the pattern of interaction between Mark and the rest of the family in the evenings, snapping a rubber band on her wrist every time she felt inclined to verbally bark at Mark for something he said. This would allow her to gather much more information on the dynamics in the family and to build a realistically positive goal for what interactions with Mark and the family could become.

In her observations, Elena would probably notice that every night she got extremely focused on the family chores—the dinner, laundry, bills, kids' homework—and that she became impatient when Mark wanted to talk about his day because they had so much to do. To become more patient and open the doors of communication with Mark, she could take the small step of listing all the family chores and thinking hard about which ones had to be done on busy weekday nights. Yes, the kids did need to do their homework, and the family needed to eat. But did they really have to deal with the pile of laundry every night? The kids had plenty of clothes to get through a week. They could survive if their favorite pair of jeans or T-shirt wasn't always clean. Elena and Mark could catch up on bill paying on Saturdays and not worry about that during the week. More important, Elena needed to step back and recognize that the high priority was to create a less pressured atmosphere in the evenings, so that family members had time to talk with one another and the stress level was reduced.

To increase her patience in the evenings, Elena also needed to find ways to wind down between the end of work and when Mark and the kids came home. She currently worked right up until the second she had to rush out and pick up one of the kids or get home to begin making dinner. She would arrive home harried and often carrying the weight of work stress on her shoulders. She needed to build in time between work and home and develop better ways to manage her stress and emotions. During this cushion period, Elena might practice meditative exercises, or run on her treadmill, or just sit with a cup of tea and a magazine. By taking the small step of relaxing before everyone arrived home, she would be better equipped to be patient with everyone else as they wound down from their days.

Elena did carry through with these exercises and when she listened intently to what was going on in the family for a few days, she heard her own voice criticizing Mark continuously for his ways of interacting with the children, for his annoying habits, and for his boring tales of woe at work. She recognized that much of her frustration and anger with Mark came from these thoughts in her head as much from anything he actually said or did. She was surprised how harsh and unreasonable her own silent criticisms had become and could see how they made her overreact to Mark. She let one frustration bleed into others, leading her to find fault with Mark over what were really innocent acts or comments. Elena wrote down these negative thoughts on cards. For some of the cards, she came up with counter-thoughts. For example, she had the thought "He only finds fault with the kids" and then generated the counter-thoughts: "He actually also praises them often" and "What they do *is* wrong sometimes, and they should be called on it." She felt her emotions shift from annoyance and anger to appreciation and understanding as she generated these counter-thoughts.

For other criticisms, though, her counter-thought was simply "I don't want to think this way." For example, Mark had the annoying habit of talking with his mouth full. He'd always done this, but it drove Elena crazy these days, for reasons she didn't entirely understand.

She'd tense up at dinner, ranting and raving at him in her head, and her irritation would interfere with her ability to listen to Mark or the kids, or cause her to make a snide comment about something completely unrelated to Mark's talking with his mouth full. When she'd tell Mark that his eating with his mouth full annoyed her, he'd get angry and defensive, so she knew it was unlikely he'd drop this habit. So she told herself, "This is relatively trivial, and I don't want my annoyance over it to balloon into some big problem. I am going to choose not to be as bothered by it anymore, because it is a low priority compared to improving the family atmosphere." In this way, Elena effectively got around an obstacle she had created in her head—she had been telling herself that she couldn't relax at dinner if Mark kept talking with his mouth full, but she chose to go down a different path by declaring she would focus on her larger goal of improving their family life. Elena also shifted her focus away from getting her way (getting Mark to stop talking with his mouth full) to getting the job done (making herself less irritable and the family less tense).

All these small steps helped Elena gain patience and perspective, and begin to respond to Mark more in line with her positive image of him than her previous negative image. She was calmer and more relaxed when he got home and thus less likely to get combative if he said something potentially provocative. She created the space for him to wind down by telling her about his day and worked to take his perspective and communicate caring about him. When Mark did act in an objectively unreasonable way toward the kids, Elena would take a deep breath and try to validate his concerns, then redirect the conversation to problem solving rather than accusations. Previously, if Mark yelled at one of the kids, "You're always acting disrespectfully to your mother!" Elena would have typically said something like "You just don't understand teenagers! Stop harping on him!" Now Elena might say, "I know this bothers you a lot and you're right that he is often disrespectful. I don't think yelling will do much good. Let's think of something concrete we can do to make it clear to him that he needs to stop being rude." Mark would then calm down and be more likely to focus on solving the problem rather than venting his anger.

In this case, Elena was practicing what I described earlier as *accommodative behavior*—small acts of validation, perspective-taking, and forgiveness that diffuse conflict between a couple. Instead of feeding the argument by responding to Mark's remarks with her own hostile comments, Elena expressed understanding of his concerns. This stopped Mark's hostility in its tracks and changed the momentum of the argument. Then Elena practiced her mental strength of focusing on a pathway to their goal (getting their son to behave more respectfully) rather than winning the argument with Mark.

Finally, Elena realized that the balance in her relationship with Mark had all but disappeared. Six out of seven days of the week were spent busily running around and doing chores, the seventh day they tried to pack in all their family time, and they no longer reserved any time just to be a couple. Even on Saturday nights, they typically collapsed, exhausted, on the couch and watched a movie on television. Elena proposed that they carve out one night a week, probably Saturday night, to do something as a couple, away from the kids and the television. This might be as simple as going out to dinner, or maybe seeing a play. She even thought about starting a wine-tasting club that would meet once a month, so they could socialize with people other than the parents of their kids' friends who also liked wine and good food. Mark loved the idea. Even more, he loved that Elena was taking concrete steps to recover some of the joy and fun they'd had early in their marriage. He noticed that Elena had become markedly less cantankerous, and this motivated him to practice a bit more patience and understanding in his interactions with the kids and with her.

Too often when we want to change our relationships, we focus only on what's wrong with them, specifically what is wrong with the other person. We think that by complaining about his or her behavior, or punishing it in some way, we will stop it. But most often our complaining and hostility only creates resistance and resentment. I believe we are much more likely to change our relationships, and bring out the best in our partners, if we commit to using and improving our mental, identity, emotional, and relational strengths to change our own behavior in the relationship.

Elena did this by first asking herself when and where she and Mark were having the most trouble. After identifying the situations in which conflict most often arose, Elena conjured positive images both of what she'd like their interactions to look like and what Mark's best attributes were. Then she took many small steps to bring out his best self and to make real her positive image of relaxed, supportive family evenings. Elena used her relational strengths of perspective-taking and listening to better understand the forces driving Mark's behavior, and to recognize the ways her own behaviors and thoughts were contributing to the hostility between them. She chose to practice patience, and took steps to enhance her ability to be patient and better manage her frustrations, by creating time between work and home to engage in relaxing, wind-down activities.

Elena countered the raging negative thoughts she had about Mark by either acknowledging those that were unreasonable or rejecting those that were petty and trivial. She also redirected her energies away from pointing out Mark's annoying habits to ignoring those habits and getting the job done of improving the family atmosphere. Elena found ways to redirect escalating conflicts by validating Mark's concerns and then focusing the couple's attention on solving the problem at hand rather than arguing about it. She also took steps to create a better balance between work and play in their life as a couple.

Creating a Healthy Personal-Relational Balance

Creating a healthy balance between your personal needs and interests and the needs and interests of your partner and family is one of women's most common problems or concerns. Women most often sacrifice personal concerns too much in favor of relational concerns. They may compromise on their jobs and careers for the sake of their partner's career. They may carry too much of the burdens of household and child-care duties. They may give in to their partner's wishes too often, and let their partner make all the important decisions in the family.

We all do this to some degree, and sacrificing personal needs for our partner and family is something many women choose freely and willingly to do. But some of us fall into the habit of always putting others first, all the while developing resentments and feeling slighted. This can be toxic for women, as their self-esteem and feelings toward their partners and families grow more negative. As discussed in chapter 5, research shows that women who chronically sacrifice their own needs to keep peace in their relationships are more likely to become depressed and anxious, have lower self-esteem, and suffer poorer health. It can also be toxic for women's relationships with their partners, as their resentments spill over into their interactions. Relationships don't last as long when the personal-relational balance is off for one or both members of a couple.

Let's examine how one woman marshaled several of her mental, identity, emotional, and relational strengths to create more equilibrium between her personal life and her relational life. Marie, thirty-two, and her husband, Elias, are first-generation Mexican Americans whose parents immigrated to Arizona thirty years ago. Although Marie had finished college, her parents had always emphasized that women should stay home with their children, and the only reason they sent her to college was so she could raise smart children who would be successful. Marie had majored in business administration, and right out of college she had taken a job as a mid-level manager in a large manufacturing plant near Phoenix. Shortly after that, she met Elias, who was an engineer at the plant, and they married within a year. Their first child, Raymond, was born on their second wedding anniversary. Marie happily quit work to care for Raymond full-time. Over the next five years, two more children were born, and Elias was transferred from Phoenix to the company's plant in North Carolina.

Marie kept busy caring for their three children, but often felt adrift and alone in their home in Charlotte. The people were friendly, and she had a nice house, but Marie greatly missed her family and the friends she had grown up with in Phoenix.

Meanwhile, the demands on Elias from his job seemed to grow

every day. He frequently worked sixty to eighty hours per week, missing the children's soccer games and recitals, even their birthday parties and dinner dates with Marie. Occasionally she would complain, but most of the time she just suffered in silence, feeling a combination of bitterness against Elias and sadness and anger for the kids' disappointment. She also felt guilty for being angry with Elias and a self-loathing around her own inadequacies and weaknesses. She had gained considerable weight with the pregnancies and hadn't been able to lose it yet. She also felt stupid when Elias talked about the successes he was having at work and the interesting people he talked to each day.

By the time Marie and her family had lived in Charlotte for two years, she was chronically depressed, not wanting to get out of bed in the morning, having trouble keeping up with caring for the children, and increasingly irritable in her interactions with her family. Because she had slowed down so much, she gained more weight, which just damaged her self-esteem that much more. She consulted the priest at the church they attended, but didn't find him very sympathetic or helpful. While the children were in school one day, Marie was flipping through television channels when she stumbled on a show on which women were discussing depression. As one woman told her story, Marie felt as though she was hearing herself talk. This woman said she had been feeling angry at her husband for not paying attention to the family, and she felt increasingly unattractive and useless. She didn't care about taking care of herself or her home any longer, and even playing with her children didn't make her happy. As tears streamed down Marie's face, she waited for the woman to hand her the answers to her problems. Should she just try to be a dutiful wife, as her mother kept telling her? Should she take pills, as everyone seemed to be doing these days? Should she leave Elias and go home to live with her family in Phoenix?—but she could never do this!

The answer offered by the woman on the TV was not the one Marie had expected. She said, "I realized I had to turn myself into the woman I wanted to be, and the woman I was meant to be." The audience clapped enthusiastically and the woman beamed. Then the woman talked about enrolling in college and exploring lots of courses before she found her true love in graphic art. She completed her degree and was now working in a great job. It turned out the show was about women going back to college.

Marie turned off the television, thinking, "Well, that wouldn't work for me. I've already finished college." She went about vacuuming the floor until the children returned home from school. For the rest of the day, however, she kept hearing the words of the woman on the TV: "I realized I had to turn myself into the woman I wanted to be, and the woman I was meant to be." What did that really mean? What would it mean for her? Wasn't she exactly what she was meant to be—a full-time mother and homemaker? That's what her parents always told her she was supposed to be. But was that who she really wanted to be? The possibility that the answer to this question might be "no" frightened Marie.

As she lay awake in bed that night, waiting for Elias to come home, Marie thought back to her years in Phoenix, when the children were younger. She had been happy there, busy with the children and activities with her extended family, and helping out in their local church. When the family moved to Charlotte, Marie had lost a chunk of her identity, that part of herself that was tied to her parents, siblings, and extended family, and to their large and vibrant Hispanic church. Phoning her family back in Phoenix wasn't enough, and the church they belonged to in Charlotte had few Hispanic families.

At first this realization only made Marie cry with sadness and despair. She didn't see how things could change—Elias's career was thriving here in Charlotte so there was little chance he'd agree to move the family back to Phoenix, where the company's plant had been downsized. But again the words of the woman on the TV came to her: "I realized I had to turn myself into the woman I wanted to be, and the woman I was meant to be."

Marie tried to muster an image of who that woman would be for her. After a moment, she saw herself interacting with others, helping them as she used to in her old church. She was smiling and feeling good about herself for being of assistance. Her children were around, watching her be competent and effective, and she was proud of herself for showing them she had talents in addition to baking and cooking. She also saw herself with her parents and siblings, and although she accepted that she could not live with them any longer, she knew she needed to see them more often than the annual visits she had made since they moved to Charlotte.

When Marie began to think about how she could make this image come true, she first felt a sense of defeat. She heard herself saying, "This will never happen, I don't have anything to offer other people, I can't just be flying me and the kids to Phoenix all the time." But she conjured the face of the woman she'd seen on TV and told herself, "I've got to find ways. I can find ways to make some of this happen. I can't just stay the way I am and I don't want to."

When Marie asked herself what aspects of herself had been left behind in Phoenix, the answers were *connections* and *competence*. She had lost connection with her extended family, which was dear to her and very much a part of her identity. She had also lost the sense of competence she had received from her work with elderly and needy people in their church. She knew she had to find some ways to regain her sense of connections and competence here in Charlotte.

The next day Marie called her sister Yvonne to tell her about her newfound motivation for change. Yvonne, who was a successful attorney in Phoenix, was thrilled to hear that Marie had decided to take action—she had been encouraging her to do so for months, every time Marie called to complain that she was unhappy. Marie worried that she didn't know what to do next to begin making changes in her life. Yvonne decided to grab the opportunity to strengthen her sister's motivation, and said that since Monday was a holiday, she was flying out to Charlotte to spend the long weekend with Marie and her family. Marie was ecstatic, and spent the rest of the week cleaning the house and cooking for Yvonne.

When Yvonne arrived, she told her sister, "Marie, the first thing you've got to do is to stop thinking everything has to be perfect for everyone in your life. You've got to work on you, not on making the house spotless or baking endless cookies." Marie's face fell, but Yvonne continued, "I know that's how Mom always has been, but it wasn't necessary and I don't think it was healthy for you or for me. You've turned into a clone of her. I rebelled and became resentful of her. You don't want these outcomes for your children, do you?"

Marie shuddered to imagine her daughter ever becoming as unhappy and trapped as she currently felt, and to think that either of her kids would find her as controlling as she often found her own mother. She said to Yvonne, "Help me think of ways to make things better here in Charlotte. I know I want to do something that makes me feel good about myself, like what I was doing back at our church in Phoenix. I've also got to see you and the rest of the family more often."

The two sisters started brainstorming how Marie could feel more competent and fulfilled. They listed Marie's past experience at work and volunteering and she noted what she enjoyed and didn't enjoy about each position. Marie also noted that she didn't want to work in a full-time job until the children were at least in high school, so whatever she did had to involve flexible hours and commitment. They had the idea of Marie working in a church or volunteer agency, using her skills at business administration. Yvonne helped Marie put together a résumé of her past experience and qualifications. Then they went through the Yellow Pages and city Web sites to identify possible targets for Marie to inquire about jobs.

The next day the two sisters thought about how Marie could spend more time with her family. "This one is easy," said Yvonne. "It was obvious last night at dinner that Elias wants you to be happy. And you guys are making enough money to afford some airline tickets. You just have to get over being afraid to tell him you want to go to Phoenix more often, and take the kids."

Marie knew she was right, but she was terrified of talking with Elias about this. She imagined him getting angry with her and telling her she was selfish to spend his hard-earned money on visiting her family. When she told Yvonne this, her sister replied, "What do you mean *his* hard-earned money? It's your money, too. You and he have made the choice that you will stay home with the kids, and you can't be punished by not having a say over how the family's money is spent."

This was a revelation to Marie, and she felt stupid that it was. Of course it was her money also. Elias wanted her to be a full-time mom, and valued her doing it. She should be able to use some of the money for herself. Still, Marie was so unaccustomed to asking for what she wanted and needed that she didn't know how to begin. So Yvonne role-played with her. Yvonne played Elias, and Marie practiced what she would say to him about wanting to go back to Phoenix more often. It took about a dozen tries, but eventually Marie was able to say, "Elias, I know you know how close I am to my family. Since we've moved to Charlotte, I miss them terribly and the kids do, too. I'd like to fly the kids and me back to Phoenix more often than just once a year."

That night, with Yvonne waiting in the guest bedroom, Marie tried this approach with Elias. He said simply, "Sure. You might want to fly your parents out here once and a while also." Marie kissed him, then went to the guest bedroom, where she jumped up and down like a school girl with Yvonne.

Within a couple of months, Marie had taken a volunteer position with a different church in Charlotte, one that had a much larger Latino congregation, helping indigent and elderly parishioners deal with legal and business documents. She made her own hours so she could pick up the children at school every day. Her self-esteem was soaring and she was feeling much more connected to this church than the previous one. Marie and the children flew out to Phoenix three times a year on school vacations, and her parents came to visit for a month each spring in Charlotte. Marie enjoyed showing her parents around the city, and being their host gave her a much greater appreciation for the history, food, and culture of the region.

Marie had a major identity weakness after moving to Charlotte—her sense of self had not been stable and flexible enough to withstand the move, and she had left a big chunk of herself back in Phoenix. She used many of her strengths, bolstered by her sister, to reestablish her feelings of connection and competence. Marie evaluated what she had left behind in Phoenix, then came up with ideas for expressing and fulfilling her interests and needs in Charlotte. She took small but concrete steps toward the solutions she generated, which eventually led to her new position of helping people at the new church. When she felt pessimistic about improving her life, she tuned in to her thoughts and countered them to remain persistent and find ways around the obstacles she saw. She enlisted the help of her sister, who gave her motivation and helped her tap in to all her strengths. Her sister also coached her to develop more assertive ways of communicating her needs and desires to Elias and to others.

Women use their mental, identity, emotional, and relational strengths to tremendously enrich the relationships and people in their lives. In turn, they are rewarded with broad networks of others who love them, trust them, and will go to the ends of the earth for them. Women's mental and physical health are greatly supported by these relationships, and their quality of life is increased by leaps and bounds. People who have close relationships with women also benefit in endless ways from women's expertise in bringing out the best in them.

14.

Aging Like a Woman

It might seem ironic to suggest that we would all do well to age like a woman. Popular culture dictates, after all, that aging is a woman's absolute archenemy. Women spend billions of dollars each year to overcome the physical aging process through botox, liposuction, face creams, hair dyes, and health clubs. Freud and other early twentieth-century psychologists espoused that once a woman could no longer reproduce, she grew despondent, recognizing that her usefulness in life was now over. When her children grew up and left home, she was said to suffer from "empty-nest syndrome." There was once even a special psychiatric diagnosis for the kind of depression that women purportedly experience after menopause: melancholia.

Fortunately, none of this is true—at least for most women. Yes, many try to slow the aging process through expensive moisturizers and alpha-hydroxy treatments, but on average, women's body images actually become more positive as they move from their twenties and thirties into middle age.[1] As my friend Lori recently said, "I finally stopped comparing myself to fashion models and realized I had a pretty great body for a fifty-year-old!"

Women's overall mental health and life satisfaction also improve with age. Rates of depression, anxiety, and suicide in women go down, not up, as they grow older.[2] Women's general life satisfaction increases with age, and marital satisfaction goes up considerably when women's children leave home.[3] Women feel less lonely as they grow older and feel more affirmed and appreciated in their marriages.

Figure 2. Women's Lives Get Better with Age

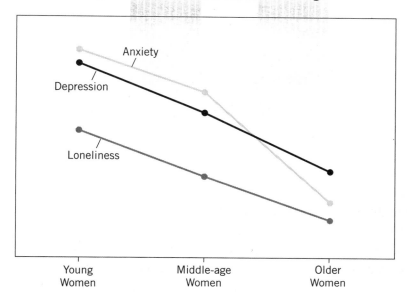

Women's rates of depression, anxiety, and loneliness decline with age. Unpublished data adapted from S. Nolen-Hoeksema and C. Ahrens, "Age Difference and Similarities in the Correlates of Depressive Symptoms," *Psychology and Aging* 17 (2001): 116–24.

In our study of over 1,300 women and men from the San Francisco Bay Area, we saw many signs that life gets better with age. In particular, levels of depressive symptoms, anxiety symptoms, and feelings of loneliness were lower among women in middle age (forty-five to fifty-five years old) and older age (sixty-five to seventy-five years old), compared to those in young adulthood (twenty-five to thirty-five years old), as seen in the figure above.

Women's lives get better instead of worse as they grow older because of their tremendous psychological strengths. Women use their mental strengths to tackle the new problems that arise as they age, such as navigating the health care system or living on less income in retirement. They draw upon their identity strengths to manage the many changes that come with aging in their roles and capabilities, lifestyles, and living arrangements. Because of their relational strengths, women enter older age with a strong network of close relationships with people they trust and who want to reciprocate their empathy, patience, listening, and care. Women apply their emotional strengths to handling distress, which empowers them to weather the crises and losses that come more often as we grow older. Women's full complement of strengths give them the mindset to celebrate older age as a time of joy, love, and fulfillment for all they have worked for and grown to be over their lifetimes.

Women's strengths help them to not only be happier in old age but to live longer and more healthy lives. Psychologist Carol Ryff of the University of Wisconsin has found that older women who have developed many personal strengths show better immune system functioning, healthier cholesterol, and better regulation of the neuroendocrine systems, all of which play a critical role in physical health.

As women have had more opportunities for education and work outside the home, their sense of mastery and their ability to be assertive have increased markedly. As a result, women are living vibrant, productive lives well into older age. One of my role models for optimal aging, renowned psychologist Eleanor Maccoby, illustrates this beautifully. Born in 1917 in Tacoma, Washington, Maccoby earned her bachelor's degree from the University of Washington in 1939 and her doctorate from the University of Michigan in 1950—a time when it was rare for women to pursue higher education. Her sharp intellect and advanced research skills earned her a teaching position at Harvard. Yet Maccoby sensed that Harvard was unlikely to promote a woman to a professorship. She cultivated a keen belief in her mission in life—to provide useful research on children's development—and resolved to pursue that mission wherever she could, overcoming any obstacles that arose. When she was offered a faculty position at the more progressive and still relatively young Stanford University in 1958, she took it. Over the next thirty years, Maccoby became one of the world's leading experts on child development, writing seminal books on the effects of parents on their children and on differences in the personalities of boys and girls. When she retired in 1987, she could easily have rested on the legacy of her major contributions to the field of developmental psychology.

Instead, Maccoby decided that retirement gave her more time to do the research she loved, and she began what many consider her most important work, on the effects of divorce and different custody arrangements on children. This research project culminated in two books, *Dividing the Child* in 1992 and *Adolescents After Divorce* in 1996. In these award-winning books, Maccoby refuted the assumption that joint custody is usually best for children, showing that when parents are unable to set aside their conflicts, it can be better for children to be under sole custody of one parent. Her evidence and thinking revolutionized how courts approached custody disputes between divorcing parents. Still not satisfied that she had completed her life's work, Maccoby published *The Two Sexes* in 1998, synthesizing fifty years of research by herself and her colleagues on the differences and similarities between girls and boys, and women and men.

Eleanor Maccoby is not simply notable for her scholarly accomplishments over the years. As a pioneer among women in academia, she was, and still is, a vocal supporter of family-friendly policies and equal treatment of women faculty. Her teaching and mentorship of undergraduate and graduate students, even after her retirement, has won her teaching awards and scores of advisees who credit her with inspiring their careers. I had the privilege of serving on the Stanford faculty with her from 1986 to 1995, and came to know her as a challenging and motivating mentor—and a supportive and stimulating friend. She and her husband, Nathan (whom most people called Mac), frequently hosted dinner parties that created opportunities for junior faculty to get to know senior faculty in a relaxed atmosphere, full of good food and humor. Eleanor and Mac also lent my husband and me their house on the waterfront in Mendocino for weekend getaways. With her terrific perspective-taking skills, Eleanor saw that the young faculty at Stanford needed time to retreat from the intense career pressures but generally couldn't afford the pricey California lifestyle that was right in front of their faces. So she and Mac gave up some of their own resources to improve the lives of others.

When Mac died in 1992, Eleanor was devastated, but because she had given so much to so many other people over her lifetime, she had amassed a vast network of support from scores of friends. She eventually moved forward with her life, publishing two more books and a dozen more articles. Now in her nineties, Eleanor has slowed physically but can still wrestle any intellectual competitor to his or her knees with her piercing debate skills and vast knowledge of social science—all the while maintaining a sly smile on her beautiful face. The saying goes, "growing old is not for sissies"—but whoever said it can't have been a woman. Eleanor is proof positive that aging like a woman is a compliment indeed.

People are living longer today than at any previous time in history. So the odds are now great that our lives, especially in our later years, will be punctuated by significant challenges: a serious and prolonged health problem, such as cancer, or the death of someone we love. Short of these tragedies, we will face many changes in social role and in lifestyle, from retiring from a job to moving to a new community to allowing our grown children to take the lead in family matters. Women's psychological strengths are perfectly suited to meet these challenges. Women grow as individuals, and develop their relation-ships with others, as a response to these experiences.

In this chapter, we'll explore how women's strengths help them age not only gracefully but triumphantly. Women's strengths carry them through the difficulties and traumas that become more frequent as we grow older and allow them to continue to grow as they age, reaching their greatest potential as human beings. I'll discuss how to improve strengths so that we can deal with all of these challenges effectively and look forward to the future not with fear and dread, but with courage and hope.

Facing the Ultimate Loss

Almost every woman will experience the death of one or both of her parents during her lifetime. Many will lose a sibling during adulthood and many will be widowed. Increasingly, the death of a loved one is preceded by months, or even years, of illness, during which women often serve as caregivers to family members.

Although women's identities are intimately tied to their relationships with others and they have deep relationships with many people in their lives, women actually fare better than men after a loss.[4] For example, women show less decline in their physical and mental health following the death of their spouse than men do. Because women live longer than men, they may expect their spouses to die before them, whereas men do not expect this. Thus the death of a spouse may not be as much of a shock for women as it is for men, and expected losses tend to be easier to cope with than unexpected losses.

Yet I also believe that women's strengths make them exceptionally good at dealing with the losses that come with aging, and there is plenty of evidence for this belief. In our San Francisco Bay Area study, we asked people how they tended to cope with the inevitable stresses of life. In all three age groups—younger adults, middle-aged adults, and older adults—women said they coped by trying to look at the situation from a new perspective (that is, reappraisal), finding solutions to the problems they faced, and reaching out to others for support. Among the older adults, who were facing the adversities that come with aging, the men showed less inclination to use these important coping skills compared to the women. In other words, older women were more likely than older men to tap their mental, emotional, and relational strengths to deal with adversity, which in turn left them less vulnerable to depression and anxiety in the face of difficulty.

In my studies of women caregivers and terminally ill family members, I was continually astonished at the strength and fortitude the women exhibited. They relentlessly sought to ensure that their loved one attained a satisfactory quality of life to the end and prepared themselves to cope with the eventual loss.[5] Women didn't just "get through" these events, many of them felt they grew personally as a result of the experience. Over and over, we heard comments such as this one from Vera, sixty-five, whose ninety-year-old father died of leukemia:

> Thinking back on it, if I had not done this, look at all I would have missed—all this growth, all this understanding.[6]

And from Nora, forty-six, whose husband died:

> There were plenty of positive things. Even on a day-to-day basis
> right now, I feel a lot stronger and a lot more capable of dealing with
> life in general and the sadness. Life is joyous and life is sad. Instead
> of getting depressed and overwhelmed by its sadness, I'm able to put
> it in what for me is its proper perspective.[7]

Despite the realities of their situations, Vera and Nora embraced a
determined optimism, which motivated them to do the best they
could while their loved one was alive, and then to take the positive
thoughts from the experience forward into the future once their
loved one had passed away.

Similarly, Christine, a seventy-four-year-old widow, chose to focus
on what went right, instead of what went wrong, as her husband
suffered through his cancer:

> We were really lucky because he didn't suffer a lot of pain. He only
> took morphine the last two days. So with all those millions of things
> to be grateful for, all you can do is, when you get down, kick your-
> self in the rear end and say, "Get going!"[8]

Another widow, Joy, called upon her optimism and her mental
strength of focusing on finding new paths around obstacles to rebuild her life after her husband died. She declared, "Every day's a little learning experience for myself, of doing new things and learning
new things as a single person."[9]

Optimistic women exercise their other psychological strengths in
many ways to cope effectively. Like Joy, they call upon their mental
strengths to reprioritize their goals and calculate new paths to those
goals. They employ their emotional strengths to reappraise their loss as
an opportunity. Using mental and relational strengths, they enlist others'
support, both for practical help—for example, in handling their loved
one's estate—and especially for moral and emotional support. Rather
than wallowing in their grief or trying to hold it in, they express their

feelings of grief with their friends and family members, who in turn make them feel loved and valued, and help them rebuild their lives. Not surprisingly, all these strengths help women avoid prolonged depression after a loss and help them recover a sense of purpose and well-being.

Women also draw upon their identity strengths to deal with caregiving and loss. Ida, who lost her sister to cancer, worked hard to maintain a stable sense of herself despite the upheaval her sister's illness and death caused in her life. She put her sister's needs first when she had to, but also recognized when she had to put her own needs first to remain healthy. Her advice:

> Be very patient with yourself because you're going through things that you don't even understand. I'd say no matter what you're feeling, just take it easy, be patient with yourself. Give yourself pep talks. Say, "You're doing just fine." I feel you will learn and grow and be different because of it. . . . The thing that helped me the most going through my sister's illness and then the death was just doing whatever I could to take care of me. I would treat myself a lot of times, as a way of getting through things. Even if it was a New York Peppermint Patty, it was something to say I was still okay, although it seemed my world around me was crashing down.[10]

Indeed, many women in our study reported that their relational strength of patience was enhanced through the experiences of caregiving and bereavement. As Angel, sixty, who lost her husband, said, "I learned patience. I learned compassion. I learned forgiveness. I learned that my priorities were worthless. And I learned that, no matter how bad things can be, there's still love and humor in the world. . . . You learn your own strengths."[11]

Women's tremendous relational strengths mean that they have a broad and deep network of close relationships that hold them up and bring them through crises such as illness and loss. The love and care women show others, and others show them, enhance these relationships even further, causing them to flourish and grow in the midst of tragedy. Jan, whose sister died of breast cancer, said:

It seemed like when situations would come up that I didn't know how to handle or didn't have the answers to, when things were really the darkest, the very next day there would be someone there, a phone call or someone would stop by or I'd run into someone in the store. Whatever that problem was, the next day someone was there with an answer and solved my problem for me, or at least showed me how to handle it.[12]

And Fiona, who lost her father to cancer, said:

I've always been close to my sister, but we became even more close. We relied on each other. She makes me laugh, she makes me feel good. It's great. She's been there for me during my real down periods, and she'll understand, but she doesn't always give me great sympathy, which is exactly what I need—she comes right out there with it, punches me in the nose with it, and that's great too.[13]

Of course, not all the women coped well with their loss. Those who were unable to marshal their strengths were more likely to feel acutely depressed and to remain depressed over months and years following their loss. One such woman was Karyn, a fifty-five-year-old, full-time homemaker who lost her sister, fifty-nine, to colon cancer. Karyn and Melanie had been extremely close throughout their lives. They lived in the same town and saw each other almost every day from the time they were each married in their twenties. Their kids grew up together, and once all the kids had gone off to college and jobs, Karyn and Melanie spent even more time with each other. They enjoyed the same activities—both were avid tennis players and handbag shoppers. They could tell each other anything, and were each other's greatest sources of support.

When Melanie was diagnosed with colon cancer, Karyn felt as though she'd been shot in the chest. When she thought about losing Melanie, Karyn often felt as though she couldn't breathe and was going to have a heart attack. Karyn went with Melanie to her doctor's appointments, holding Melanie's hand and peppering the doctor with questions about treatments. Karyn was with Melanie through all the surgery and chemotherapy, trying to keep Melanie's spirits up while feeling lost and hopeless herself. Finally, the doctors said that they were not able to stop the progression of Melanie's cancer into other parts of her body, and she had only two months to live.

Karyn was Melanie's caregiver through those tough months. As Melanie grew weaker, Karyn fed her, helped her bathe and dress, and spent every waking hour just being with her. Melanie often wanted to talk with Karyn about her death—what she believed about an afterlife, what she was proud of in her life, and what she regretted. These conversations were very hard for Karyn, and she had difficulty tolerating her upsetting feelings when Melanie insisted on talking about these subjects.

Karyn was also not taking care of herself in other ways. She was drinking more than usual, which was driving her blood pressure up. Spending so much time with Melanie meant that she was neglecting her family. Her family tried to be supportive and understanding, but when Karyn's husband Chris expressed concern that she was not taking any time away from Melanie to take care of herself or spend time with him or their kids, she became angry and accused him of being heartless.

Once Melanie died, Karyn retreated into herself. She spent hours in the bedroom, door closed, crying. She felt as though there was a black hole in her universe, first sucking Melanie in and now sucking her life force from her. Karyn couldn't imagine anything that would ever make her feel good again. She was debilitated by her grief.

After a few months, Chris knew that Karyn needed professional help to cope with her loss. He did some research, discovering through recommendations an outstanding grief counselor, Dr. Laura Nelson. Chris set up an appointment with Dr. Nelson and insisted that Karyn keep it, nearly dragging her out of bed to take her to Nelson's office.

Nelson immediately recognized that Karyn's identity had been so tightly wound around her relationship with Melanie that a big chunk of her own definition of self had died when Melanie died. Rather than having a stable sense of self that could carry her beyond Melanie's death, she couldn't see past the death to ways she could rebuild her life.

Being happy meant being with Melanie, and Karyn couldn't draw on her mental strengths to find new ways to be happy.

From what Chris had told her of Karyn's behavior before Melanie's death, Nelson also suspected that Karyn had not developed her strengths in other areas, even before Melanie died. Karyn had been unable to tolerate her distress when Melanie wanted to talk about her death. Without a strong foundation of mood-management skills, Karyn had turned to unhealthy ways of turning off her emotions, such as alcohol, after Melanie died. Karyn understood that her depression was due to grief, but she was unwilling to express her grief to others or take the help and support her family was offering to her.

It's difficult to help someone rebuild their sense of self if they won't get out of bed, so Dr. Nelson concentrated at first on getting Karyn out of the bedroom and back into life. She cajoled Karyn into making a list of simple things she used to do that made her feel good, things she hadn't exclusively done with Melanie, such as baking cookies for her family and volunteering at the local soup kitchen. Then Nelson asked Karyn to make a contract that she would do each of these things at least once in the week before her next appointment. Karyn protested that the activities didn't have a chance any longer of helping her feel better, but Nelson insisted she carry through with them anyway. She also told Karyn to write down her thoughts and reactions after she finished each of her tasks.

With a lot of prodding from Chris, Karyn did bake cookies and spent an evening helping out at the soup kitchen. When she took time to reflect on her thoughts and feelings afterward, Karyn noted that the phrases "This won't help" and "I wish Melanie was here" kept going through her head before each task. As she got involved in actually doing the task, however, these thoughts diminished, particularly at the soup kitchen, where people were frequently asking questions and looking for assistance. She had to admit she felt a little better, although she doubted it would last, and knew it would never be enough to compensate for Melanie not being there.

When Karyn showed her notes to Dr. Nelson the following week, Nelson picked out certain thoughts and wrote them on a separate sheet of paper: "This won't help." "I wish Melanie was here." "This improvement in my mood won't last." Nelson helped Karyn see that these thoughts were contributing to her depressed mood. Then she said, "Tell me how true each of these are."

Karyn was a bit puzzled at the request—they were her thoughts, what did it matter if they were true? They felt true to her. Dr. Nelson persisted, so Karyn said, "Well, it's absolutely true that I wish Melanie was here, but she's not. I guess it was only partly true that baking the cookies or working in the soup kitchen wouldn't help my mood. I felt a little bit better while I was doing those things. But the lift in my mood didn't last—after a while I was feeling really depressed again."

"Okay," Nelson said, "so some of your thoughts are absolutely true, and some of your thoughts are only partly true. Whether they are true or not, they are pulling you down. Can you step back and imagine if a friend of yours was having these thoughts and you were trying to help her? Close your eyes and imagine how you might help her respond to these thoughts."

Karyn closed her eyes and imagined that her friend Sharmin had experienced a loss and was having thoughts like hers. It took her a while, but Karyn finally said, "Well, the wish that Melanie was here, I'd probably tell Sharmin that it's okay to long for her, but she wouldn't want your life to end because she was gone. I would tell her to appreciate what she had with her sister, but then spend time focusing on what could help her feel better now.

"With the thoughts that doing things won't help her mood, I'd point out that they did help her mood, and that it felt good to be a little less depressed, even for a while. And I'd tell her that even though the better feelings didn't last long, that doing more things that feel good will make the depressed feelings go away more and more."

Dr. Nelson smiled broadly. "That's great advice. Why don't you write down that advice for yourself next to each of your statements." By getting Karyn to distance herself a bit from her own thoughts and feelings through this imagination exercise, Dr. Nelson helped her generate counter-thoughts to her depressing thoughts. The counter-thoughts Karyn generated prompted her to accept the loss of Melanie and her own grief, choose to try to feel better, and focus her time and attention on doing things that helped her feel better. Karyn's counter-thoughts also challenged her pessimistic predictions that baking cookies or helping at the soup kitchen wouldn't help her feelings for long and focused her on getting to her goal of feeling better.

Nelson then asked Karyn to take the sheet of paper with her thoughts and counter-thoughts home with her, and to do two more activities in the next week that might make her feel a bit better. When she heard herself having negative thoughts, she was to pull out this sheet of paper. If the thoughts were similar to the ones on the paper, she should look at the counter-thoughts and practice them in response. If Karyn was having new negative thoughts, she was to write them down, and then try to generate counter-thoughts to them, perhaps by invoking the distancing exercise that Dr. Nelson had taught her.

Over the next week, Karyn decided to help at the soup kitchen again because this had been the most rewarding thing she'd done the previous week. She also decided to ask her friend Sharmin to play tennis with her. This was an especially brave move, since it was Melanie she'd usually played tennis with in the past. But in her work with Dr. Nelson and conversations with her husband, Karyn had made a commitment to get back into life, and she knew if she could play a game of tennis without breaking down, that would be a major accomplishment for her. She also knew that Sharmin was a warm and trustworthy friend who could help her if she did break down.

The soup kitchen experience was even more rewarding that week as Karyn worked hard to focus on the people she was serving and the good feelings her service gave her. After she finished her shift, she wrote down all the positive thoughts and feelings she was having, to reinforce them and capture them on paper.

The tennis experience wasn't quite so successful. Karyn met Sharmin at the tennis court and by her second serve was crying so much she couldn't continue playing. She and Sharmin sat on a nearby bench, and Sharmin let Karyn cry softly on her shoulder. After a while, Karyn said, "I'm sorry, this is not fair to you. I just miss her so, and I was stupid to think I could do this—play tennis—without losing it."

Sharmin laughed a bit and said, "Well, I thought you were pretty crazy to try it, too. It's going to take time and you probably need to take smaller steps rather than big leaps to getting on with your life. But I'm proud of you for wanting to try."

"I just miss her so much! And I feel so empty without her."

"Yeah, she was great and you two were great together. But Karyn, you're great on your own, too. You're a good friend and a wonderful mother. You do—or at least did—great things at the soup kitchen. All those things are still true even though Melanie is gone."

Sharmin's words made Karyn start to cry again, but mixed in with the grief was relief. What Sharmin said was true. She was a good mother and her work at the soup kitchen and other volunteer agencies was important. Karyn and Sharmin sat on that bench talking for another couple hours, some about Melanie, and a lot about what Karyn could do to move on with her life. The two of them made another date to get together, not for tennis this time, but to go to an art exhibit that had just opened.

After hearing about her conversation with Sharmin, Dr. Nelson asked Karyn to list what her interests, talents, and activities were before Melanie died and what was important to her about each of these. Then they developed plans for Karyn to get involved in the most important of these slowly. On her list of "most important" Karyn included the soup kitchen and work she had done with the food pantry that collected packaged goods from grocery stores and restaurants to distribute to the needy. She also noted how important her kids and husband were to her. In the next week, Karyn called the director of the soup kitchen and committed to organizing the cooking and service every Wednesday night. She also showed up at the food pantry, where they greeted her with open arms and worked an afternoon shift that day.

Dr. Nelson then asked Karyn a much harder question—what were the qualities of her relationship with Melanie that she most missed. After much tears and quite a bit of time, Karyn was able to say that she missed the emotional closeness, the sense that they could read each other's minds, the fact that she felt so totally loved and accepted by Melanie. Just expressing these thoughts and feelings was a huge release for Karyn. She hadn't consciously admitted these losses to herself, and certainly hadn't had the courage to voice them to anyone else. Acknowledging that they were there, and they were true, freed Karyn to begin to accept them. Karyn also realized that she had been judging all her remaining relationships—with Sharmin, with her other friends, and with her family members—by the standard that her relationship with Melanie had set. With Dr. Nelson's encouragement, she wrote down these thoughts, and next to them wrote: "I'll never replace Melanie. But I can still have good friendships if I don't judge them by my relationship with Melanie."

After a few weeks of treatment, Dr. Nelson began working with Karyn to build her emotional strengths. Karyn had already come a long way in expressing her grief. She was still avoiding places and activities that reminded her of Melanie, and still drinking alcohol when she got upset. Nelson taught Karyn some relaxation exercises she could use when she felt upset, instead of drinking. She also helped Karyn identify the situations that most often triggered her upset feelings and drinking. These included evenings alone at home, when Chris was at a meeting or late at work. Karyn would sit and think about Melanie, start to cry, and then get a drink to drown her feelings. Dr. Nelson and Karyn generated some ideas for alternative things to do in these evenings, such as calling a friend to go to a movie when Chris was going to be gone all evening, or brewing herself some tea and writing down her thoughts about Melanie in a diary.

Karyn also got upset when she did things that reminded her very much of Melanie, like going shopping at Macy's or playing tennis. Nelson talked about the importance of Karyn gradually exposing herself to these upsetting reminders, little by little, and using her relaxation exercises to tolerate her upsetting feelings at each stage. They made a plan for Karyn to start out by driving to the garage adjacent to the Macy's and parking there, but not going in. She was to use her relaxation exercises if she felt upset, until she felt calm and could stay in the garage for a few minutes without the feelings flooding back. The next step was to step inside the Macy's, but not go far into the store, again using her relaxation exercises to quell her upset feelings until she was calm and could tolerate being there. Eventually, Karyn went into Macy's with Sharmin and walked around for a while, then at the next step stayed long enough to purchase a sweater, then finally went in on her own and did some shopping.

It took about six months of working with Nelson to build her strengths, but Karyn emerged not only without the depression that had been devastating her but feeling as though she was moving into a new and positive phase of her life. She still thought about Melanie often and missed her terribly, but those feelings no longer disabled her.

Karyn needed professional help because her grief-related depression had become so severe that she was not able to make changes on her own. Fortunately, most of us do not experience that level of depression following a loss. You can use many of the exercises described in Part II of this book to bolster our strengths to cope with our loss and grief.

Grabbing the Riches of Retirement

Women generally have an easier time than men dealing with the transitions in life roles that come with older age. Writer Gail Sheehy observes, "When men reach their sixties and retire, they go to pieces. Women go right on cooking." Men's identities are so often wrapped up in their job that when they retire, particularly if they are forced to retire, they lose their sense of self. The transition from different roles in life is generally smoother for women because of their identity strengths. They find new ways of expressing who they are and exercising their talents and interests as their life circumstances change with age. In addition, men are more likely than women to become despondent over health problems or losses in bodily function that so often occur in older age. Again, being seriously ill or incapacitated strikes at the center of a man's sense of himself as strong and competent. This is a major reason that the rate of suicide goes up dramatically in men as they age, but doesn't go up at all for women.

Women's multiple roles and strong relationships also carry them gracefully into retirement. Studies of older adults find that those with multiple roles have more positive well-being, fewer health disabilities, and fewer chronic conditions.[14] Women's multiple roles after retirement often include work in their religious community, involvement in a local organization, taking care of grandchildren, and visiting friends. Moreover, many women going into retirement have been doing these activities long before retirement, so they have long-standing associations with organizations and the people in them. In contrast, because men are so much more focused on the workplace many have not been involved in community organizations and family activities to the same degree, and may have to initiate these involvements anew upon retiring.

Having a broad network of close relationships is one of the best protections against declines in well-being and health in older age.[15] While men's friends may be tied to their work, women tend to have broader and deeper social networks, and this is a huge asset to them as they move away from the workplace into a new phase of their life. Moreover, men's relationships outside their families tend to revolve around activities such as bowling leagues or civic organizations. Women's relationships are more intimate, focused on the personal connections between them and their friends and families rather than on shared activities. This makes it easier for women to turn to others for emotional support and to admit they need help in times of stress.

Some women find retirement challenging and unfulfilling, however, as did seventy-two-year-old Rose, a retired homemaker in Kansas City. Rose welcomed her husband's retirement when they were both seventy, envisioning it as a time during which they could travel, putter around the house, and visit their grandchildren across town. But the first years of John's retirement had not lived up to Rose's vision. She and John had not saved enough money for retirement and could not afford to travel to the exotic places Rose longed to see. Instead of finding things to do around the house, John spent much of the day watching television or going to the American Legion hall to drink coffee with his old buddies. And Rose's grandchildren were so busy with school activities and sports that they were rarely at home to be visited.

Rose was becoming increasingly morose, and she started manifesting signs of hypochondria: if she felt an ache or pain, she would run to the doctor, sure she had cancer or some other fatal illness. She called her daughter Luisa several times a day to talk about her health or to ask Luisa what the children were doing, or just to hear Luisa's voice. Finally, as they sat talking about Rose's latest doctor's appointment over coffee one evening, Luisa lost it and said, "Ma, you gotta do something. You're driving me crazy. You're bored, you're depressed. You're not sick now but you're going to make yourself sick."

Rose crumpled in her chair and started crying. Luisa was ashamed of herself for being so harsh with her mother, and started stroking her hair softly. She said, "Ma, I'm sorry. I'm just worried about you and I don't think it's doing you any good to continue supporting the way you're living your life. You're a healthy, smart woman who happens to be seventy-two years old. God willing, you've got lots of years left. I want to help you figure out how to enjoy them."

It took Rose a long time to stop crying, not only because she was hurt by Luisa's outburst but also because she knew Luisa was right. She felt bored and boring, and was angry that this phase of her life was not turning out as she had imagined it would. She had dutifully raised her children and kept house all her life, expecting that once she and John retired, she could finally experience all of the adventures she had been missing out on. Instead, she felt trapped in a life that was less interesting than the one she had had before retirement, when she was heavily involved in her children's schooling and took classes in literature at the local community college. Eventually, Rose composed herself and found a way to share these thoughts and feelings with Luisa.

Luisa responded, "Okay, Ma, let's make a plan." They talked at length and agreed that Rose's depression and hypochondria stemmed from the fact that her vision of retirement was not coming true and was probably not possible given their financial constraints. Luisa and Rose resolved to use their mental strengths to identify ways Rose could have her adventures and learn new things within the financial constraints she faced in retirement. Rose noticed that the times during the week she felt most interested and exhilarated were when she was watching the Travel Channel on television or when she listened to presentations at her church by people who had gone abroad to aid people in disadvantaged nations. Rose and Luisa brainstormed three steps that Rose could take to create opportunities for affordable travel for herself (and John, if he would go along). First, Rose would find out whether she was eligible to go on one of these trips with her church. Second, she would look into the cost of trips organized by the local senior center. Third, she would ask John to come with her to see a financial counselor, who might be able to help them stretch their money further, allowing them to do some traveling on their own.

Rose had already enlisted Luisa's aid, but she also called her friend Gladys, who was very involved in the senior center, to get more ideas for inexpensive travel and to see if she had information on financial counselors. Gladys came through with the name of a counselor and put Rose in touch with the person at the center who organized trips overseas. Over the course of the next four weeks, Rose realized that she felt much more vibrant and alive than she had in two years and that she had no desire to go to the doctor. Within two months, Rose and John had worked with the financial counselor to reposition their savings and cut some daily costs of living; as a result, they found a way to finance a trip to Europe through the senior center. John was initially resistant, having grown accustomed to being a couch potato, but Rose enlisted Luisa's help to persuade him to go, and he ended up enjoying the trip immensely. By the end of the year, Rose had been on a trip with her church to Nicaragua to help build a school and had gotten a job at the senior center as a travel guide, which provided her with free airfare and hotel for two trips per year. She was living her dream of having adventures through travel, and feeling as though she was doing good things for other people at the same time.

Rose and Luisa used many of their strengths as women to improve Rose's quality of life in retirement and to pull her out of a sinking depression. Their mental strengths helped them find alternative paths to Rose's goal of travel that overcame the financial obstacles she was up against. They enlisted many kinds of help, from financial counseling to advice on how to get less expensive trips. Luisa's emotional strengths helped her see the situation from her mother's perspective and identify what was driving her depression. Then she was able to express her emotions to her mother to jolt her into taking action.

Women's many strengths are the reasons they can go through the many hardships and tragedies that aging can bring, and not only maintain a positive sense of themselves and their lives, but often grow and blossom as a result of the experience. Women also help to carry others—their husbands, their children, their friends—through these hardships and tragedies. As a result, women's strengths benefit both them and everyone else around them as they grow old together.

Coming Into Your Own Later in Life

Old age is not just about surviving, it's about flourishing. There is increasing evidence that most people feel a greater sense of fulfillment, self-actualization, reaching their peak—or whatever you wish to call it—as they grow older. For example, psychologist Abigail Stewart of the University of Michigan studied women who graduated from high school or college in the 1950s and '60s and found that as they grew older, they were more certain of their identity ("I have a sense of being my own person." "I feel my life is moving well."), felt more productive and generative ("I feel a new level of productivity or effectiveness." "I have influence in my community or area of interest.") and were more confident in their power ("I feel I have the authority to do what I want." "I feel confident."). These women talked about having "come into their own," reaching a level of maturity, confidence, and competence that was not just satisfying but exhilarating.[16]

Similarly, Carol Ryff and Princeton researcher Burton Singer have studied what they call "personal well-being" in people as they grow older.[17] They define personal well-being not just as a vague sense of being content and happy but use six critical dimensions: self-acceptance—an awareness of both your strengths and weaknesses, and an acceptance of both as part of who you are; positive relations with others; a sense of personal growth; a purpose in life; environmental mastery—the sense that you can craft your surroundings to meet your needs and capacities; and autonomy—a sense of independence and self-determination.

Dimensions and Definitions of Personal Well-Being

Dimension	Qualities of High Scorers	Qualities of Low Scorers
Self-acceptance	Possesses a positive attitude toward the self; acknowledges and accepts multiple aspects of self including good and bad qualities; feels positive about past life	Feels dissatisfied with self; is disappointed with what has occurred in past life; is troubled about certain personal qualities; wishes to be different than what he or she is
Positive relations with others	Has warm, satisfying, trusting relationships with others; is concerned about the welfare of others; capable of strong empathy, affection, and intimacy; understands give-and-take of human relationships	Has few close, trusting relationships with others; finds it difficult to be warm, open, and concerned about others; is isolated and frustrated in interpersonal relationships; not willing to make compromises to sustain important ties with others
Personal growth	Has a feeling of continued development; sees self as growing and expanding; is open to new experiences; has sense of realizing his or her potential; sees improvement in self and behavior over time; is changing in ways that reflect more self-knowledge and effectiveness	Has a sense of personal stagnation; lacks sense of improvement or expansion overtime; feels bored and uninterested in life; feels unable to develop new attitudes or behaviors
Purpose in life	Has goals in life and a sense of direction; feels there is meaning to present and past life; holds beliefs that give life purpose; has aims and objectives for living	Lacks a sense of meaning in life; has few goals or aims; lacks sense of direction; does not see purpose of past life; has no outlook or beliefs that give life meaning
Environmental mastery	Has a sense of mastery and competence in managing the environment; controls complex array of external activities; makes effective use of surrounding opportunities; able to choose or create contexts suitable to personal needs and values	Has difficulty managing everyday affairs; feels unable to change or improve surrounding context; is unaware of surrounding opportunities; lacks sense of control over the external world

Autonomy	Is self-determining and independent; able to resist social pressures to think and act in certain ways; regulates behavior from within; evaluates self by personal standards	Is concerned about the expectations and evaluations of others; relies on judgments of others to make important decisions; conforms to social pressures to think and act in certain ways

Adapted from D. Ryff and B. H. Singer, "Know Thyself and Become What You Are: A Eudaimonic Approach to Psychological Well-Being," *Journal of Happiness Studies* (2008): 25–26.

Women show increases in personal well-being as they go from their forties to their fifties to their sixties and beyond. Women are particularly likely to show increases in mastery, autonomy, personal relations, and self-acceptance. Moreover, older women who show higher levels of personal well-being as defined by Ryff and Singer are both more mentally and physically healthy in many ways.[18] Their bodies fight disease better. They sleep better. They report being more happy, and their brains show more activity in areas associated with happiness.

Women exercise their many strengths to flourish in older age. Women's mental strength of optimism motivates them to reject or ignore the cultural messages that their future is bleak in favor of building a future that is fun and fulfilling. They know there may be hardships ahead, but they also know they have the wherewithal to cope with those hardships, to do what needs to be done to take care of themselves and their loved ones, and that there is the potential for growth even in hardship.

Women's mental strength to see many pathways to their goals bring them an increasing sense of competence and confident power as they grow older. They have had much practice by the time they are middle-aged or older in overcoming obstacles and lack of resources to accomplish their goals and provide for themselves and their family. As their resources and capabilities narrow, they can adjust their lifestyles and their goals for themselves so that they can still feel satisfied and fulfilled, just as Rose found ways to travel even though money was tight.

Because they don't worry about getting their way, the loss of social status or power that sometimes comes with leaving the workplace, and generally with growing older, doesn't faze women as much as it does men. Women's ability to enlist others empowers them to get the help they need—medical help, financial help, practical help from their children or others—to deal effectively with challenges such as illness or financial trouble. That is, women aren't afraid to ask for help, so they get it when they need it, greatly improving their quality of life in older age.

Several studies provide evidence that women's identity strengths continue to grow into older age. They have learned to maintain a stable sense of themselves through the many transitions of life and move into old age fully accepting and respecting themselves, and are thus able to contend with the cascade of role transitions that come with aging. Successfully dealing with older age requires that people recognize that some of their capabilities may decline but that they'll be able to find ways to continue to pursue their interests within their new constraints. For example, you may have tended a huge, one-acre garden when you were a young adult and middle-aged, but as you grow older, the physical labor of maintaining that garden may become burdensome, so you scale back to a good-size plot in your backyard. As you move into your seventies, the plot becomes even smaller, and in your eighties, your garden is now a window box. Yet you have always been a gardener, through all these changes. Women's stable but flexible sense of self helps them move from the one-acre plot to the window box, retaining the sense of joy and satisfaction they get out of gardening, while coping with the realities of their shifting physical ability.

Women's multiple roles are critical to their personal well-being as they age.[19] Women who have multiple roles have a greater sense of life satisfaction, less negative emotions, and a greater sense of self-acceptance, personal growth, and purpose in life. Being actively involved in your children's lives, in volunteer activity, and often still in the paid workforce keeps women intellectually vibrant, socially connected, physically moving, and personally moving. Women's strength of seeing themselves in relation to others means that they have built rich social networks that continue into old age, giving women roles in many people's lives, as well as many people to play important roles in their own lives as they age.

In later years, women's emotional and relational strengths also develop in interesting ways. Although women are generally good at managing their emotions when they are young, they get even better at it in older age. When they experience a negative event, older women perceive it as less stressful, and have less negative emotional reactions to the event, compared to younger women.[20] For example, a study of people whose homes were severely damaged or completely destroyed in a flood found that older women were less distressed than younger women.[21]

Laura Carstensen of Stanford University argues that as we grow older, we put more stock in maintaining a positive emotional balance. We basically know that time is increasingly short, and we're motivated to increase the happy times and decrease the unhappy times in our lives as much as we can. We employ many strategies to do this. We avoid people who make us unhappy, and spend more time with people who make us happy. Close friends and trusted family members will make us laugh, understand our needs, support us when we are stressed, and affirm our value in their lives. As we grow older, we spend more time with these kinds of people and less time trying to make new friends, who may or may not be good for our well-being. Women's understanding of their emotions and their ability to read whether other people are going to bring their emotions down or buoy them up help them optimize the selection of whom they want to be with, thereby optimizing their moods. Further, because women have broad networks of friends they are emotionally close to they are especially likely to have the kind of friends who bolster their emotions instead of bring them down.

When they are interacting with others, older women employ their strengths of patience and perspective-taking to avoid getting angry and upset when others act inappropriately. With increasing age, we are less likely to get into an argument or interpersonal conflict with others—it's just not worth it.[22] When we do get into a conflict with others, we get less angry over it than we did when we were younger, and tend to be more sympathetic toward the person we were in conflict with.[23] We also let interpersonal slights roll off our backs more easily. In one study, a group of adults in their mid-sixties to mid-eighties and a group of adults under age forty both listened to tapes of people apparently making disparaging remarks about them.[24] For instance, one of the tapes depicted two family members of the person talking in another room about how boring the person's conversation was. Compared to the younger people, the older people reported less anger and were generally less emotional about the disparaging remarks they heard about themselves. The older adults also made fewer negative remarks about the individuals on the tapes than the younger people. The older adults tended to say, "You can't please all of the people all of the time!" while the younger adults tended to say "How dare they say that about me! What gives them the right!" The strengths of perspective-taking, patience, and forgiveness provide women with a powerful tool for maintaining a positive emotional tone to their relationships and their lives overall.

I'll end with one more story of a woman who used her strengths to glide through the changes that come with aging and to flourish in older age. Along with her husband, Murray, Helen ran a small grocery store on a busy corner in Atlanta, Georgia. When they first opened the store in the 1950s, it had been the only grocery store in the area. Helen and Murray provided high-quality products at good prices; they also knew and welcomed everyone who came into the store. They were an institution in the neighborhood, where they were frequent contributors to food banks and other local charities. Although the store kept them very busy, they raised two children, Sam and Delia, sponsoring their baseball teams, attending every band recital, and generally showering them with affection and wise counsel.

By the 1980s, big supermarket chains had been established close enough to Helen and Murray's shop to cause substantial declines in their business. They just couldn't compete with the prices the supermarkets could offer. Murray would spend hours each day ranting and raving about the demise of the neighborhood and society in general.

Helen, on the other hand, knew they had to reframe their services to the neighborhood or they would go broke, or at the very least not have enough money to see the kids through college and see themselves into retirement. Using her mental strengths, she looked for new ways they could be successful and read everything she could get her hands on about marketing trends in the grocery business, enlisting the help of industry experts to determine how they should position their business. The craze on the West Coast of America at the time seemed to be organic produce and imported cheeses. Young people were making lots of money in the new computer industry and spending it on high-end groceries. Would the same trends come to Atlanta?

Helen dragged Murray to city council meetings to learn about plans for new developments in and around the Atlanta. One mile north of their grocery store a new office complex was going up, and the city was actively recruiting technology-related companies into the complex with tax incentives. A few miles east of their grocery store, two new housing developments, specializing in what some people called "McMansions," were going up.

It took all her persuasive powers, and almost two more months of lively discussion with Murray, before Helen convinced him they should begin revamping their store to focus more on organic produce and imported foods. Murray wanted to believe that the way they had always run the grocery store was still good, but Helen was convinced they had to forge new paths to continued success. She listened patiently as Murray insisted his way was the right way, but then showed him the information she had gathered and the budgets for the transition to the new products she had created. Murray finally relented.

As soon as the office complex opened, young families began moving into the nearby housing developments, and word spread about Helen and Murray's "gourmet" grocery store. By 1990, the store was thriving again. Sam and Delia were out of college and eager to play a role in their parents' vibrant new business. Helen and Murray were ready to retire, tired of the daily grind of the business.

Helen was adamant, however, that she wanted to stay mentally and physically active. She saw an opportunity to continue being the businesswoman and mother she had always been, but in a different way now that she was retired. She struck a deal with Sam and Delia that she and Murray would combine their personal traveling around Europe with researching new products for the store. Helen loved visiting the artisans who made cheeses and cured meats, tasting their wares, negotiating prices. She would listen as they would insist on some outrageous price for their products, smiling patiently, then offer a considerably lower but fair price for the goods. She had done her research before the visit to know exactly what it cost to produce a given cheese or salami, and argued expertly with the merchants for her price. They eventually appreciated her preparation and her fairness, and she usually got the price she wanted.

Arthritis eventually put a stop to Helen's traveling. She found it too hard to sit on airplanes for transatlantic flights and found the hotels in Europe too uncomfortable. Helen wouldn't let this change in circumstances get her down, though. She refused to focus on what she couldn't do, or how unfair it was that she couldn't travel even though she had the money. Instead, she found other ways to continue helping Sam and Delia with the store. Helen took a course at the community college on how to use the Internet, and her ability to find unique products at good prices thrived, but this time online.

Staying home more allowed Helen to get involved again in the local Better Business Bureau and the charity organizations she and Murray had helped so often in years past. She became secretary of the local BBB, and volunteered often at a soup kitchen, helping improve storage practices so that the food remained safe and usable for longer periods. Many of the people Helen knew through these organizations had been friends for over fifty years, and she relished the opportunity to talk about grandchildren, old times, and new community projects the organizations were launching. Whenever she got tired of browsing the Internet or thinking about cheese, or listening to Murray complain, she would go do something related to her other roles. She felt a sense of connectedness to a wide network of people, of mastery and competence in advising the soup kitchen, and of giving back to others in all she did. Helen often went to sleep at night smiling.

Staying home also allowed Helen to spend more time with her grandchildren. Sam, Delia, and their respective spouses were extremely busy with the business. The kids never came right out and said they were unhappy about not seeing their parents enough, but Helen listened "between the cracks" of what the kids did say, took their perspectives, and surmised that they were dissatisfied. She understood the pressures Sam and Delia were under with the business, but she also knew that the attention they paid their own children was more important than the profit margin of the store. In a loving and nonconfrontational way, she expressed her concerns to Sam and Delia, and they conceded that they needed to work harder on the balance they created between work life and family life.

Helen's emotional strengths were greatly tested when Murray had a heart attack in 2004. Although she and Murray had had their conflicts, they loved each other deeply, and Helen hated to see him suffer. She forced herself to remain optimistic and to quell her worried thoughts with counter-thoughts that Murray was getting good care. She also did everything she could to ensure that Murray was getting the best medical care available. Helen was at his side through the bypass surgery and as he recovered in the hospital. When Murray came home, the doctors said he was physically okay, but Helen knew he was not psychologically okay. It seemed as though the life had been sucked out of him. Murray no longer wanted to visit with his buddies at the Rotary Club or see the grandchildren. He seemed afraid to move, and sat in front of the TV all day instead of doing the exercises the doctor had prescribed. Helen could read Murray like an open book, and knew he was depressed. The doctors poo-pooed the idea, but Helen persisted until they put him on an antidepressant. Murray was back to himself in a couple of weeks.

The changes that Helen encountered as she grew older were not remarkable. Her community developed, forcing adaptations in her business. Retirement and health challenges brought changes in her lifestyle. Her relationship with her own children evolved as she and they grew older. No, the circumstances Helen faced were not remarkable, but Helen's strengths in dealing successfully with these circumstances were remarkable. In dealing with the changes thrust upon her business, and then the changes in her roles upon retirement, Helen employed her mental strengths to focus on accomplishing the goal of being successful by flexibly going around obstacles that arose. Similarly, Helen found a way around the limitations her arthritis imposed to continue her participation in the business and remain mentally active. Helen's identity as a businesswoman and mother remained strong and stable through all these changes. Helen wasn't afraid to enlist help—from marketing experts, from the city council—to determine what the best path to her goals was. And she always remained optimistic that she would find ways around the roadblocks that hung up Murray so much.

Helen employed her relational strengths throughout her life to build a network of customers and fellow businesspeople that were loyal to her and respected her. She also clearly had the respect and love of her children, who could trust her to lovingly tell them hard truths when they needed to hear them. Helen worked hard to develop multiple roles throughout her life, and these roles brought her support, gratification, and relief well into her so-called retirement. Finally, Helen's emotional strengths carried her through the changes in her roles and circumstances, her own health difficulties, and Murray's heart attack and depression so that she remained able to cope effectively and continue to grow as a person.

I began this book heralding the new revolution in the definition of womanhood, a definition that spotlights women's strengths instead of their weaknesses. Mental prowess, a strong but flexible identity, extraordinary emotional insights, and relational expertise have been women's tools for surviving and prospering for millennia. What's new is that the world is finally able and willing to recognize women's strengths. Indeed, the world is realizing that it absolutely must capitalize on women's strengths to cope with the extraordinary challenges we all face—at home, in the office, in our communities, and in our halls of power.

Women are up to the challenge.

Notes

1. The Self-Help Revolution

1. Center for Women's Business Research, "Key Facts About Women-Owned Businesses," 2009, http://www.nfwbo.org/facts/index.php.
2. Center for American Women and Politics, "Women in Elective Office 2008," 2008, http://www.cawp.rutgers.edu.
3. Winifred Robinson, "The REAL gender gap scandal", *Daily Mail*, August 2009.
4. Higher Education Statistics Agency, Press Release 139, http://www.hesa.ac.uk/index.php/content/view/1521/161.
5. A. J. Stewart, J. M. Ostrove, and R. Helson, "Middle Aging in Women: Patterns of Personality Change from the 30s to the 50s," *Journal of Adult Development* 8 (2001): 23–37. C. D. Ryff and B. H. Singer, "Know Thyself and Become What You Are: A Eudaimonic Approach to Psychological Well-Being," *Journal of Happiness Studies* 9 (2008): 13–39.
6. W. Wood and A. Eagly, "A Cross-Cultural Analysis of the Behavior of Women and Men: Implications for the Origins of Sex Differences," *Psychological Bulletin* 128 (2002): 699–727.
7. J. M. Twenge, "Changes in Women's Assertiveness in Response to Status and Roles: A Cross-Temporal Meta-Analysis, 1931–1993," *Journal of Personality and Social Psychology* 81 (2001): 133–45.
8. "Moving Beyond Rhetoric," in *Women: Looking Beyond 2000* (New York: United Nations, 1995), 121, quoted in Estelle B. Freedman, *No Turning Back: A History of Feminism and the Future of Women* (New York: Ballantine Books, 2002), 346–47.
9. Audre Lorde, *The Cancer Journals* (San Francisco, Calif.: Aunt Lute Books, 1980), p. 15.

2. Genius Redefined

1. Estelle B. Freedman, *No Turning Back: A History of Feminism and the Future of Women* (New York: Ballantine Books 2003).

2. See Women for Women International, http://www.womenforwomen.org.

3. Quoted in Deborah Sontag, "Israel Honors Mothers of Lebanon Withdrawal," *New York Times*, June 3, 2000.

4. Higher Education Statistics Agency, Press Release 131, http://www.hesa. ac.uk/index.php?ophon=com_content&task=view&id=1397&Itemid=161.

5. Catherine Woods, "Women Entrepreneurs: the statistics", May 2008, www.real-business.co.uk/business-comment/5266986/womenentrepreneurs-the-statistics. thtml.

6. Center for American Women and Politics, "Women in Elective Office, 2009," http://www.cawp.rutgers.edu/fast_facts/index.php; accessed May 5, 2009.

7. MPs by gender, www.parliament.uk/mpslordsandoffices/mps_and_lords/ gender.cfm.

8. R. J. Sternberg, "The Theory of Successful Intelligence," *Review of General Psychology* 3 (1999): 292–316.

9. Caliper Corporation, "The Qualities that Distinguish Women Leaders," 2005, http://www.caliperonline.com/womenstudy/WomenLeaderWhitePaper.pdf.

10. A. H. Eagly and L. L. Carli, "The Female Leadership Advantage: An Evaluation of the Evidence," *Leadership Quarterly* 14 (2003): 807–34.

11. B. M. Bass, *Transformational Leadership: Industry, Military, and Educational Impact* (Mahwah, N.J.: Erlbaum Publishers, 1998).

12. L. D. Steinberg, "Transformations in Family Relations at Puberty," *Developmental Psychology* 17 (1981): 833–40.

13. Hugh Allen, "CARE International's Village Savings Programmes in Africa," 2002, https://www.msu.edu/unit/phl/devconference/CAREVillSavLoanAfr. pdf.

14. Womensphere, "The formation of village savings and loan associations has reduced cases of domestic violence in Uganda," 2008, http://womensphere. wordpress.com/2008/08/10/.

15. E. Anyango, E. Esipisu, L. Opoku, S. Johnson, M. Malkamaki, and C. Musoke, "Village Savings and Loan Associations: Experience from Zanzibar," MicroSave, 2009, http://www.microsave.org.

16. Jean M. Twenge, *Generation Me* (New York: Free Press, 2006).

17. Susan Nolen-Hoeksema and Judith Larson, *Coping with Loss* (Mahwah, N.J.: Erlbaum Publishers, 1999), 78.

18. Caliper Corporation, "Qualities that Distinguish Women Leaders."

19. C. S. Carver and M. F. Scheier, "Optimism," in *Handbook of Positive Psychology*, ed. C. R. Snyder and S. L. Lopez (New York: Oxford University Press, 2002), 231–43.

20. V. Helgeson, "Unmitigated Communion and Adjustment to Breast Cancer: Associations and Explanations," *Journal of Applied Social Psychology* 33 (2003): 1643–61.

21. Vital Voices, "The Troubles: Inez McCormack Remembers over 24 Years of

Conflict in Northern Ireland," http://www.vitalvoices.org/desktopdefault.aspx
?page_id=676.

22. See Vital Voices, http://www.vitalvoices.org.

23. P. Williams and R. Williams, *How to Be Like Women of Influence: Life Lessons from 20 of the Greatest* (Deerfield Beach, Fla.: Health Communications, 2003), 179.

3. Resilient Selves

1. American Association of University Women, *Shorthchanging Girls, Shortchanging America* (Washington, D.C.: American Association of University Women, 1991).

2. Carol Gilligan, *In a Different Voice: Psychological Theory and Women's Development* (Cambridge, Mass.: Harvard University Press, 1982); Mary Pipher, *Reviving Ophelia: Saving the Selves of Adolescent Girls* (New York: Putnam, 1994).

3. See U.S. Girl Scouts, "Uniquely Me!: The Girl Scout/Dove Self-Esteem Program," http://www.girlscouts.org/program/program_opportunities/leadership/uniquelyme.asp.

4. J. M. Twenge and W. K. Campbell, "Age and Birth Cohort Differences in Self-Esteem: A Cross-Temporal Meta-Analysis," *Personality and Social Psychology Review* 5 (2001): 321–44.

5. Josephson Institute Center for Youth Ethics, "Character Counts," http://charactercounts.org/pdf/reportcard/2008/data-tables_gender-demographic-breakdowns.pdf.

6. S. Harter, P. L. Waters, and N. R. Whitesell, "Lack of Voice as a Manifestation of False Self Behavior Among Adolescents: The School Setting as a Stage Upon which the Drama of Authenticity Is Enacted," *Educational Psychologist* 32 (1997): 135–73: S. Harter, P. L. Waters, N. R. Witesell, and D. Kastelic, "Level of Voice Among Female and Male High School Students: Relational Context, Support, and Gender Orientation," *Developmental Psychology* 54 (1998): 892–901.

7. J. M. Twenge, "Changes in Masculine and Feminine Traits Over Time: A Meta-analysis," *Sex Roles* 36 (1997): 305–25.

8. A. Feingold, "Gender Differences in Personality: A Meta-Analysis," *Psychological Bulletin* 116 (1994): 429–55.

9. A. H. Eagly and S. J. Karau, "Role Congruity Theory of Prejudice Toward Female Leaders," *Psychological Review* 109 (2002): 573–98.

10. "Women in the Armed Forces", http://mod.uk/DefenceInternet/FactSheets/WomenintheArmedForces.htm.

11. FT Weekend Magazine, "The great pay divide", September 2009.

12. P. Sellers, "Power: Do Women Really Want It?" *Fortune* 148 (October 13, 2003): 80–111.

13. K. Pickert, "Lilly Ledbetter," *Time,* January 29, 2009; http://www.time.com/time/printout/0,8816,1874954,00.html. Quote from Ledbetter originally reported by Agence France Presse, June 7, 2007.

14. Anita Doberman, "Interview: Michelle Obama," Babble.com, August 25, 2008;

http://www.babble.com/Michelle-Obama-on-the-campaign-her-career-and
-raising-kids-in-the-public-eye/index.aspx.

15. Binyamin Appelbaum, "FDIC Conductor Wields a Steady Hand," *Washington Post*, October 2, 2008; http://www.washingtonpost.com/wp- dyn/content/story/ 2008/10/01/ST2008100103624.html.

16. Charles Duhigg, "Fighting Foreclosures, F.D.I.C. Chief Draws Fire," *New York Times*, December 10, 2008; http://www.nytimes.com/2008/12/11/business/ 11bair.html.

17. Neil A. Lewis, "A Friendship in Tatters Over Policy," *New York Times*, September 13, 1996; http://www.nytimes.com/1996/09/13/us/a<->friendship-in-tatters -over-policy.html.

18. See http://womenshistory.about.com/od/quotes/a/marian_edelman.htm.

19. S. E. Cross and L. Madson, "Models of the Self: Self-Construals and Gender," *Psychological Bulletin* 122 (1997): 5–37.

20. R. Goode, "A Theory of Role Strain," *American Sociological Review* 25 (1960): 483–96.

21. H. T. J. Bainbridge, C. Cregan, and C. T. Kulik, "The Effect of Multiple Roles on Caregiver Stress Outcomes," *Journal of Applied Psychology* 91 (2006): 490–97.

22. R. C. Barnett and G. K. Baruch, "Women's Involvement in Multiple Roles and Psychological Distress," *Journal of Personality and Social Psychology* 49 (1985): 135–45.

23. E. A. Vandewater, J. M. Ostrove, and A. J. Stewart, "Predicting Women's Well-being in Midlife: The Importance of Personality Development and Social Role Involvements," *Journal of Personality and Social Psychology* 72 (1997): 1147–60.

24. O. Sullivan and S. Coltrane, "Men's Changing Contribution to Housework and Childcare," discussion paper distributed by the Council on Contemporary Families, 2008, http://www.contemporaryfamilies.org/ subtemplate.php?t=briefingPapers&ext=menshousework.

25. M. A. P. Stephens, M. M. Franks, L. M. Martire, T. R. Norton, and A. A. Atienza, "Women at Midlife: Stress and Rewards of Balancing Parent Care with Employment and Other Family Roles," in *How Caregiving Affects Development: Psychological Implications for Child, Adolescent, and Adult Caregivers*, ed. K. Shifren (Washington, D.C.: American Psychological Association, 2009), 147–67.

4. Emotions as Tools

1. P. Salovey and J. D. Mayer, "Emotional Intelligence," *Imagination, Cognition, and Personality* 9 (1990): 185–211.

2. J. Mayer, P. Salovey, and D. Caruso, "The Mayer, Salovey, Caruso Emotional Intelligence Test"; http://www.emotionaliq.org/MSCEIT-Sample.htm.

3. M. A. Brackett, S. E. Rivers, S. Shiffman, et al., "Relating Emotional Abilities to

Social Functioning: A Comparison of Self-Report and Performance Measures of Emotional Intelligence," *Journal of Personality and Social Psychology* 91 (2006): 780–95.

4. See notes 1 and 2 above and M. A. Brackett, J. D. Mayer, and R. M. Warner, "Emotional Intelligence and the Prediction of Behavior," *Personality and Individual Differences* 36 (2004): 1387–402; C. M. Martin, "A Meta-Analytic Investigation of the Relationship Between Emotional Intelligence and Leadership Effectiveness," Ph.D. diss., East Carolina University, Greenville, N.C., 2008; J. D. Mayer, D. Perkins, D. R. Caruso, and P. Salovey, "Emotional Intelligence and Giftedness," *Roeper Review* 23 (2001): 131–37; D. Rosete and J. Ciarrochi, "Emotional Intelligence and Its Relationship to Workplace Performance of Leadership Effectiveness," *Leadership & Organization Development Journal* 26 (2005): 388–99; M. M. Rubin, "Emotional Intelligence and Its Role in Mitigating Aggression: A Correlational Study of the Relationship between Emotional Intelligence and Aggression in Urban Adolescents," Ph.D. diss., Immaculata College, Immaculata, Penn., 1999.

5. J. A. Hall, "Gender Effects in Decoding Nonverbal Cues," *Psychological Bulletin* 85 (1978): 845–57; and *Nonverbal Sex Differences: Communication Accuracy and Expressive Style* (Baltimore: Johns Hopkins University Press, 1984).

6. E. B. McClure, "A Meta-Analytic Review of Sex Differences in Facial Expression Processing and Their Development in Infants, Children, and Adolescents," *Psychological Bulletin* 126 (2000): 424–53.

7. Ibid.

8. J. Dunn, I. Bretherton, and P. Munn, "Conversations about Feeling States Between Mothers and Their Young Children," *Developmental Psychology* 23 (1987): 132–39; R. Fivush, "Exploring Sex Differences in the Emotional Content of Mother-Child Conversations About the Past," *Sex Roles* 20 (1989): 675–91; R. Fivush, "Gender and Emotion in Mother-Child Conversations About the Past," *Journal of Narrative and Life History* 4 (1991): 325–41.

9. American Psychiatric Association, *The Diagnostic and Statistical Manual of the American Psychiatric Association*, vol. 4, rev. (Washington, D.C.: American Psychiatric Association, 2000).

10. Temple Grandin, *Thinking in Pictures: And Other Reports from My Life with Autism* (New York: Vintage Books, 1995), 132.

11. Paul Ekman, *Emotions Revealed: Recognizing Faces and Feelings to Improve Communication and Emotional Life* (New York: Times Books, 2003).

12. K. Byron, "Male and Female Managers' Ability to 'Read' Emotions: Relationships with Supervisors' Performance Ratings and Subordinates' Satisfaction Ratings," *Journal of Occupational and Organizational Psychology* 80 (2007): 713–33.

13. J. Bajgar, J. Ciarrochi, R. Lane, and F. P. Deane, "Development of the Levels of Emotional Awareness Scale for Children (LEAS-C)," *British Journal of Developmental Psychology* 23 (2005): 569–86.

14. K. McLaughlin, "A Public Health Approach to the Study and Prevention of Adolescent Depression and Anxiety," Ph.D. diss., Yale University, 2006.

15. S. Nolen-Hoeksema and C. Rusting, "Gender Differences in Well-Being," in *Foundations of Hedonic Psychology: Scientific Perspectives on Enjoyment and Suffering*, ed. D. Kahneman, E. Diener, and N. Schwarz (New York: Russell Sage Foundation, 1999), 330–52.

16. J. M. Gottman and R. W. Levenson "How Stable Is Marital Interaction Over Time?" *Family Processes* 38 (1999): 159–65.

17. A. L. Stanton, S. Danoff-Burg, C. L. Cameron, et al., "Emotionally Expressive Coping Predicts Psychological and Physical Adjustment to Breast Cancer," *Journal of Consulting and Clinical Psychology* 68 (2000): 875–82.

18. J. J. Gross "Antecedent- and Response-Focused Emotion Regulation: Divergent Consequences for Experience, Expression, and Physiology," *Journal of Personality and Social Psychology* 74 (1998): 224–37.

19. A. L. Stanton, S. Danoff-Burg, C. L. Cameron, and A. P. Ellis, "Coping Through Emotional Approach: Problems of Conceptualization and Confounding," *Journal of Personality and Social Psychology* 66 (1994): 350–62.

20. K. G. Niederhoffer and J. W. Pennebaker, "Sharing One's Story: On the Benefits of Writing or Talking about Emotional Experience," in *Handbook of Positive Psychology*, ed. C. R. Snyder and S. J. Lopez (New York: Oxford University Press, 2002), 573–83.

21. J. C. Barefoot, W. G. Dahlstrom, and R. B. Williams, "Hostility, CHD Incidence, and Total Mortality: A 25-Year Follow-up Study of 255 Physicians," *Psychosomatic Medicine* 45 (1983): 59–63.

22. Carol Tavris, *Anger: The Misunderstood Emotion* (New York: Touchstone Books, 1989).

23. See my books: *Women Who Think Too Much* (New York: Henry Holt, 2003); and *Women Conquering Depression* (New York: Henry Holt, 2010).

24. F. Fujita, E. Diener, and E. Sandvik, "Gender Differences in Negative Affect and Well-Being: The Case for Emotional Intensity," *Journal of Personality and Social Psychology* 41 (1991): 427–34.

25. B. L. Fredrickson, "Positive Emotions," in *Handbook of Positive Psychology*, ed. C. R. Snyder and S. J. Lopez (New York: Oxford University Press, 2002), 120–34.

26. A. H. Eagly and S. J. Karau, "Role Congruity Theory of Prejudice Toward Female Leaders," *Psychological Review* 109 (2002): 573–98.

27. For example, see A. A. Grandey, "Emotion Regulation in the Workplace: A New Way to Conceptualize Emotional Labor," *Journal of Occupational Health Psychology* 5 (2000): 95–110.

28. P. Totterdell and D. Holman, "Emotion Regulation in Customer Service Roles: Testing a Model of Emotional Labor," *Journal of Occupational Health Psychology* 8 (2003): 55–72.

5. Valuable Links

1. For an excellent discussion of this debate, see A. H. Eagly and W. Wood, "The Origin of Sex Differences in Human Behavior: Evolved Dispositions versus Social Roles," *American Psychologist* 54 (1999): 408–23.

2. T. Charman and W. Clements, "Is There a Gender Difference in False Belief Development?" *Social Development* 11 (2002): 1–10.

3. S. L. Bosacki, "Theory of Mind and Self-concepts in Preadolescents: Links with Gender and Language," *Journal of Educational Psychology* 92 (2000): 709–17.

4. D. L. Ames, A. C. Jenkins, M. R. Banaji, and J. P. Mitchell, "Taking Another's Perspective Increases Self-referential Neural Processing," *Psychological Science* 19 (2008): 642–44.

5. L. J. Lundell, J. E. Grusec, K. E. McShane, and M. Davidov, "Mother-Adolescent Conflict: Adolescent Goals, Maternal Perspective-Taking and Conflict Intensity," *Journal of Research on Adolescence* 18 (2008): 555–71.

6. A. Galinsky, W. W. Maddux, D. Gilin, and J. B. White, "Why It Pays to Get Inside the Head of Your Opponent: The Differential Effects of Perspective-Taking and Empathy in Negotiations," *Psychological Science* 19 (2008): 378–84.

7. Chief Executive.net, "Chief Executive of the Year: 2008," *Chief Executive*, press release June 3, 2008; http://www.chiefexecutive.net/ME2.

8. Adam Bryant, "Corner Office: The Keeper of That Tapping Pen," *New York Times*, March 21, 2009; http://www.nytimes.com/2009/03/22/business/22corner.html?pagewanted=2&_r=1.

9. T. Fassaert, S. van Dulman, F. Schellevis, and J. Bensing, "Active Listening in Medical Consultations: Development of the Active Listening Observation Scale (ALOS-Global)," *Patient Education and Counseling* 68 (2007): 258–64.

10. C. Rusting and S. Nolen-Hoeksema, "Regulating Responses to Anger: Effects of Rumination and Distraction on Angry Mood," *Journal of Personality and Social Psychology* 74 (1998): 790–803.

11. Ibid.

12. J. Orathinkal, A. Vansteenwegen, and R. Burggraeve, "Are Demographics Important for Forgiveness?" *Family Journal: Counseling and Therapy for Couples and Families* 16 (2008): 20–27.

13. M. E. McCullough and C. V. O. Witvliet, "The Psychology of Forgiveness," in *Handbook of Positive Psychology*, ed. C. R. Snyder and S. J. Lopez (New York: Oxford University Press, 2002), 446–58.

14. C. V. O. Witvliet, T. Ludwig, and K. Vander Laan, "Granting Forgiveness or Harboring Grudges: Implications for Emotion, Physiology, and Health," *Psychological Science* 121 (2002): 117–23.

15. M. E. McCullough, P. Orsulak, A. Brandon, and L. Akers, "Rumination, Fear, and Cortisol: An In Vivo Study of Interpersonal Transgression," *Health Psychology* 26 (2007): 126–32.

16. M. E. McCullough, G. Bono, and L. M. Root, "Rumination, Emotion and

Forgiveness: Three Longitudinal Studies," *Journal of Personality and Social Psychology* 92 (2007): 490–505.

17. S. Walker, "Gender Differences in the Relationship Between Young Children's Peer-Related Competence and Individual Differences in Theory of Mind," *Journal of Genetic Psychology* 166 (2005): 297–312.

18. R. J. Sternberg, "A Balance Theory of Wisdom," *Review of General Psychology* 2 (1998): 347–65.

7. Cultivating Genius

1. V. E. Frankl, *Man's Search for Meaning* (New York: Washington Square Press, 1963), 104.

8. Multiplying Adaptability

1. G. Downey, A. L. Freitas, B. Michaelis, and H. Khouri, "The Self-fulfilling Prophecy in Close Relationship: Rejection Sensitivity and Rejection by Romantic Partners," *Journal of Personality and Social Psychology* 75 (1998): 545–60; H. L. Fritz and V. S. Helgeson, "Distinctions of Unmitigated Communion from Communion: Self-Neglect and Overinvolvement with Others," *Journal of Personality and Social Psychology* 75 (1998): 121–40; V. S. Helgeson, "Relation of Agency and Communion to Well-Being: Evidence and Potential Explanations," *Psychological Bulletin* 116 (1994): 412–28.

2. S. Nolen-Hoeksema and B. Jackson, "Mediators of the Gender Difference in Rumination," *Psychology of Women Quarterly* 25 (2001): 37–47.

3. T. Joiner and J. C. Coyne, *The Interactional Nature of Depression: Advances in Interpersonal Approaches* (Washington, D.C.: American Psychological Association, 1999).

4. See also research by K. A. Reynolds, H. Seltman, V. S. Helgson, et al., "Impact of Interpersonal Conflict on Individuals High in Unmitigated Communion," *Journal of Applied Social Psychology* 36 (2006): 1595–1616.

5. V. Helgeson, "Unmitigated Communion and Adjustment to Breast Cancer: Associations and Explanations," *Journal of Applied Social Psychology* 33 (2003): 1643–61.

9. Sharpening Emotional Attunement

1. Robert Sapolsky, *Why Zebras Don't Get Ulcers*, 3rd ed. (New York: Henry Holt, 2004).

2. These exercises are adapted from D. C. Rimm and J. C. Masters, *Behavior Therapy: Techniques and Empirical Findings,* 2nd ed. (New York: Academic Press, 1979); W. Schafer, *Stress Management for Wellness* (Fort Worth, Tex.: Holt, Rinehart & Winston, 1992).

3. E. Kross and O. Ayduk, "Facilitating Adaptive Emotional Analysis," *Personality and Social Psychology Bulletin* 34 (2008) 924–38.

4. For a summary of studies, see S. D. Hollon, K. L Haman, and L. L. Brown, "Cognitive-Behavioral Treatment of Depression," in *Handbook of Depression,* ed. I. H. Gotlib and C. L. Hammen (New York: Guilford Press, 2002).
5. Ibid.

11. Leading Like a Woman

1. B. M. Bass, *Transformational Leadership: Industry, Military, and Educational Impact* (Mahwah, N.J.: Erlbaum, 1998).
2. B. J. Avolio, B. M. Bass, and D. I. Jung, "Re-examining the Components of Transformational and Transactional Leadership Using the Multifactor Leadership Questionnaire," *Journal of Occupational and Organizational Psychology* 72 (1999): 441–62.
3. K. B. Lowe, K. G. Kroeck, and N. Sivasubramaniam, "Effectiveness Correlates of Transformational and Transactional Leadership: A Meta-Analytic Review of the MLQ Literature," *Leadership Quarterly* 7 (1996): 385–425; T. DeGroot, S. D. Kiker, and T. C. Cross, "A Meta-Analysis to Review Organizational Outcomes Related to Charismatic Leadership," *Canadian Journal of Administrative Sciences* 17 (2000): 356–71.
4. A. H. Eagly, M. C. Johannesen-Schmidt, and M. L. van Engen, "Transformational, Transactional, and Laissez-faire Leadership Styles: A Meta-Analysis Comparing Women and Men," *Psychological Bulletin* 129 (2005): 569–91.
5. Caliper Corporation, "The Qualities that Distinguish Women Leaders," 2005, http://www.caliperonline.com/womenstudy/WomenLeaderWhite Paper.pdf.
6. National Public Radio, "Parks Recalls Bus Boycott: Excerpt from a 1992 Interview with Lynn Neary," October 25, 2005; http://www.npr.org/templates/story/story.php?storyId=4973548.
7. See http://www.rosaparks.org.
8. Quoted in P. Williams, R. Williams, and M. Mink, *How to Be Like Women of Influence: Life Lessons from 20 of the Greatest* (Deerfield Beach, Fla.: Health Communications, 2003), 335–36.
9. C. M. Martin, "A Meta-Analytic Investigation of the Relationship between Emotional Intelligence and Leadership Effectiveness," Ph.D. diss., East Carolina University, Greenville, N.C., 2008.
10. Caliper, "Qualities That Distinguish Women Leaders."
11. Ibid.
12. House of Commons Library, "Women in Parliament and Government", June 2009, http://www.parliament.uk/commons/lib/research/briefings/snsg-01250.pdf.
13. Center for American Women and Politics, "Women in Elective Office 2009," http://www.cawp.rutgers.edu.
14. K. Holtfreter, "Is Occupational Fraud 'Typical' White-Collar Crime?: A Comparison

of Individual and Organizational Characteristics," *Journal of Criminal Justice* 33 (2005): 353–65.

15. Female Entrepreneurship: General Statistics and Facts, http://www.prowess.org.uk/facts.htm.

16. Center for Women's Business Research, http://www.nfwbo.org/facts/index.php.

17. FT Weekend Magazine, "FT top 50 women in world business," September 2009.

18. Parent Teacher Association, http://www.pta.org.

19. Quoted in V. Ruiz, *From Out of the Shadows: Mexican Women in Twentieth-Century America* (New York: Oxford University Press, 1998), 143.

12. Parenting Like a Woman

1. N. Hasan and T. G. Power, "Optimism and Pessimism in Children: A Study of Parenting Correlates," *International Journal of Behavioral Development* 26 (2002): 185–91.

2. C. S. Dweck, "The Development of Early Self-Conceptions: Their Relevance for Motivational Processes," in *Motivation and Self-Regulation Across the Life Span*, ed. J. Heckhausen and C. S. Dweck (New York: Cambridge University Press, 1998), 257–80.

3. J. G. Bachman, K. N. Wadsworth, P. M. O'Malley, et al., "Marriage, Divorce and Parenthood During the Transition to Young Adulthood: Impacts on Drug Use and Abuse," in *Health Risks and Developmental Transitions During Adolescence*, ed. J. Schulenberg, J. L. Maggs, and K. Hurrelmann (New York: Cambridge University Press, 1999), 246–79.

4. N. Eisenberg, Q. Zhou, S. H. Losoya, et al., "The Relations of Parenting, Effortful Control, and Ego Control to Children's Emotional Expressivity," *Child Development* 74 (2003): 875–95.

5. L. Steinberg, R. Dahl, D. Keating, D. J. Kupfer, et al., "The Study of Developmental Psychopathology in Adolescence: Integrating Affective Neuroscience with the Study of Context," in *Developmental Psychopathology*, vol. 2, ed. D. Cicchetti and D. Cohen (New York: Wiley, 2006), 710–41.

6. J. P. Allen, S. T. Hauser, C. Eickholt, et al., "Autonomy and Relatedness in Family Interactions as Predictors of Expressions of Adolescent Affect," *Journal of Research in Adolescence* 4 (1994): 535–52.

7. M. D. Wood, J. P. Read, R. E. Mitchell, and N. H. Brand, "Do Parents Still Matter? Parent and Peer Influences on Alcohol Involvement Among Recent High School Graduates," *Psychology of Addictive Behaviors*, 18 (2004): 19–30.

13. Loving Like a Woman

1. Susan Nolen-Hoeksema and Judith Larson, *Coping with Loss* (Mahwah, N.J.: Erlbaum Publishers, 1999).

2. Ibid., 84.

3. For a review of this literature, see H. T. Reis, W. A. Collins, and E. Berscheid, "The

Relationship Context of Human Behavior and Development," *Psychological Bulletin* 126 (2000): 844–72.

4. Ibid.

5. J. K. Monin, M. S. Clark, and E. P. Lemay, "Communal Responsiveness in Relationships with Female versus Male Family Members," *Sex Roles* 59 (2008), 176–88.

6. For a review, see T. F. Robles and J. K Kiecolt-Glaser, "The Physiology of Marriage: Pathways to Health," *Physiology and Behavior* 79 (2003): 409–16.

7. J. C. Coyne, M. J. Rohrbaugh, V. Shoham, et al., "Prognostic Importance of Marital Quality for Survival of Congestive Heart Failure," *American Journal of Cardiology* 88 (2001): 526–29.

8. A. L. Geers, S. P. Reilley, and W. N. Dember, "Optimism, Pessimism, and Friendship," *Current Psychology: Developmental Learning, Personality, Social* 17 (1998): 3–19.

9. C. S. Carver, L. A. Kus, and M. F. Scheier, "Effects of Good versus Bad Mood and Optimistic versus Pessimistic Outlook on Social Acceptance versus Rejection," *Journal of Social and Clinical Psychology* 13 (1994): 138–51.

10. F. D. Fincham, "Optimism and the Family," in *The Science of Optimism and Hope*, ed. J. E. Gillham (Radnor, Penn.: Templeton Foundation Press, 2000), 271–98.

11. S. Srivastava, K. M. McGonigal, J. M. Richards, et al., "Optimism in Close Relationships: How Seeing Things in a Positive Light Makes Them So," *Journal of Personality and Social Psychology* 91 (2006): 143–53.

12. D. Belle, "Gender Differences in the Social Moderators of Stress," in *Gender and Stress*, ed. R. C. Barnett, L. Biener, and G. K. Baruch (New York: Free Press, 1987), 257–77; H. T. Reis, M. Senchak, and B. Solomon, "Sex Differences in Intimacy of Social Interaction: Further Examination of Potential Explanations," *Journal of Personality and Social Psychology* 48 (1985): 1204–17.

13. J. K. Monin, M. S. Clark, and E. P. Lemay, "Communal Responsiveness in Relationships with Female versus Male Family Members."

14. M. Kumashiro, C. E. Rusbult, and E. J. Finkel, "Navigating Personal and Relational Concerns: The Quest for Equilibrium," *Journal of Personality and Social Psychology* 95 (2008): 94–110.

15. S. M. Graham, J. Y. Huang, M. S. Clark, and V. S. Helgeson, "The Positives of Negative Emotions: Willingness to Express Negative Emotions Promotes Relationships," *Personality and Social Psychology Bulletin* 34 (2008): 394–406.

16. N. L. Collins and L. C. Miller, "Self-Disclosure and Liking: A Meta-Analytic Review," *Psychological Bulletin* 11 (1994): 457–75.

17. K. Dindia and M. Allen, "Sex Differences in Self-Disclosure: A Meta-Analysis," *Psychological Bulletin* 112 (1992): 106–24.

18. S. L. Gable, H. T. Reis, E. A. Impett, and E. R. Asher, "What Do You Do When Things Go Right? The Intrapersonal and Interpersonal Benefits of Sharing Positive Events," *Journal of Personality and Social Psychology* 87 (2004): 228–45.

19. S. M. Graham, J. Y. Huang, M. S. Clark, and V. S. Helgeson, "The Positives of Negative Emotions: Willingness to Express Negative Emotions Promotes Relationships," *Personality and Social Psychology Bulletin* 34 (2008): 394–406.

20. J. C. Coyne, "Depression and the Responses of Others," *Journal of Abnormal Psychology* 85 (1976): 186–93.

21. J. Gottman, "Psychology and the Study of Marital Processes," *Annual Review of Psychology* 49 (1998): 169–97.

22. C. E. Rusbult, J. Verette, G. A. Whitney, et al., "Accommodation Processes in Close Relationships: Theory and Preliminary Empirical Evidence," *Journal of Personality and Social Psychology* 60 (1991): 53–78.

23. X. Arriaga and C. E. Rusbult, "Standing in My Partner's Shoes: Partner Perspective Taking and Reactions to Accommodative Dilemmas," *Personality and Social Psychology Bulletin* 24 (1998): 927.

24. W. Ickes, P. R. Gesn, and T. Graham, "Gender Differences in Empathic Accuracy: Differential Ability or Differential Motivation?" *Personal Relationships* 7 (2000): 95–109.

25. S. D. Kilpatrick, V. L. Bissonnette, and C. E. Rusbult, "Empathic Accuracy and Accommodative Behavior Among Newly Married Couples," *Personal Relationships* 9 (2002): 369–93.

26. Ibid.

27. W. B. Stiles, L. M. Lyall, D. P. Knight, et al., "Sex Differences in Verbal Presumptuousness and Attentiveness," *Personality and Social Psychology Bulletin* 23 (1997): 759.

28. A. E. Fruzzetti and N. S. Jacobson, "Toward a Behavioral Conceptualization of Adult Intimacy: Implications for Marital Therapy," in *Emotions and the Family: For Better or Worse*, ed. E. A. Blechman (Hillsdale, N.J.: Erlbaum Publishers, 1990), 117–35.

29. J.-A. Tsang, M. E. McCullough, and F. D. Fincham, "The Longitudinal Association Between Forgiveness and Relationship Closeness and Commitment," *Journal of Social and Clinical Psychology* 25 (2006): 448–72.

30. F. D. Fincham, S. R. H. Beach, and J. Davila, "Longitudinal Relations Between Forgiveness and Conflict Resolution in Marriage," *Journal of Family Psychology* 21 (2007): 542–45.

31. S. M. Drigotas, C. E. Rusbult, J. Wieselquist, and S. W. Whitton, "Close Partners as Sculptor of the Ideal Self: Behavioral Affirmation and the Michelangelo Phenomenon," *Journal of Personality and Social Psychology* 77 (1999): 293–393.

32. Ibid.

14. Aging Like a Woman

1. J. C. Chrisler, "Body Image Issues of Women over 50," in *Women over 50: Psychological Perspectives*, ed. V. Muhlbauer and J. C. Chrisler (New York: Springer, 2007), 6–25.

2. A. Fiske, J. L. Wetherell, and M. Gatz, "Depression in Older Adults," *Annual Review of Clinical Psychology* 5 (2009): 363–89.

3. M. Argyle, "Causes and Correlates of Happiness," in *Well-Being: The Foundations of Hedonic Psychology*, ed. D. Kahneman, E. Diener, and N. Schwarz (New York: Russell Sage Foundation, 1999), 353–73.

4. M. S. Stroebe and W. Stroebe, "Who Suffers More? Sex Differences in Health Risks of the Widowed," *Psychological Bulletin* 93 (1983): 279–301.

5. About 75 percent of the caregivers were women, and my comments here are focused on the trends in the study pertaining specifically to them. For full details of this study, see Susan Nolen-Hoeksema and Judith Larson, *Coping with Loss* (Mahwah, N.J.: Erlbaum Publishers, 1999).

6. Ibid., 143.

7. Ibid., 149.

8. Ibid., 77.

9. Ibid., 78.

10. Ibid., 82–83.

11. Ibid., 147.

12. Ibid., 84–85.

13. Ibid., 105.

14. C. J. C. Ahrens and C. D. Ryff, "Multiple Roles and Well-Being: Sociodemographic and Psychological Moderators," *Sex Roles* 55 (2006): 801–15; P. K. Adelmann, "Multiple Roles and Physical Health Among Older Adults," *Research on Aging* 16 (1994): 142–67.

15. H. T. Reis, W. A. Collins, and E. Berscheid, "The Relationship Context of Human Behavior and Development," *Psychological Bulletin* 126 (2000): 844–72.

16. A. J. Stewart, J. M. Ostrove, and R. Helson, "Middle Aging in Women: Patterns of Personality Change from the 30s to the 50s," *Journal of Adult Development* 8 (2001), 23–37.

17. C. D. Ryff and B. H. Singer, "Know Thyself and Become What You Are: A Eudaimonic Approach to Psychological Well-Being," *Journal of Happiness Studies* 9 (2008): 13–39.

18. C. D. Ryff, B. H. Singer, and G. D. Love, "Positive Health: Connecting Well-Being with Biology," *Philosophical Transactions of the Royal Society of London* B359 (2004): 1383–94.

19. Ahrens and Ryff, "Multiple Roles and Well-Being."

20. S. T. Charles and L. L. Carstensen, "Emotion Regulation and Aging," in *Handbook of Emotion Regulation*, ed. J. J. Gross (New York: Guilford Press, 2007), 307–27.

21. J. F. Phifer, "Psychological Distress and Somatic Symptoms After Natural Disaster: Differential Vulnerability Among Older Adults," *Psychology and Aging* 5 (1990): 412–20.

22. D. M. Almeida, "Resilience and Vulnerability to Daily Stressors Assessed via

Diary Methods," *Current Directions in Psychological Science* 14 (2005): 64–68; D. M. Almeida and M. C. Horn, "Is Daily Life More Stressful During Middle Adulthood?" in *How Healthy Are We? A National Study of Well-Being at Midlife*, ed. O. G. Brim, C. D. Ryff, and R. C. Kessler (Chicago: University of Chicago Press, 2004): 425–51.

23. K. S. Birditt and K. L Fingerman, "Do We Get Better at Picking Our Battles? Age Group Differences in Descriptions of Behavioral Reactions to Interpersonal Tensions," *Journal of Gerontology: Psychological Sciences* 60B (2005): P121–28.

24. S. T. Charles and L. L. Carstensen, "Unpleasant Situations Elicit Different Emotional Responses in Older and Younger Adults," *Psychology and Aging* 23 (2008): 495–504.

Acknowledgments

Writing this book was pure joy for me. In this joyous endeavor, I have been given intellectual, practical, and emotional support from many people. First, I would like to express my great appreciation to two women who were the primary inspirations for this book, my late mother, Catherine Sims Nolen, and my mother-in-law, Marjorie Coombs Hoeksema. My mother was one of those women whose strength was quiet and reserved but absolutely unflappable, especially when it came to taking care of her children. She taught me that you can have a major impact on the world by sticking to core values no matter what, showing others you believe in them, and believing in yourself. My mother-in-law, Marjorie, taught me that everything in life is an adventure—and you don't have to just go along for the ride. Your job is to find how you can contribute to that adventure. I also wish to thank the rest of my family, my husband, Richard, and son, Michael, my father, John Nolen, and my father-in-law, Renze Hoeksema, for their stalwart support of me as I put long hours into this book. Special thanks to my sister-in-law, Terri Lawyer Nolen, for letting me tell her story of strength.

When I first suggested this book to my literary agent, Todd Shuster, he was as excited as I was, which is always a good sign. Todd shepherded the book proposal expertly, and then handed me off to Robin Dennis, my editor for this book. Robin's experience, intelligence, and good humor were major reasons both for my enjoyment in writing the book and its final quality.

Many colleagues in the academic world have contributed the science on women's strengths I cite, and many have served as mentors and friends, including Joan Girgus, Judi Larson, Abby Stewart, Janet Malley, Laura Carstensen, Ellen Markman, Eleanor Maccoby, Marcia Johnson, Teresa Treat, Barbara Fredrickson, Margaret Stroebe, Margaret Clark, and Woo-kyoung Ahn. I also wish to thank the women students who have shown me the future of women's strengths. Over the years I have known many other strong women, some of whom appear in this book either overtly or masked. My deep thanks to those who let me tell their stories.

I hope every reader learns as much from reading this book as I did in writing it about the tremendous strengths of women and about their own strengths. The world will be a better place for it.

Index

(page numbers in italics refer to tables and other illustrations)